Success on Your Certificate Course in English Language Teaching

A Guide to Becoming a Teacher in ELT/TESOL

Caroline Brandt

SAGE Publications
London • Thousand Oaks • New Delhi

SAGE Publications Ltd
1 Oliver's Yard
55 City Road
London
EC1Y 1SP

SAGE Publications Inc.
2455 Teller Road
Thousand Oaks, California 91320

Sage Publications India Pvt Ltd
B-42, Panchsheel Enclave
Post Box 4109
New Delhi 110 017

British Library Cataloguing in Publication data

A catalogue record for this book is available from the British
Library

ISBN 10 1-4129-2059-0   ISBN 13 978-1-4129-2059-9
ISBN 10 1-4129-2060-4   ISBN 13 978-1-4129-2060-5

Library of Congress Control Number: 2006921463

Typeset by Pantek Arts Ltd, Maidstone, Kent
Printed in Great Britain by Athenaeum Press, Gateshead
Printed on paper from sustainable resources

Contents

Chapter 4: Knowing your certificate course   44

Chapter 5: Getting started   64

Acknowledgements

Many people contributed towards the research on which this book is based.

I owe my greatest debt to the numerous course participants and tutors around the world who provided me with frank descriptions of their experiences of English Language Teaching certificate courses. I am particularly grateful to Rod Pryde, Regional Director of the British Council in India and Sri Lanka, for his support and enthusiasm for the project during its early phase. The research would also not have been possible without the encouragement and scholarly guidance of Dr Rob McBride, former Director of International Education, School of Education, University of East Anglia, United Kingdom.

I would also like to thank the following colleagues and friends for their critique, clarifications, and contributions:

David Bowker, University of Paisley, United Kingdom; Professor Christopher Dixon, Abu Dhabi University, United Arab Emirates; Tamsin Haggis, University of Stirling, United Kingdom; Rachel Launay, British Council, United Kingdom; Vicky McWilliam, St Giles College, United Kingdom; Professor David Prescott, University Of Brunei, Brunei Darussalam; Patricia Prescott, University of Brunei, Brunei Darussalam; Jenny Pugsley, Trinity College London, United Kingdom; Alison Standring, London School of Economics, United Kingdom; Lyn Strutt, former teacher and CELTA tutor, British Council; and Steve Tait, American University Alumni Language Center, Thailand.

On the publishing side, I would particularly like to thank Helen Fairlie, SAGE Publications, United Kingdom, for her tireless advice and criticism, in the most useful sense of the word, of successive chapter drafts; Jeanette Graham, for managing the production; Lyn Strutt, for painstakingly editing the manuscript, and ensuring that our friendship survived the process; and Sarah Wimperis, of Sarah Wimperis Illustrations, for adding a light touch with her amusing cartoons.

These acknowledgments would not be complete without mention of my daughters Zoë, Ellie and Jessica. Their interest in the project, and all their questions about it, were at once thought-provoking and motivating.

All of the above have helped to make this a better book.

Except in a few cases where full names are supplied, pseudonyms have been used throughout.

You will find a printable glossary of key abbreviations and terms used in this book on the companion website www. Words that are included in the glossary are printed in **bold** when they are first used in this book.

*All things are difficult before
they become easy.*
Fuller, 1732

Chapter 1

Setting the scene

In this chapter you can learn about:

- English Language Teaching and the kind of people the profession suits
- who this book is for
- why people take certificate courses
- the four aims of this book: to clarify the field of ELT/TESOL; to enable you to identify a good certificate course; to help you to succeed on your certificate course; and to help you to prepare for employment in ELT/TESOL
- the background of the author
- how to use this book.

▶ ENGLISH LANGUAGE TEACHING

English Language Teaching is a profession that is also known as **Teaching English to Speakers of Other Languages** or **Teaching English as a Foreign Language**. All three labels are abbreviated, so you will come across **ELT**, **TESOL** and **TEFL**. The abbreviation ELT/TESOL is used throughout this book.

As a profession, ELT/TESOL offers a wide variety of interesting possibilities, including the opportunity to teach children or adults. This book is concerned in particular with English Language Teaching to adults.

A career in ELT/TESOL could suit you if:

- you like the thought of a job that involves working with language (though you do not need to speak English as a first language to become qualified to teach it; nor do you need to know a lot about English **grammar** before you begin)
- you would like a job that involves meeting and working with adults from other countries and cultures
- you like the idea of living and working in another country (though a career in ELT/TESOL does not necessarily mean you have to work abroad – you might well be able to stay in your home town).

If this description fits you, then you should read on. This book will tell you more about all of these aspects, and it will also tell you about how to become a qualified teacher in ELT/TESOL by taking one of the many certificate courses available.

WHO THIS BOOK IS FOR

This book is for anyone who is:

- interested in learning about ELT/TESOL and what the field has to offer
- considering applying for a place on a certificate course with a view to gaining an initial ELT/TESOL qualification
- currently taking an ELT/TESOL certificate course.

Certificate courses are taken each year by thousands of adults of all ages and from a wide range of backgrounds. These courses are open to anyone who has a standard of education that would enable them to find a place in a higher education institution. This means that you do not need to be a university graduate to get a place on a certificate course.

WHY DO PEOPLE TAKE ELT/TESOL CERTIFICATE COURSES?

People take certificate courses for very many reasons. For example, perhaps you:

- are interested both in teaching and in English language
- want to support yourself during a 'gap year', before you continue with higher education
- are a recent university or college graduate, and see ELT/TESOL as a temporary career, until you decide what you want to do
- want to work in a country or countries other than your own
- have retired after a career in a different area but would like to continue working – ELT/TESOL can be a flexible and interesting choice
- are dissatisfied with your current job, or have been made redundant, and are seeking a change of career
- are a qualified teacher, and would like to expand your range of skills and qualifications to include an ELT/TESOL qualification
- are well qualified in another area, but living in a country where it is difficult to find employment in your field – you might be in this position if you accompany your partner overseas
- have children to take care of and would like flexible part-time work with opportunities for full-time employment and career development in the future.

If you take an ELT/TESOL certificate course, you will be working alongside people who are taking the course for any of the above reasons, and others besides.

❱ THE AIMS OF THIS BOOK

This book has four main aims:

1. To clarify the field of ELT/TESOL

If you are interested in ELT/TESOL, you may well have typed 'English Language Teaching', 'ELT', 'TESOL', or something similar, into the search engine of your internet browser. This will have resulted in hundreds of thousands of results; an unmanageable figure. You will also have come across further abbreviations such as **EFL, ESL, ESOL**, and **TESL** in the process, as well as some jargon, such as 'explicit grammar instruction'. And this is before you have even visited one of the websites that your search produced.

If you then perhaps refined your search to include the word 'certificate', you would have received tens of thousands of results this time, and a brief glance at only the first page of results might well tell you that you can take a certificate course over a weekend, online, by distance-learning, full-time, part-time, in the UK, in Thailand and in New Zealand. If you explored some of the sites further, you would probably have come across further abbreviations and jargon, such as **CELTA, RSA, CertTESOL, UCLES, Cambridge ESOL**, and **guided observation**.

You might also have visited websites where visitors have expressed their confusion and uncertainly about which certificates are recognized and which are not, and what is meant by 'recognized'. You will almost certainly find some discussion about the meaning of the word '**validation**', and you might also have read about people who have had bad experiences with certificate courses.

Such an initial encounter with the field of ELT/TESOL can be overwhelming, bewildering and discouraging. But help is at hand. This book clarifies ELT/TESOL in general. It will tell you what all those abbreviations mean, and what goes on under the auspices of the profession. It will also explain the terms 'validation' and 'recognition'.

2. To enable you to identify a good certificate course in order to become a qualified teacher of ELT/TESOL with excellent employment potential

Two qualifications in particular are widely-recognized by employers internationally. These are:

- the **Cambridge ESOL CELTA** (Certificate in English Language Teaching to Adults)
- the **Trinity College London CertTESOL** (Certificate in Teaching English to Speakers of Other Languages).

While there are some differences, these two courses are sufficiently similar to allow them to be seen as representing one model or approach. This approach is referred to here as the 'CELTA/CertTESOL approach'. It is both described in detail and used as the reference base for this book, because:

- CELTA and CertTESOL courses and qualifications enjoy significant popularity and are widely recognized and accepted by employers internationally.
- Many alternative courses, available all over the world, take a comparable approach.

CELTA and CertTESOL courses, being widely accepted, are excellent options, but many courses that follow the same approach or a similar one could be good alternatives. There are too many such courses to be able to include them in a book of this kind, and little purpose would be served in doing so in any case, because of their close resemblance to CELTA/CertTESOL courses. This book therefore does not set out to compare and contrast alternatives to CELTA or CertTESOL courses, since reading the information about CELTA/CertTESOL courses will help you to distinguish between good alternative courses, and those that may be less useful because they lack certain key features. Reading this book, therefore, you will learn about the many features that a good alternative course should have, such as a minimum of six hours of teaching practice with classes of **language learners**.

3. To help you to succeed on your certificate course

Certificate courses are challenging experiences. Regardless of whether you opt for a part-time course or a full-time one, you will probably find the experience an intense and demanding one, because there is a great deal to cover in a short time. Research has shown that the people who do well are those who:

- are prepared
- understand their course very well
- know both what to expect and what is expected of them
- can implement a range of skills and strategies to help them to learn more effectively.

For these reasons, certificate courses are described in detail in this book. You will read about what happens during all the various certificate course components, such as teaching practice, **feedback** and **guided observation**, including what is expected of you at each stage. You will also read about the experiences of many former **course participants** and tutors, and you will learn about many skills and strategies that have been used in the past by successful participants.

'Success' in this context means:

- enjoying the experience and benefiting from it on a number of levels
- being certain at the end of your course that you have given your personal best
- graduating with a qualification that will enable you to find good employment with a reputable employer wherever you want to work.

4. To help you to prepare for employment in ELT/TESOL

The last chapters of this book will provide you with information that can help you make the move from being a certificate course participant to being a qualified, practising, teacher. You will learn about:

- how to find a good position with a reputable employer
- what a good job should provide you with
- how to survive the first few weeks in your new teaching job
- how to continue to develop professionally
- how to practise 'good practice'.

Armed with all of the above information, you can be sure that your investment of time, money and effort into an ELT/TESOL certificate course will be rewarded with success.

▶ ABOUT THE AUTHOR

I took a certificate course in English Language Teaching 24 years ago, and in doing so opened the door to a wide variety of experience in many countries, including the United Kingdom, the United Arab Emirates, New Zealand and Hong Kong. This experience includes teaching small groups of **multilingual** learners in English language schools such as International House, and teaching centres run by the **British Council**; lecturing large groups of **monolingual** undergraduates at national universities; designing national examinations; and developing teachers on certificate, diploma, PGCE, B.Ed. and Masters programmes.

Teacher education is one of my key interests, and initial teacher education in ELT was the focus of my Ph.D. research. This book is based upon that research.

Throughout my career, I have found that my professional practice has been informed more by a developing set of values and beliefs than by current trends in methodology. These values are reflected in my understandings of the qualities of a good English language teacher.

A good teacher in an ELT/TESOL context is:

- a democrat: equal to his or her students, but different from them as they are different from each other
- an enthusiast: for language, teaching, learning and people
- a pragmatist: able to adapt to the local context
- a guide: able to create learning opportunities and allow learning from mistakes
- a humanist: aware of his or her own foibles and weaknesses, as well as those of others, but free of cynicism
- an optimist: believing that he or she usually has a small but positive effect on learners' views of language, learning and culture

- a collaborator: needing colleagues for their views, ideas, opinions, arguments and experience
- a communicator: believing in the need to share rather than harbour ideas.

Such values as those outlined above underpin this book.

USING THIS BOOK

It is likely that you will be reading this book during a very busy period in your life – while you are preparing to take a certificate course or while you are actually taking one. This book has been written with that in mind.

The content has been organized to reflect the process that you, as a potential certificate course participant, are likely to experience (from having an early general interest in the field, to wanting to know detailed information about the course and how to survive it, to career options upon graduating from the course), but there is no need to read it from cover to cover if you do not have the time to do so. It is recognized that readers will be at various stages in relation to the course, and you are encouraged to turn straight to whichever part of the book relates most closely to your interests and needs at the time.

Certain features of the book will help you to find the information you need:

- The contents and index pages provide you with detailed information about what is included in the book, and where to find it.
- The bullet points at the start of each chapter tell you what you will read about in the chapter.
- Each chapter is followed by a 'takeaway' section, which summarizes the main points made. If you have very limited time, try reading just these 'takeaway' sections.

As mentioned earlier, the icon **www** in the text directs you to the companion website at http://www.sagepub.co.uk/brandt. This website provides additional information and resources for anyone interested in becoming a teacher in ELT/TESOL, including:

- suggested reference texts and teaching aids
- links to websites, bookstores, professional organizations, journals and magazines
- blank **lesson plan** forms that you can print out to use on your course and after you have qualified
- a printable glossary of key abbreviations and terms used in this book and which you will be likely to encounter in the early stages of a career in ELT/TESOL – words that are included in the glossary are printed in bold when they are first used in this book
- quizzes related to each chapter, giving you the opportunity to check your understanding of what you have read.

It is suggested that you visit the website now, and print out a copy of the glossary. You can keep it with you and refer to it throughout your course and early career.

Another valuable feature of this book is the focus on the key strategies that will enable you to survive the course and enjoy the experience. However, this book is aimed at helping you not only to survive, but to succeed. In the introduction to Chapter 9, 'Succeeding', you will find sixteen strategies for success, drawn from the research on which this book is based. It would be a good idea to turn to this list now, and start to think about which ones you might want to address. The introduction is followed by a description of each strategy and a set of steps to help you to develop each.

It is recommended that you carry this book round with you when you are on your course so that you can turn to it when you need to, or if you have a few free minutes. Mark it up with a highlighter; scribble notes in the margins as they occur to you; turn over page corners – anything that will help you to learn from it, or help you to return to a particular point that you would like to follow up on. In other words, do whatever you need to do to get the most from it, when you need it. *Success on Your Certificate Course in English Language Teaching: a Guide to Becoming a Teacher in ELT/TESOL* has been designed to support you through a challenging experience. Make it work for you.

Chapter 2

Introducing English Language Teaching

In this chapter you can learn about:

● common abbreviations, acronyms and terms in English Language Teaching, such as ELT and TESOL

● the difference between EFL and ESL and what this means for English Language learners and teachers

● the people involved in English Language Teaching

● why people want or need to learn English language

● English Language Teaching and what the profession includes

● the relationship between English Language Teaching and Applied Linguistics

● some common misconceptions about grammar in English Language Teaching, including how much you need to know about it in order to apply for a place on a certificate course

● the term 'native speaker' and what level of English proficiency you need to have if English is not your first language.

❱ ELT, TESOL, EFL? A LOOK AT THE LANGUAGE

Anyone interested in English Language Teaching will first of all encounter a bewildering range of abbreviations simply to talk about the subject. Among the most common are ELT, TESOL, TEFL and EFL.

ELT (which is pronounced as three separate letters) is the abbreviation for English Language Teaching, while TESOL (an acronym, pronounced as a single word, with the first syllable sounding like 'tea') stands for Teaching English to Speakers of Other Languages. TEFL (which, like TESOL, is pronounced as a word. The vowel sounds like the vowel in 'tell') is an abbreviation of Teaching English as a Foreign Language; EFL (said as three separate letters) stands for English as a Foreign Language. These acronyms and abbreviations have one thing in common: they all tell you that the field or *profession* is essentially about *people and language*. But this use of abbreviations does not stop at terms used to talk about the area, because you will also find an enormous range relating to all aspects of the field, for reasons that might be connected to its recent development and expansion. Beginning with the profession itself, you have the four acronyms above, plus others; then there are various labels and terms that are used to talk about its people; and you will also find a number of ways of referring to, or describing, English language.

What follows is a brief discussion of the terms you will encounter if you are considering moving into ELT/TESOL. I will deal with the *profession* first, and follow this with a description of terms used to refer to the *people* in the field and to describe the *language* that learners study.

> ELT = English Language Teaching
>
> TESOL = Teaching English to Speakers of Other Languages
>
> TEFL = Teaching English as a Foreign Language

The profession

Anyone entering the profession will encounter a bewildering range of abbreviations

ELT is a useful, neutral, and widespread umbrella abbreviation for the field. It is perhaps more common in the United Kingdom than the term TESOL, which has tended to be associated more closely with the industry in the United States. While

ELT and TESOL both refer to the same broad areas of activity, the acronym TESOL is particularly useful because dropping the 'T', allows for a focus on the *language* and its *learners* rather than just the *teaching* of it.

The acronym TEFL (Teaching English as a Foreign Language) is also common, but its use appears to be declining in favour of ELT or TESOL. This is probably because it gives the impression of referring only to those who *choose* to learn English, rather than to those who need to learn it in order to survive or succeed in an English-speaking country. This distinction is at the heart of the difference between English as a Foreign Language (EFL) and English as a Second Language (ESL), the abbreviations for both of which are pronounced as separate letters, not as words. Very broadly, these two terms refer to the same thing: learning the English language. However, EFL is generally understood to refer to the English that people learn for eventual social, educational or professional gain, and it will not necessarily be widely used in the community in which it is being studied. ESL on the other hand refers to the English learned when people find themselves, or expect to find themselves, living and working or studying in a country where English is the first or official language, or where it is used as a language-in-common; in these circumstances English is spoken in the community in which it is being studied. ESL classes in the United Kingdom usually take place in state colleges or institutions where there is a significant proportion of speakers of other languages in the region. Another less common acronym that you may find in place of ESL is EAL (English as an Additional Language).

Outside the United Kingdom, you may find that ESL is used to refer to situations in which English is the 'lingua franca', or language-in-common, for groups of speakers of different languages in a single country, as is the case in Singapore. Or it may be used to refer to those contexts in which English is taught at school and university level in order to enable members of the workforce to function at an international level for purposes of trade or diplomacy, for example.

A distinction is made between EFL and ESL because such issues as those touched on above affect the kind of English that is taught, and also how it is taught. These issues help teachers to decide what their priorities in the classroom should be. For example, consider the position of a teenage boy, recently arrived in London with his family. He speaks Farsi as his first language and has little knowledge of English. As English is the main language of the community, he will have a pressing need for some knowledge of it to help him to survive: he will need to be able to buy some food or catch a bus, and fill in forms giving personal information. He may need to be able to take a book out of his local library, or buy a stamp at a post office. He is motivated by immediate, tangible needs; for him, English is a 'need to have'.

Compare this Iranian boy with an Italian second-year Economics undergraduate at the University of Pavia, in Italy, who takes a month-long intensive course in English during her summer vacation, in her home town in Italy. She wants to do this because she knows that improving her English will help both her studies and her future career prospects. She is motivated by possible long-term benefits. Her needs are rather different from those of the young Iranian boy, partly because English is not the main language of the community in which she lives and studies. While the Iranian student has immediate survival needs, our Italian student, who may want to read some English textbooks, for example, may prefer to study the kind of English that is likely to help her with her studies – what has become known as academic English or **EAP** – English for Academic Purposes. Or perhaps she will choose to study English for Business, with an eye on her future career. For her, English is 'nice to have'. Such differences can have an impact on the classroom: on how the teacher decides to use the available time and what he or she sets as home-work, for example.

The EFL–ESL distinction is the subject of current debate. The term ESL has a long history in the United Kingdom in relation to immigrants and asylum seekers, and for many years ESL teaching was considered to be very different to EFL teaching. In the United Kingdom, the government is currently setting targets for the teaching of English to asylum seekers and refugees, and is establishing guidelines against which examination boards are developing new TESOL qualifications.

> ESL = Need to have
>
> EFL = Nice to have

However, there are those who believe that that the EFL–ESL distinction no longer serves a useful purpose, because the situations in which English is taught and learned, and the reasons that people have for learning English, are enormously varied and nuanced, and the distinction can begin to blur. On the other hand, many believe that the distinction is a useful one as it represents two broad areas of English language teaching and learning.

Part of the profession is of course concerned with the subject of this book: learn-ing to teach. This has led to a variety of courses with their own abbreviations, acronyms, terms, and jargon, as you may be discovering. You may be considering a certificate in Teaching English to Speakers of Other Languages (TESOL); in Teaching English as a Second Language (TESL); in Teaching English as a Second Language to Adults (**TESLA**); in Teaching English as a Foreign Language (TEFL); in Teaching English as a Foreign Language to Adults (**TEFLA**); in English Language Teaching (ELT); or in English Language Teaching to Adults (ELTA). An 'A' (for Adults) is sometimes added when the organization also offers a certificate aimed at those who want to teach children, sometimes known as 'Young Learners' in the industry, because a distinction is made between teaching adults and teaching children. This book is particularly concerned with teaching adults. You may also find courses in Teaching English as an Additional Language (**TEAL**) and Teaching English as an International Language (**TEIL**).

The people

The people at the heart of ELT/TESOL are its language learners and its teachers. The field is a rich and varied one and you will come across a range of different roles, jobs and titles, such as 'director of studies', 'operations manager', '**assessor**', or '**IELTS** student'. Some terms used to describe people in ELT/TESOL that are of immediate relevance and use to anyone embarking on a certificate course are considered here.

Probably one of the first that you will come across is 'trainee'. This is widely used in the profession, particularly in the United Kingdom. However, the term (course) participant is used throughout this book as it suggests an active involvement in the learning process which is in accord with the values and aims of this book. 'Tutor' is also preferred to the widespread 'trainer'.

The people who study English language are often referred to as 'students', but the alternative 'language learner' is becoming increasingly common, and the term is preferred here, once again because of the emphasis on learning.

The language

The term 'English' will often be used in this book to refer to 'English language'. 'English language' is more accurate, however, because it helps to distinguish the field from English as a content subject in schools and universities, where it may include the study of literature and **discourse**, and where language is studied as a subject area, rather than learned as a medium or a skill. But, because it is common practice in the profession, and because it is more succinct, the term 'English' alone will frequently be used here.

People have any number of reasons for wanting to learn English; and perhaps because of this, as well as many courses in general English, you can now find courses that offer learners the opportunity to study more narrowly focused areas, sometimes coming under the umbrella term ESP – English for Specific Purposes. For example, learners can choose to study English for Law, English for Medicine, or English for Tourism. In each case, the intention is not that they should learn the content of the subject, but rather that they should learn English in – or through – a particular context, with an emphasis on the kind of language needed in that particular context. Students can also elect to study EAP (English for Academic Purposes), which is similar in that the focus will be less on content and far more on developing the kind of English skills that a college or university student needs in order to study his or her chosen major through the medium of English.

It is also possible to find courses that focus on one area or skill required in learning a language. For example, you may come across 'conversation classes', or classes to develop 'writing skills'. These areas lend themselves less easily to acronyms and abbreviations – fortunately for us all, perhaps!

The discussion above has focused on some of the more common terms in use on the field. To summarize, in this book I will be making extensive use of the following terms:

- (T)ESOL
- ELT
- English (language)

- (English language) teacher
- (English language) learner
- (Course) participant
- Tutor

The names given to certificate courses have created further complexity, as you might expect, and these are explored in Chapter 3; see in particular 'The development of initial English language teacher training'.

ELT AS A PROFESSION

ELT is far from new. It has been in existence as long as people have wanted, needed, or been required to learn the language. However, the idea of ELT/TESOL as a profession is relatively recent, having developed only over the last 35 to 40 years. Until the 1960s, it was assumed that anyone who could speak English could also teach it, and ELT/TESOL was not viewed as an independent academic discipline. Consequently few were able to turn it into a career (Gray, 1997).

Since the 1960s, however, various domestic and international political, economic, technological and social developments and pressures have led to changes in the functions of English worldwide. English, once a language of colonial administration and imperialism, has become an international 'lingua franca', the language-in-common for people in science, technology, commerce, finance, and communications. This development has created a specific, wide scale and immediate need for instruction towards **proficiency** in English language. This has contributed to the development of a global industry devoted to the selling and promotion of the English language. Such activities include the teaching of English language as well as the designing, setting and marking of tests and examinations, the placement of overseas students in institutions in English-speaking countries and the pre-service and in-service training of English language teachers. The scale and scope of such activities have helped to establish ELT/TESOL as a profession.

ENGLISH AS A MEDIUM OF INSTRUCTION

If your first language is English and you studied a modern foreign language such as French, German or Spanish while at school, as I did, you may remember attending language classes in which both languages – English as well as the new language – were used. This is still the approach taken in some schools. For example, my daughters are all learning French at school, but they are all doing it partly in, or through, English. Their French teacher (who is English) explains some things about French to them in English. They all have notebooks that are sprinkled with translations from French into English: French words, phrases and grammar, alongside their English counterparts. This is quite different to how they learn French when they go to their evening class at the local Alliance Française. There, their teacher is French, and, although she speaks English well, she never uses English in class. Instead, all of her lessons are conducted in the medium of French, and her students' notebooks are all in French: there is not a word of English in sight. This is how much English language instruction is carried out – through the medium of English.

As a teacher you may have no choice but to approach the task through the medium of English, because you may find that you do not know your learner's first language (or *all* of your learners' first *languages*: think about a class of French, Spanish, Turkish and German people, or any of the other possible class compositions that exist). Fortunately for the profession, this approach is generally understood to be beneficial for all concerned: not only for the teachers, but also for the learners, who will be exposed to more English in an English-medium classroom than might otherwise be the case.

▶ THE SCOPE OF ELT

ESOL is taught to children ('Young Learners'), teenagers, young adults such as university undergraduates, and adults of all ages, in a wide variety of contexts all over the world, including:

- private language schools
- quasi-governmental organizations such as the British Council, which has English language teaching centres around the world
- state and private primary schools, secondary schools, and sixth form colleges
- colleges of further education
- universities
- charities and volunteer agencies such as Volunteer Service Overseas (VSO) and the Workers' Educational Association (WEA) in the United Kingdom
- home tutoring
- online courses
- companies, as part of staff training and development.

There is therefore a wide variety of possible teaching situations in which you might find yourself. Examples include:

- Small classes (up to around 15) of adults of all ages and language backgrounds, attending intensive classes in a private language school in an English-speaking country. Classes are therefore likely to consist largely of speakers of different languages (this is known as a **multilingual** class).
- Small classes (up to around 15) of adults of all ages, attending intensive classes in a private language school in their own country. Classes are therefore likely to consist largely of speakers of the same language (this is known as a **monolingual** class).

- Large classes (30 or more) of undergraduates, preparing to study their degree subjects through the medium of English, or taking English to support their studies, in an English-speaking country or in their home countries.
- Classes of just one student, known as one-to-one classes, often privately arranged or through a home tutoring arrangement.
- Classes for women only, possible in Islamic states such as the United Arab Emirates, Kuwait and Saudi Arabia.

However, ELT/TESOL as a field is not limited to the teaching and learning of ESOL. It encompasses a wide range of related activities, including for example:

- development and administration of internal tests, such as those needed to place students in a language programme or to assess progress
- development and administration of national and international examinations and tests of proficiency, including those such as **TOEFL** (the Test of English as Foreign Language) and IELTS (the International English Language Testing System)
- development and publication of **materials** and textbooks for class use and for teachers' reference
- owning and managing private language schools
- management and administration of departments within schools, colleges and universities
- training and development of English language teachers at all stages: pre-certificate, certificate, diploma, Masters, Ph.D.; and for specializations such as EAP or Young Learners
- training of ELT/TESOL trainers or tutors
- moderation and assessment of teacher training courses such as those validated by Cambridge ESOL and **Trinity College London**
- management and promotion of international associations such as **IATEFL** and **TESOL**
- organizing and running conferences, seminars and workshops
- research and publication of journals and research papers
- publication of newsletters and magazines for teachers and language learners
- design and operation of websites including chat rooms and discussion forums
- recruitment
- marketing and promotion of courses and materials.

It is therefore easy to make a rich and diverse career in ELT/TESOL, including any or all of the above contexts, situations and activities.

▶ LINGUISTICS, APPLIED LINGUISTICS AND ELT

Linguistics is a social science, but it involves the scientific study of language as a phenomenon. Linguists try to answer the questions: What is language? How is it managed by the brain?

As a Linguistics undergraduate, you would study phonetics and **phonology** (the production, perception and patterns of sounds); **semantics** (the **meanings** of words in languages); morphology (how words are formed and their structure); and syntax (how sentences are formed). You would also be able to study other areas such as the relationship between language and society (sociolinguistics); or between language and the brain (neurolinguistics).

> 'Linguistics is the scientific study of language: structurally, phonetically, socio-culturally and biologically.'
>
> Poster, Department of English Language and Linguistics, University of Brunei Darussalam

Applied Linguistics, on the other hand, is less abstract. Because language conveys social, cultural and political aspects of life, Applied Linguistics looks at the language-related concerns of individuals and groups, including, for example, teachers, immigrants, policy-makers and refugees. Fields of study in Applied Linguistics therefore include: language policy and planning; language acquisition; bilingualism; second and foreign language learning; and teaching and assessing (together often known as second language pedagogy). ELT/TESOL may therefore be seen as part of the broader field of Applied Linguistics, and so can be studied as part of a degree in this subject.

> As a Linguistics student, I was frequently asked 'So how many languages do you speak?'
>
> In fact, students of Linguistics learn about languages. They don't learn to speak languages as such.

Some terms in common use in ELT/TESOL have their source in Applied Linguistics. One of the most common of these is the **L2** learner, which simply means someone who is learning a second language. This person may be referred to elsewhere as a language learner, as described above. A related term that is also useful is **L1**, which simply refers to a person's first language, sometimes known as his or her mother tongue.

▶ SNAPSHOTS OF A CAREER IN ELT

A career in ELT/TESOL can offer surprising variety. In the course of our careers, my current ELT/TESOL colleagues and I have:

- taught small groups of multilingual language learners in a private school in Hastings, United Kingdom

- taught adult literacy classes as a volunteer in Canada
- set up and run CELTA courses in the Arabian Gulf
- been a visiting assessor for CELTA courses in the Sultanate of Oman, Kuwait, New Zealand, Thailand, Hong Kong, and Australia
- attended management development courses in Greece and Egypt
- taught on an Intensive English Language Programme for Form 5 and 6 students preparing to sit 'O' Level in Hong Kong
- trained teachers to use a new language laboratory in Korea
- examined IELTS students in Guangdong Province, China
- lectured MA students on Language Policy and Planning in New Zealand
- tutored students taking the 'Adult Learning' module of the University of Sheffield's distance learning M.Ed. programme in Hong Kong
- researched and written articles and academic papers for publication
- attended conferences and given presentations
- reviewed ELT/TESOL textbooks for publishers prior to publication
- taught IELTS preparation courses in Japan
- designed a multi-level language programme for a language school in Korea
- established a small lending library in a language school in Brunei
- taught social English on a one-to-one basis to the wife of a foreign ambassador to Brunei to prepare her for royal audiences
- worked one-to-one with the national delegate to a world conference on forest conservation to prepare him for participation in discussion groups and interaction with other delegates
- designed a course which uses folk tales to develop writing skills for adult immigrant English learners in a multinational class in Australia
- supervised the teaching practice of PGCE and B.Ed. TESL students in Brunei
- taught the language of safety to factory workers in Australia
- taught English for basic car maintenance to a group of immigrant women on a course at a vocational college
- taught refugee women the language they need to talk about their health care with health professionals
- ran classes for Thai gardeners working in a six-star resort in Brunei, to teach them how to greet guests lost in the grounds and get them safely back on track
- worked with Indonesian computer programmers on a United Nations project to introduce computer assisted language learning in Indonesian schools
- taught business English courses in the evenings in Singapore
- chaired a panel of judges for an inter-schools public speaking competition

- given impromptu lessons to college students while on holiday in Bali
- learned to eat all kinds of food and attended all kinds of cultural events and celebrations!

Such activities span a period of time – months or even years. On a more day-to-day level, the teachers above have found themselves occupied by such tasks as the following:

- teaching the present perfect for the nth time
- teaching a class at no notice and so having nothing prepared
- assessing students' **oral** performance for Cambridge ESOL's First Certificate in English
- negotiating understanding between Serbian and Bosnian students in a multinational class
- dealing with an uncooperative or overly demanding student (that is, one who does not conform to expected classroom behaviour)
- listening to and trying to support a teacher with personal problems
- creating timetables for 60 teachers and 2,000 students
- marking scripts for various public and institutional examinations and tests
- finding a substitute teacher at the last minute to cover for someone who has just phoned to say that she is unwell
- dealing with the furious parents of a youth who has failed his first-year university English language course, and cannot proceed with his studies until he has repeated (and passed) the same course
- developing teaching material at home, to a deadline
- meeting educational publishers' representatives
- accompanying a group of language students on a day trip to the Tower of London
- taking the minutes of a staff meeting
- observing a teacher as part of his performance appraisal
- invigilating a 3-hour examination, spotting and trying to prevent cheating
- placing orders for books and materials
- taking an inventory of materials in a resource centre.

Such a range of activities is far from uncommon and has led to, for me, a career with few dull moments. This kind of variety can be yours too in your career in ELT/TESOL.

I once found a university student in his final examination with the 'answers' written neatly on the underside of the peak of his cap.

I still have that cap.

▶ WHAT KIND OF PEOPLE GO INTO ELT?

The website of one organization that offers certificates in ELT, the **School for International Training (SIT)** in the United States, responds to the Frequently Asked Question 'What kind of people take this course?' with the following information:

> Many are college-age students who are interested in travelling and working overseas. There are also working professionals preparing to enter TESOL as an alternative career or in retirement. Non-native English speakers with strong English skills also take the course so they can teach English in their own countries or elsewhere. Many experienced teachers find the Certificate course a valuable introduction to SIT's model of reflective practice.
>
> *School for International Training, 2005a*

To give you some idea of the variety of people who take certificate courses, below are brief biographies from several participants and course graduates.

> I grew up in a suburb of New York. I've always wanted to travel and live abroad. And so, after gaining a BA in Speech and Hearing Sciences from the University of California in Santa Barbara in 2001, I moved to Rome to take a CELTA. I don't plan to leave for a long time!
>
> *(David)*

> I'm from Taiwan, but I've lived in California in the United States for most of my life. I have a Bachelor of Arts in Social Anthropology. I took a TESOL certificate course in 1999, and I've been teaching ESOL ever since.
>
> *(Carol)*

> I grew up in Australia, but I didn't go to university. I'd heard about someone who was recruiting young people to work in remote parts of China. All you needed for this job was a TESOL certificate. So I took one, passed it, and I've been in China since January.
>
> *(Brendan)*

> After a ten-year career in publishing in the UK I decided I needed a change. I went to Prague in the Czech Republic (because I had a friend there) and took a full-time certificate in ELT. I began teaching there immediately afterwards.
>
> *(Jack)*

> I have a B.Sc. (Hons) in Applied Biological Sciences from Manchester Metropolitan University, UK. Before taking a TESOL certificate I was a trainer in the pharmaceutical industry!
>
> *(Sylvia)*

> I've been working in the entertainment business, on the ticketing side, which I've done in Melbourne where I'm from. But I've spent most of my working life not being terribly happy in doing what I was doing. When I left my last job the only thought I had was that I actually wanted to work with either the written or the spoken word. A friend of mine here's a school teacher. I asked her if she knew of any courses I could do and she mentioned the CELTA. So here I am.
>
> *(Brian)*

I started out, thousands of years ago in North America, working on a degree in music. But then, for various reasons, I switched from music to education. After I graduated I taught primary for about 22 years before suffering teacher burnout. Then I focused again on music, and so for the last 15 years or so, I've been teaching music in one form or other. But it's hard to get work here teaching music, and so when I heard about the course, I thought – that's for me! I'm hoping the certificate will be useful to me when I retire next year.

(Jenny)

I did teacher training years ago. I've already got a postgraduate teaching certificate and a diploma in education, which I did immediately after I graduated. But I didn't pursue teaching then as a career, I went into working in investment, which is how I ended up in Hong Kong – I came here to work for the Securities and Futures Commission in fact. However, teaching is what I love to do, so when I was more financially set up I decided to go back to teaching. I'm doing this course because a lot of my students – I'm teaching at secondary level – have English as a Foreign Language problems.

(Kathy)

From this, you will be able to see that the field appeals to a wide range of people. But is it for you?

▶ IS ELT FOR YOU?

Having read the above, you will already have a very good feel for the field. And will probably have reached a decision about whether or not to follow up on your idea of taking an ELT/TESOL certificate. Nevertheless, as with all careers, it is undoubtedly suited better to some people than others.

It helps, for example, if you like meeting and working closely with people, and if you do not mind constantly meeting new people. The field is also ideal if you like the idea of living and working in countries other than your own, as employers often look for people with experience in different countries. It also helps if you have an interest in English and other languages, in teaching, and in other peoples and cultures. You do not need, though, to be able to speak the language of the people you will be teaching (although it is certainly helpful if you do), because, as described above, much ELT is carried out through the medium of English.

> 'I enjoy people, I enjoy teaching, I enjoy exploring the conventions, intricacies and foibles of the English language. This attitude is, I think, a strength that allows me to develop a good rapport with students.'
>
> Participant, Hong Kong

ELT/TESOL can also be convenient if you want a 'stop-gap', a short-term 'temporary' career, for whatever reason. However, as suggested above, the field also provides plenty opportunities for a long-term and satisfying career.

It's a good career if you like the idea of living and working in other countries

ELT/TESOL may not suit you if you do not much like the idea of living and working in a country other than your own, particularly one in which English and/or your first language may not be widely spoken. Usually, you will have an opportunity to learn the language of your host country (and a good employer in a country other than your own should facilitate this), but if you are not interested in learning a language, it is probably not a good idea to take up a profession where you are helping others to do just that. ELT/TESOL may also not be for you if you cannot face the thought of moving from country to country, and job to job, possibly accompanied by your family. It can also be a risky business: without the funds or time to visit the country of your new employer before you sign the contract, it can sometimes be difficult to be completely certain about conditions.

If you are still in doubt after reading the above:

- Talk to an English language teacher and/or someone who has completed a certificate course.
- Observe a lesson or series of lessons if you can – visit a school or college and ask to sit in on a class. A good school will welcome you. (See Chapter 4, 'Guided observation', for a list of suggested points to look for while observing.)
- Attend an ELT/TESOL 'Taster Day' – some centres offer this.
- Browse the internet – with a critical eye. Reading this book first will help you here!

'BUT I'M NOT A NATIVE SPEAKER ...'

As you enter the profession, you will come across the phrases **native speaker** and **non-native speaker**, a distinction much like the EFL–ESL one discussed above, in the sense that it suggests a clear cut division where one does not really exist.

Many people believe that native speakers make the best teachers, perhaps a relic from the days when it was the only precondition for becoming a teacher in ELT/TESOL, besides having a first degree.

However, there are several problems with the distinction. First, it is often difficult to identify who is a native speaker and who is not. A friend of mine, born and brought up in France, learned ESOL at school from the age of seven, studied it at university in Paris and eventually moved to England where she became an English teacher. People ask her what part of the United Kingdom she comes from; they have no idea that she is fact French and that English is not her 'first' language. Another example is provided by my Malaysian colleague. She studied ESOL in primary and secondary school, and is now a fluent user of the

> The terms 'native speaker' and 'non-native speaker' suggest a clear-cut distinction that doesn't really exist. Instead it can be seen as a continuum, with someone who has complete control of the language in question at one end, to the beginner at the other, with an infinite range of proficiencies to be found in between.

language in all contexts. She makes only one 'error' (that is, a consistent mistake rather than a slip, which all speakers make from time to time): she regularly adds 'isn't it' to sentences where it does not fit grammatically. For example, while talking to some student teachers about their pupils, she commented, 'They like Milo, isn't it?', and later 'They don't have tea, is it?' This is an 'error' that she frequently makes. The distinction, like that between EFL and ESL, is often nuanced and blurred and belies a greater complexity than is suggested by the two terms.

Secondly, it may be the case that near-native speakers are actually better placed to teach ESOL, bringing a number of benefits to the classroom. For example, as a proficient near-native speaker, you will be:

- Providing an example of a successful *user* of the second language. (The native speaker teacher, often ignorant of the first language of his or her language learners, provides a restricted model of a language learner.)
- Providing an example of a successful *learner* of the second language. (The native speaker teacher can only be vicariously aware of his or her learners' experiences and difficulties.)
- More likely to be familiar with your learners' culture, background and values. (The native speaker teacher is often essentially an outsider.)

It is also the case that a great deal of communication in English occurs not between native speakers but between those who use English as a lingua franca, or language-in-common. It follows therefore that language learners need to be able to communicate with both native speakers and non-native speakers like themselves. Clearly the near-native speaker teacher of English is well placed to help language learners to develop the skills required to communicate with other non-native speakers.

> Even if you don't speak English as your first language, you can take an ELT/TESOL certificate, providing you meet the minimum entry requirements.

Anyone with a standard of education equivalent to that required for entry into higher education can learn to teach English, once their proficiency in the language has reached a certain **level**. Some centres require IELTS Band 9, others a TOEFL computer-based score of 250 (equivalent to a paper-based score of 600), or having a Cambridge ESOL Certificate of Proficiency in English – so do not be put off by people who try to tell you otherwise. Certificate courses are open to both so-called native and near-native users of English. You will find more information about certificate course entry requirements in the first section of Chapter 5.

▶ 'I DON'T KNOW THE FIRST THING ABOUT GRAMMAR ...'

Just as some people whose first language is not English may worry about their proficiency in English in relation to their ability to teach the language, there are many people who speak English as their first language but who express similar anxieties. In their cases, however, these people do not doubt their proficiency – they know they can speak, read, write and listen to English fluently – but they do doubt their ability to make this knowledge explicit. They express this by saying things such as, 'I couldn't possibly teach English. I don't know the first thing about grammar', or 'I'd like to teach English but when I was at school grammar was out of fashion, so my grammar's terrible. What's a past subjunctive, for example? I haven't got a clue.'

There are two common misconceptions about grammar related to taking a certificate course. They are:

- You need to have explicit knowledge of English grammar before you start a certificate course. In fact, this is *not* so.
- The course is largely about learning grammar because teaching English is largely about teaching grammar. This is *not* the case.

Even if you studied explicit grammar at school and you can recall what you were taught, it may not help you greatly on your certificate course, because not only have understandings of grammar changed and developed over the years, but there are also differences between the grammar that you learn about in order to account for your own language as a native speaker, and the grammar that you learn about in order to teach it to those learning a second language.

It is also worth bearing in mind that the certificate course is an *initial* qualification, and so one of the functions of the course is to introduce you to the basic **pedagogic grammar** that you will need to teach the language. Therefore, you do not in theory need to worry about how much grammar you know before you apply for a place on one of these courses, because you will learn enough, through the **pre-course tasks** that tend to be part of these courses and while on the course itself, to give you a basic grasp of the key issues. I say 'in theory' because if you happen to be applying for a place on a course at a centre where there is no shortage of applicants, then it is possible that explicit knowledge of grammar may be one of the criteria used to discriminate one applicant from another.

> 'We had our first language awareness session today – the dreaded grammar. It wasn't too bad really. I was thrown a bit though by the fact that all the names have changed since I was at school – there's no pluperfect any more!'
>
> Participant, Hong Kong

However, to address the second misconception, the course is, in any case, not by any means all about teaching and learning grammar. Grammar is one element out of many, albeit an important one. The term 'grammar' does not even equate to what is often referred to as **language awareness**, because this term includes awareness of *all* aspects of language, which extends beyond grammar to include other areas such as **pronunciation** and meaning. It is important therefore to keep 'grammar' in perspective. For an idea of the range of topics that you will study, take a look in particular at the 'example workshop schedule' in the first section of Chapter 6. You will see from this that you are in for a rich and varied experience.

Because grammatical awareness may be one of the criteria used to discriminate course applicants, the best advice to give anyone about to attend an interview for a place on a certificate course is the same as you would give someone applying for a job – *prepare*, and *prepare well*. If you were applying for a job, you would find out as much as you could about the company and the job, before the interview. Grammar can be seen as one element of this job, so it would be a good idea to do a little reading beforehand. No certificate interviewer will expect you to display a full grasp of English grammar, but he or she will be mightily impressed by your display of several relevant abilities: for example, the ability to anticipate and prepare, to recognize gaps in your knowledge, and to carry out independent research.

So, just as these courses are open to both so-called native and near-native users of English, they are open to those who think they know a lot about grammar as well as those who know their limitations with regard to their grammatical knowledge. Do not be put off by grammar – remember instead that it is just one area out of many that you will learn about on a certificate course.

Introducing English Language Teaching: Key points to take away with you

- Both TESOL and ELT are umbrella abbreviations for the industry. The term TESOL is associated more closely with the United States, while ELT is more common in the United Kingdom. TESOL allows for a focus on the language and its learners (ESOL) rather than just the teaching of the language. You may also come across TEFL: Teaching English as a Foreign Language.

- EFL is English as a Foreign Language and is 'nice to have'. ESL is English as a Second Language and is a 'need to have'.

- ESOL is taught and learned in a huge range of contexts all over the world.

- Linguistics is the scientific study of language; Applied Linguistics is concerned with language as used by individuals, groups and societies; ELT/TESOL may be seen as one aspect of Applied Linguistics.

- In ELT/TESOL, English is usually the medium of instruction in class, that is, English is taught through English, with little or no use of a learner's first language.

- ELT/TESOL can offer a varied and interesting career for people who like working with others, who like the idea of working in different countries and who are interested in language and languages.

- To be offered a place on a certificate course, you do not need to have a specialized knowledge of English grammar, nor do you need to speak English as your first language.

Check your understanding of Chapter 2 by completing the quiz available on the companion website at: www.sagepub.co.uk/brandt

Chapter 3

Becoming qualified

In this chapter you can learn about:

● why taking a certificate course is an excellent idea if you want to become an English language teacher

● the development of certificates in ELT, in particular the evolution of the CELTA course, from the Prep. Cert. to the RSA CTEFLA to the current CELTA

● what validating organizations such as Cambridge ESOL and Trinity College London actually do

● features to look for if you are considering taking a Cambridge ESOL CELTA or a Trinity College London CertTESOL course

● criteria to help you identify a good certificate course if the course you are considering is not a Cambridge ESOL CELTA or a Trinity College London CertTESOL

● different ways in which you can take your certificate course

● the advantages and disadvantages of full-time and part-time courses.

▶ WHY SHOULD YOU BECOME QUALIFIED?

It is still possible to find a salaried job teaching ESOL with no qualifications other than those afforded by a first degree and by speaking English as a first language. The ease with which this may be achieved depends to a large extent on local market conditions: where there are not enough qualified teachers available to meet demand, employers are more likely to accept unqualified or poorly qualified teachers.

The circumstances in which an unqualified teacher may find him or herself were described in the British press by the *Education Guardian* 'Career doctor':

> In every major city of the world there are any number of quasi-legit language schools operating out of a few barely-furnished rented rooms, so if your only goal is to get away from the cold and make a few bob out of some unwilling students, you could probably get a decent job just on the basis of your degree.
>
> *Education Guardian, TEFL, 6 April 2004*

Besides 'barely-furnished rented rooms' and 'unwilling students' (and any other risks you may be taking by accepting employment in a 'quasi-legit' school), there are a number of other problems with choosing to remain unqualified. The first is that the range of opportunities and activities open to you is severely restricted, making as varied a career as the one described in Chapter 2, 'Snapshots of a career in ELT', very unlikely. This will increasingly be the case, because as certification becomes more easily available employers' expectations will also rise. The better jobs in ELT/TESOL, in terms of salary, working conditions, and opportunities, will of course tend to go to those with qualifications. The second is that a qualified teacher has a range of skills and techniques at his or her disposal which can greatly enhance confidence and improve the quality of the experience for all concerned. This can be a great motivator. It feels good to see things work in an ELT/TESOL classroom – there is enormous satisfaction to be gained from a learner who visibly appreciates the decisions that you have made in relation to their experience. In my own case, I find that this motivates me to try harder. I am constantly looking for different and more effective ways of doing things in relation to the context in which I find myself, which means that even teaching the present perfect **form** of verbs for the 'nth' time can be made interesting, which usually leads to more good feedback from learners, which in turn makes me feel good about my efforts – and so the cycle continues. How you would approach the present perfect form of verbs when teaching a large group of Iraqi refugees in London is quite different to how you would approach the same area if you were teaching a small class of French business people in France, or a class of thirty-five B.Ed. undergraduates at the University of Brunei. And because you are constantly thinking about your context and the different people in front of you, including their language background, no two lessons are ever the same.

Of course, it is possible to start teaching with no ELT/TESOL qualifications, gain some experience, and then take a qualification. In this case, you may be able to take a diploma, such as the **Cambridge ESOL DELTA**, never having taken a certificate. Some people do just this. But it is becoming increasingly difficult to find work in the first place without a certificate, and if you want flexible employment opportunities and to set your ELT/TESOL career on the right path from the beginning, then taking a certificate course could prove to be one of the best decisions you have ever made.

> Some people think that teaching must be boring because you are constantly teaching the same thing over and over, to different groups of students.
>
> But it's the different people that provide the variety. They mean that no two lessons are identical, even if lesson aims are identical, and the same material is being used.

▶ THE DEVELOPMENT OF INITIAL ENGLISH LANGUAGE TEACHER TRAINING

In the United Kingdom, formal initial training in ELT/TESOL has been available for only the last 25 years or so. Before this, it was expected that suitably qualified people (that is, those with a first degree and/or a teaching qualification) would work in language schools, obtain on-the-job experience and then take a post-experience qualification such as a diploma or a Master's degree, both of which were widely available. In 1967, the Certificate in the Teaching of English as a Foreign Language to Adults, known then as the Cert. TEFL, was introduced in Britain by the Royal Society of Arts (the RSA) – but this was a post-experience qualification, designed specifically for in-service training.

In recognition of the need for initial, pre-service, training in ELT/TESOL, in the late 1970s and early 1980s, International House, a charitable educational trust dedicated to raising language education standards worldwide and promoting international understanding through language education (International House, 2006) based in the United Kingdom, developed a **Preparatory Certificate** (or **Prep. Cert.**), a course designed specifically for initial

> CELTA used to be known as the Prep. Cert. and, later, as the CTEFLA.

training. This was taken over by the RSA in 1982 and – rather confusingly, given the existence of a Cert. TEFL – renamed the RSA Certificate in the Teaching of English as a Foreign Language to Adults (known as the **RSA CTEFLA**). Simultaneously, the Cert. TEFL was renamed the RSA Diploma in the Teaching of English as a Foreign Language to Adults (and known at the time as the Dip. TEFLA). In October 1996 the RSA CTEFLA was re-launched as the Royal Society of Arts/University of Cambridge Local Examinations Syndicate Certificate in English Language Teaching to Adults (the RSA/UCLES CELTA), partly to reflect the fact that the University of Cambridge Local Examinations Syndicate (UCLES) had taken over, in 1988, the RSA certificates and diplomas in this area. More recently, the university has introduced a new umbrella term for its teaching qualifications, Cambridge ESOL.

To summarize, the current Cambridge ESOL CELTA course (CELTA is an acronym, pronounced as a word to sound like 'selta') was developed therefore over a period of about 25 years, from its origin as the Preparatory Certificate in the early 1980s, through to the RSA CTEFLA, and finally emerging as the Cambridge ESOL CELTA in 1996. The in-service Cert. TEFL, begun in 1967, eventually evolved into the RSA Dip. TEFL and finally became what is known today as the Cambridge ESOL DELTA, the Diploma in English Language Teaching to Adults. This diploma remains a post-experience course and can only be taken after two years of full-time teaching experience.

At approximately the same time as the first Preparatory Certificate was made available by International House (late 1979/early 1980), Trinity College London inaugurated its Certificate in TESOL (the CertTESOL) at the Meads School in Eastbourne, United Kingdom. Since 1981 many others have been added to the list of centres that offer a CertTESOL course (Pugsley, 2005a). Pugsley describes Trinity College London as follows:

> Trinity College London is a long-established awarding body, dating back to 1877 as a provider of examinations. We offer examinations in music, drama, speech, dance, and English for speakers of other languages, and we accredit programmes for the training of ESOL teachers. Trinity is a company with charitable status that separated from the music conservatoire, Trinity College of Music, over ten years ago, although Trinity retains a developmental relationship with them. Trinity's qualifications are accredited by the Qualifications and Curriculum Authority, the national body in the UK charged by government with overseeing vocational qualifications outside the higher education sector.
>
> *Pugsley, 2005b*

Cambridge ESOL (previously UCLES) and Trinity College London are currently two of the largest organizations concerned with initial teacher training in ELT/TESOL. Their certificates are so far the only ones that are accepted by the British Council and widely known outside the United Kingdom, although there are many other effective courses available. The British Council website states that:

> Two of the best known and most widely accepted qualifications are the Cambridge ESOL CELTA and the Trinity College London CertTESOL.

> The most commonly accepted qualifications are the Certificate of English Language Teaching to Adults (CELTA) awarded by the University of Cambridge Local Examinations Syndicate (UCLES) and the Certificate in Teaching English to Speakers of Other Languages (Cert. TESOL) awarded by Trinity College London. These certificates are generally seen as a minimum qualification to teach English as a Foreign Language.
>
> *British Council, 2005*

Of these two organizations, Cambridge ESOL is the largest in terms of numbers of people trained. While around 4,000 participants per year pass a CertTESOL through approximately 120 institutions in the United Kingdom and overseas (Pugsley, 2005a) over 10,000 people graduate from over 900 CELTA courses held in 286 centre in 54 countries (Cambridge ESOL, 2005c). CELTA is described in Cambridge ESOL literature as 'the best known and most widely taken TESOL/TEFL qualification of its kind in the world' (Cambridge ESOL, 2004), while Pugsley notes that 'Trinity is particularly proud of its wide content coverage on all CertTESOL programmes and its required range of written and practical assignments that encourage reflective and self-critical thinking, even at this initial stage of training' (Pugsley, 2005c).

A QUALITY QUALIFICATION

In choosing which course to take, you will be taking into account a whole range of factors, such as cost, location, mode (full-time or part-time are the two main modes of delivery, and these are discussed further below), dates, course length, and so forth. One of the aims of this book is to enable you to make an informed decision, so that you can make the best possible choice in the context of your own personal circumstances and preferences.

Initial ELT/TESOL certification is currently available from a bewildering array of providers in countries all over the world. These providers are too numerous to mention, and, as described in Chapter 1, 'The aims of this book', my purpose is not to compare and contrast alternative certificate courses because reading the information about CELTA and CertTESOL courses will help you to distinguish between good alternative courses, and those that may be less useful because they lack certain key features.

In the United Kingdom, besides gaining a certificate it is also possible to take a Qualified Teacher Status route (becoming qualified to teach all age groups in state schools and institutions, such as through a Certificate in Education or a Postgraduate Certificate in Education), and, depending on your future employer's familiarity with state teaching qualifications and accreditation in the United Kingdom, you may find that you are able to work in language schools overseas too. You should be aware that the courses referred to in this book do not confer what is referred to above as Qualified Teacher Status, which means that while you will be able to work in private language schools around the world, you will not be qualified to teach in British state schools with an ELT/TESOL certificate alone. However, both the Cambridge ESOL CELTA and the Trinity College London CertTESOL are recognized under United Kingdom government requirements for teaching English in the Learning and Skills Sector (they are both at Level 4 of the National Qualifications Framework), and credit is given to holders of CELTA and CertTESOL who wish to enter mainstream education in the United Kingdom.

Assuming then that you are considering taking one of the many short, intensive, pre-service ELT/TESOL certificates, there are a number of criteria and issues that you need to consider in order to ensure that you make the best investment of your money, time and effort, and in order to improve your employment prospects upon qualifying. These are:

1. Validation

2. Course length and content, including in particular **supervised teaching practice** and guided observation

3. Reputation, and recognition and acceptance by employers

4. Centre staffing, including tutor to participant ratio, and centre facilities

5. Forms of assessment: do participants have to reach required standards of achievement before being awarded a certificate?

Points 1–4 above are discussed in more detail below. See Chapter 4, 'Assessment: what to expect', for more information about assessment.

There are, however, two further considerations that you may wish to bear in mind, and they are the location and the timing of your course. If you are free to do so, you may want to think about taking a course in a place where it is easier to find work once you have qualified. Countries may suffer from a shortage of qualified teachers in ELT/TESOL, for a number of reasons, and it can therefore be easier to find work in these countries than in others. Again, if you are free to choose when to take your course, you may wish to do so just before a busy period for the centre or the country, simply because the centre itself may be more likely to offer you work once you have passed your course.

For more information about both of these issues, see Chapter 10, 'The job hunt: issues and strategies'.

Validation

Validation means that the course in question has been approved by an external body after a process that ensures the course, in terms of its entry requirements, syllabus, length, assessment procedures and so forth, meets identified quality standards.

In the United Kingdom, the benchmark for quality is acceptance by the British Council, which accepts as validating bodies Trinity College London, Cambridge ESOL and any United Kingdom university. As yet, there is no international accreditation organization for ELT/TESOL.

In order to achieve external validation from either Trinity College London or Cambridge ESOL, a course has to be at least 100 hours long and will certainly include at least 6 hours of supervised teaching practice and feedback, as well as 6 hours of guided observation. A validated course will also be likely to offer a tutor to participant ratio of at least 1:6. Besides meeting such requirements, every validated course is individually moderated by a **moderator** (this is the term used by Trinity College London) or assessed by an assessor (the term used by Cambridge ESOL). The person who performs this function is an experienced tutor who visits the centre while the course is in progress, to ensure that the course is being run according to the standards supplied by the **validating organization**. A precondition to becoming an assessor or moderator is that the person should have recent or current experience of the same course, but in another centre. In other words, a CELTA assessor will have recently worked on his or her own CELTA course in another location; while a Trinity College moderator will likewise recently have been involved in a CertTESOL course.

Validation makes it much more likely that the course will be recognized by your future employers, in part because some employers only accept people with externally validated qualifications. Having passed a validated course, particularly one that has strong international recognition and acceptance, will increase your chances of finding good employment and it will improve your mobility between employers and countries.

The presence in the United Kingdom of two validated and com-

> Passing a course that is validated by an internationally recognized organization will greatly improve your chances of finding a good job afterwards. It will also improve your international mobility.

mercially highly successful certificate courses has influenced other providers, including those in other countries such as the Republic of Ireland and the United States. Consequently, you will find a whole range of courses on offer that are comparable to CELTA and CertTESOL courses in terms of course content, length and tutor to participant ratio. One such example is provided by the School for International Training (SIT) in the United States, which provides nationally recognized ELT/TESOL teaching qualifications, including a TESOL certificate. The **School for International Training TESOL Certificate** (see School for International Training, 2005b) is an example of the kind of certificate course that compares favourably with the CELTA/CertTESOL approach. For this reason, and also because it appears to be attracting growing international recognition and acceptance, it is discussed briefly here and occasionally in subsequent chapters, as a reminder of the fact that other good courses exist and to illustrate the extent to which they may be comparable. This decision – to refer to the SIT TESOL certificate – was taken to exemplify, and there is no significance to be attached to the fact that other good courses are not mentioned here.

The School for International Training differs from Cambridge ESOL and Trinity College London in that courses leading to the award of its TESOL Certificates are available at its headquarters. These courses may also be taken in 14 other locations, including 9 outside the United States. All certificate courses run under its name are evaluated through a process that is similar to the assessment/moderation process carried out by Cambridge ESOL and Trinity College London. This process is referred to in SIT documentation as 'evaluation' (and so the person with this function is known as an **evaluator**) rather than external assessment or moderation. As three courses are primarily referred to in this book, and each organization uses a different term for the person who visits a course to ensure that it is being run according to the standards supplied by the validating organization, the generic term **visiting validator** will be used instead when referring to this function.

To complicate matters further, you may also find courses that appear to be validated, but closer inspection reveals that in fact it is a parent or professional organization that is providing the 'validation' via a subscription service.

The effect this external validation has on the providers of alternative courses is that they can:

> ... feel obliged to come up with similar forms of approval and accreditation. Some of these will be genuinely beneficial, others more spurious. One misleading ruse is to become corporate members of teaching and training bodies. While membership of these is of interest, it's a red herring in terms of any sort of quality certificate.
>
> *Education Guardian, TEFL, 27 September 2004b*

In order to begin to distinguish those certificate courses which are 'genuinely beneficial' from those which are not, first consider validation. If the course you are considering is a Cambridge ESOL CELTA or a Trinity College London CertTESOL, you can be certain that the course will fall into the 'genuinely beneficial' category. If it is not one of these courses, however, do not reject it out of hand, but do confirm in the first instance that the course is at least 100 hours long, because a course length of 100 hours or more distinguishes full certificate courses from introductory courses, which are usually much shorter. Next, examine carefully the teaching practice and guided observation components.

Supervised teaching practice and guided observation

Teaching practice in the CELTA/CertTESOL approach must consist of a minimum of six hours, and must be with students who are genuine English language learners rather than your fellow participants (though such peer teaching may be offered as an additional – and useful – feature of any course). You should also look for a tutor to participant ration of 1:6, or better. To get the best return from your investment, reject any course that has no practical component. After all, would you employ a 'teacher' who had never taught?

> Reject any course that does not give you the opportunity to teach English language learners for at least six hours.

Guided observation, of which there should be at least six hours as well (if the CELTA/CertTESOL approach is being followed), must be of experienced teachers of English language. Some of your observation may be of classes that have been video-recorded, which is acceptable; for example, Cambridge ESOL specifies that of the six hours of guided observation on a CELTA course, two hours may be video-recorded. Both teaching practice and guided observation should be distributed throughout the course.

The commercial success of some validated certificate courses, combined with the growth and development of the internet and access to it, has led to the availability of certificate courses online or by distance learning. In judging such courses, the same criteria apply, so because they are online or by distance learning it is unlikely that they will readily meet the criterion of having a practical component in the form of regular teaching practice. While some may offer this at the end of the course, this is a far from ideal arrangement as one of the strengths of a good course is the opportunity it provides for you to put the ideas that you are learning about into immediate practice.

Recognition and reputation

So you have found a course you want to take, and although it is not validated by Cambridge ESOL or by Trinity College London, it does meet the criteria of course length (it is more than 100 hours long); a tutor to participant ratio of 1 : 6; teaching practice (it has 6 hours of supervised teaching practice, distributed throughout the course); and guided observation (it allows you to observe 6 hours of live classes with experienced teachers, also distributed throughout the course). You still need to consider two more critical factors.

First, is the certificate recognized or accepted by employers you would want to work for? Does it have a good reputation? In answering these questions, think about the short term as well as the long term. Where will you look for work upon qualifying? Where do you see yourself working in 10 years' time? In 20 years' time? If you are in any doubt about the value of the certificate you have in mind, contact a centre or centres where you might be interested in employment, and ask them if they would accept teachers with the qualification you are considering. Ask them if they think the centre you are considering has a good reputation. If their answers are 'no' then clearly you would be making a very poor investment indeed.

The last factors that you need to consider include the centre staff and facilities.

Centre staff, facilities and procedures

You should look for centres that have more than one certificate tutor. This is a mandatory feature of both CELTA and CertTESOL courses, for example, and for a number of good reasons. One tutor can cover for the other in the event of absence; two people provide a richer training environment in terms of offering you exposure to different experience, styles and ideas; and, in the event of interpersonal difficulties, you would always to be able to approach another tutor. Tutors must have a qualification in ELT at diploma level or equivalent as a minimum, plus significant teaching experience. For example, Cambridge ESOL documentation states that CELTA tutors are required to:

- have the Cambridge ESOL DELTA or equivalent ELT qualification at Diploma level (MAs in ELT with a strong practical focus may also be acceptable provided the following two conditions are also met)

- have substantial, recent and varied ELT experience

- be able to demonstrate professional involvement in ELT.

Cambridge ESOL, 2005b

Trinity College London documentation states that:

Course directors must have one of the following as a minimum qualification:

- Trinity College London Licentiate Diploma TESOL

- Cambridge ESOL (UCLES/RSA) Diploma (DTEFLA/DELTA)

- PGCE in TEFL or with TEFL as a main component

- a qualification in English language teaching of at least equivalent content and depth to the above, i.e. placed at Level 5 within the UK National Qualifications Framework or a recognised equivalent in or outside the UK.

Course directors must have substantial, recent English language teaching and documented teacher training experience.

Course tutors must have one of the following as a minimum qualification:

- Trinity College London CertTESOL

- Cambridge ESOL (UCLES/RSA) Certificate (CTEFLA, CELTA)

- a qualification in English language teaching of at least equivalent content and depth to the above, i.e. placed at Level 4 within the UK National Qualifications Framework or a recognised equivalent in or outside the UK.

Course tutors must have recent English language teaching and documented training experience.

Trinity College London, 2005b

Many centres, with a policy of transparency, will publish the qualifications of their tutors, so it will be easy for you to see how well they match up to the criteria presented above. If, however, you find yourself applying to a centre where they are not so readily available for scrutiny, then you should consider why this might be the case, and think carefully before applying to that centre.

As well as qualified staff, centres offering validated courses need to be able to provide you with a range of facilities and resources. Trinity College London states that these must include:

- photocopying facilities

- overhead projectors

- a suitable range of reference and teacher training materials, and teaching **course books**, including a range of periodicals [...]

- a suitable range of audio and video material and equipment

- a suitable range of **realia** for materials-making projects

- some access to word processing and internet facilities.

Trinity College London, 2005b

> 'Realia' means real objects used for teaching purposes. For example, if you are teaching the grammatical concepts of **countable** and **uncountable nouns**, you might take some food into your class in order to help you: 'an apple' and 'some rice'; or 'a grape' and 'some milk'. For each pair of words, the first is countable – 'one apple', 'two apples'; while the second is uncountable – we do not normally speak about 'two rices' or 'three milks'.

In addition to these resources, Trinity College London requires its centres to provide premises that meet local health and safety regulations, which are adequately lit, heated and ventilated (no mention is made of air-conditioning, a necessity in some countries) and in a reasonable state of repair, cleanliness and decorative order. Premises must be free from extraneous noise and must include sufficient space for workshops for all participants; quiet space for study and preparation; and private space for one-to-one tutorials. Rooms must be equipped with appropriate furniture to allow note-taking in workshops, and refreshment facilities must be pro-

> I once assessed a certificate course that took place mostly in a large windowless basement room which was in a state of some disrepair and was known to be home to a number of rats. The electricity supply was regularly interrupted and participants and tutors were left literally, rather than metaphorically, in the dark. The place was affectionately known among staff and participants as the 'TEFL dungeon'.

vided, with drinks being available on the premises as an absolute minimum. Where food is not available, you should be directed to a local source of reliable food (Trinity College London, 2005b).

Good centres should also have appeals and complaints procedures. Trinity College London documentation, for example, provides details of what to do if you are unhappy with your grade or an aspect of your course (Trinity College London, 2005a and 2005b).

Course selection criteria and process: a summary

The course selection criteria and process described above may be summarized as follows:

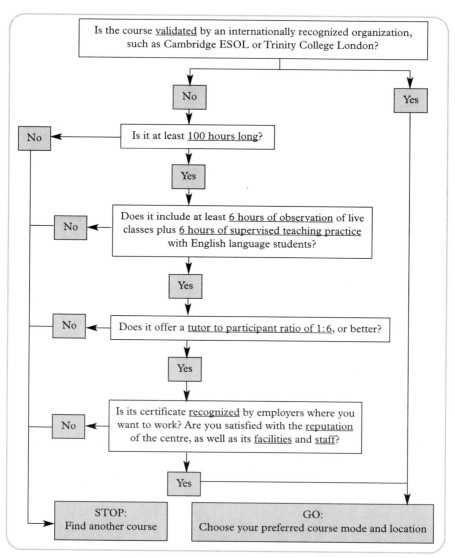

Figure 3.1 Recommended course selection criteria and process

As I have discussed earlier, two organizations currently validate the most widely accepted and recognized certificates. Statements such as the following are common:

> The most widely-accepted 'industry-standard' entry-level qualifications are the Cambridge Celta and Trinity CertTesol. These are both recognised by the Qualifications and Curriculum Authority (QCA) and are the minimum qualifications accepted by the British Council in the UK. Overseas these two have the widest possible appeal, and will be mentioned the most in job ads as something like 'Celta, Trinity or equivalent'.
>
> *Education Guardian, 27 September 2004a*

The CELTA and CertTESOL are without question widely recognized and accepted. They are also comparable, and many other good 'equivalent' courses model themselves on these. For these reasons, the model provided by these two courses is the broad focus of the remainder of this book.

▶ TAKING A CERTIFICATE COURSE: SOME ALTERNATIVES

Having established that your course fulfils the criteria described here, you are now in a good position to consider the mode of delivery that you would prefer. Choosing a course delivery mode that suits your personality and preferences is vitally important, to the extent that it can affect your enjoyment of the experience and the outcome. Before you are in a good position to choose, however, you should familiarize yourself with the range of options that are available to you.

It used to be the case that ELT/TESOL certificate courses were only available as four-week, full-time courses. Now, partly because there is a great deal of competition among institutions for participants, and partly because there is also a growing appreciation of learners' different learning styles, needs and preferences, once you begin to make enquiries you will find that providers offer courses in a wide variety of delivery modes. For example, you will be able to choose from courses that are:

- part-time
- full-time
- modular (e.g. in a two-week block; followed at a later stage by another two-week block)
- by distance learning or with a distance learning component
- online.

Remember, however, that some course delivery modes make a teaching practice component more difficult to arrange. Distance learning and online modes are both examples that fall into this category, and it is recommended that you think twice before committing yourself to a course offered in either of these modes.

Full-time courses

Taking a full-time, intensive course is a little like taking on a new full-time job, plus homework. You have all the stresses, strains and excitements of a new job plus assignments and/or preparation for the next day, still to be done at the end of what would be, for most people, a normal but very tiring working day. Former participants have described the full-time experience as extremely tough. They have described it as physically and mentally one of the hardest things they have ever had to do, observing, for example, that while on the course they often did not get enough exercise or sleep and they failed to eat well, as they tended to snack or skip meals. Several have said that they or their fellow participants eventually became run down and caught colds or influenza, or developed stress-related minor ailments. However, former participants have also enjoyed the intensity of a full-time course and appreciated being able to complete it in a comparatively short time.

> Trainees have described their full-time courses as giving them 'a short, sharp shock to the system' and 'a real buzz'.

Why should a full-time course be quite so demanding? The answer is straightforward. Not only do you have a considerable amount to learn as a participant on a full-time course, consisting of fundamental concepts, skills and techniques (described in Chapter 4), but – and this understanding is crucial to much of what this book is about – you also have to demonstrate that you have learned these concepts, skills and techniques to your tutor's satisfaction. Consequently, as well as learning a great deal in a very short time, there is the additional pressure of having your work evaluated for much of that time, while you do it. 'Work' in this context has a broad definition: as you might expect, it includes every hour of your teaching practice and all of your written work. But it also includes your overall course participation, such as how you interact with your fellow participants and your learners, how you respond to the new ideas presented in **input** sessions, how capable you are of identifying your own strengths and weaknesses after a teaching practice class, and how receptive you are to the feedback you receive from both fellow participants and your tutor. It would be safe to assume that you are under close scrutiny for much of the time!

> Not only is there a great deal to learn in theory, but it has to be put immediately into practice, too, and while tutors are observing. Moreover, it needs to be carried out to a satisfactory standard.

The intensity of a full-time course means that you may find you have little time in which to reflect upon your day, and all that you have been presented with. Participants on full-time courses have often reported that they frequently wanted to 'just sit and mull over the day's events', as a participant once put it, but they have felt unable to make time for this because of the pressure of the other things that they need to do. **Reflection**, according to specialists in adult education, is an important part of the learning process, because it can bridge the gap between understanding something in theory and being able to apply it in practice. This participant described these two aspects of learning – theory and prac-

> Reflection can help to bridge the gap between understanding something in theory and applying it in practice.

tice – graphically when she said, 'I know what I have to do to pass this course, but when I'm up there teaching it has a tendency to fly out the window.' Reflection is something that is considered in more detail in Chapter 9, where you will find several steps that you can take to support your learning, related to reflection.

Hang on to your lesson plan

However, reflection tends to be squeezed out in a full-time mode, as there is so much else to attend to. Somehow, with all the lessons that need to be planned, the liaison with fellow participants that you need to do, the **portfolio** that has to be maintained and the assignments that need to be written, reflection fails to be a priority. Lack of sufficient reflection can be an issue on full-time courses, because it can interfere with your ability to absorb new ideas and,

> 'The tight schedule – study, teach, study – meant that we did what we needed to do to get the teaching or assignments done. There was not much time for reflecting until it was all over.'
>
> Full-time course participant, Spain

therefore, your ability to demonstrate what you have learned to your tutors. This can be very frustrating, particularly if you are the kind of person who needs more time than others in which to digest new ideas. You may leave the course with the feeling that you would have enjoyed the experience more or earned a better grade, if only you had had more time in which to think about it all.

But the intensity and pressure of a full-time course suit many people. Many former participants have said that they loved the charged atmosphere, and that they responded positively to it by putting all their energy into the course. So if you are the kind of person that thrives under pressure, can cope with having little time during the course for reflection (there is, after all, likely to be much more time for reflection once the course has finished), and you love challenges that are at once physically and mentally demanding (think in terms of needing physical, mental and emotional stamina), then a full-time course may well suit you.

Such full-time courses often particularly suit people who want to return to, or start, full-time work as fast as possible, or who are willing to move away from home to a centre – possibly overseas – perhaps because they find the location interesting, or there is the possibility of employment in the centre or the country afterwards, or the price is more affordable.

If on the other hand you feel that you would prefer to have more time in which to reflect and prepare, and you cannot or do not want to put the rest of your life on hold, then you should be considering taking a part-time course.

Part-time courses

It is possible to find part-time courses held over periods of time ranging from 12 weeks to an academic year of 32 weeks or longer. The choice is yours. Some courses may offer a brief full-time period (typically, this will be the first week) followed by 11 weeks of part-time study. This can suit people who are able to take a week off work, but would not want to take much longer; and from the tutors' perspective, an intensive period of contact at the start of the course can be good for the dynamics of the group, as everyone has a good opportunity to get to know one another. It is also useful to be able to

> 'There are substantial advantages for me in having the course over 2.5 months with the ability to continue with some work. The main one is financial, with the monthly pay cheque.'
>
> Part-time course participant, Hong Kong

cover a significant amount of fundamental material, before, for example, teaching practice gets underway. However, not all part-time courses offer a full-time first week, and the arrangement may not suit you in any case.

Depending on the local conditions, and your own preferences, you may be able to find a part-time course near where you live that will allow you to continue working and living at home. Clearly, the experience of taking a part-time course while you continue to live at home near family and friends, possibly continuing in employment, is going to be rather different from taking a full-time course which may entail giving up work, moving to another town or country, finding your way around, getting temporary accommodation and making new friends.

It is a common misconception to think that taking a part-time course is easier than taking one full-time. In whichever mode you are considering taking a CELTA or a CertTESOL course, for example, you will cover the same syllabus and be expected to meet the same criteria, and, while different, both modes are challenging. On a full-time course, you are under a lot of pressure, but you may find it easier to give your full attention to the course; in part-time mode, on the other hand, you may have far more time in which to reflect and think, but you may well have more distractions from other areas of your life.

> Don't fall into the trap of believing that a part-time course is easier than a full-time one.

Although having more time in which to reflect is one of the main benefits, there are other advantages to taking a part-time certificate course. One of the most significant is more time in which to research and prepare for teaching practice and assignments. You may even have enough time available to allow you to practise your lessons with the help of family or friends, before you 'go live', so to speak. You could also find that you are able to get to know your learners, your fellow course participants and your tutors better. And of course, many people find that it is financially easier to be able to continue to work while taking a part-time course.

However, many participants have reported a significant disadvantage to taking the course part-time. They have observed that the work of the course tends to expand to fill all of the available time. In other words, while someone on a full-time course might take 30 minutes to prepare a lesson, someone on a part-time course could find that they take 2 hours to prepare a

> Stay vigilant with regard to how you use your time on a part-time course. Remember the old adage: 'Work tends to expand to fill the available time', and make sure that you are using all of your time effectively.

similar lesson, simply because they have more available time. There is therefore a greater need on a part-time course to monitor how you are using your time, to ensure that it is being used effectively: it may be better, for example, to plan your lesson in one hour and use the rest of the time to read. The important thing is to be proactive about your use of time, to set yourself targets and to manage your study time, rather than letting it manage you. See Chapter 6, 'A time for all things', for more useful advice and strategies for time management in this context.

Other ways of taking a certificate course

Part-time and full-time courses dominate the ELT/TESOL certificate market. However, it is possible to find other course modes, including semi-intensive courses, held, for example, four days a week for five weeks. Less common are modular courses, which may differ from full-time, semi-intensive and part-time modes in that they are run in blocks of time spread over a longer period. For example, you may find a course which is held in four week-long blocks, spread over six months or longer. Or you may find a course that is offered in two-week blocks over a four-month period.

To summarize, regardless of whether the course you are considering is full-time and intensive, semi-intensive, part-time, modular or by distance or online – and regardless of where in the world the course is located – to ensure value for money the most important factors to look for remain:

- validation by an internationally recognized organization
- course content, including 6 hours of supervised teaching practice with language learners and 6 hours of guided observation of live classes
- total course length of at least 100 hours
- recognition and acceptance by employers, and the reputation of the centre and its certificate
- centre staffing, including tutor to participant ratio of 1 : 6
- centre facilities, resources and procedures.

In Chapter 4, you can read about why a good certificate course is designed with the features described above.

Becoming qualified: Key points to take away with you

- You will find it easier to get a better job, in terms of salary, working conditions, and opportunities if you have a good initial qualification. You will also increase your mobility between employers.

- The current CELTA course, administered by Cambridge ESOL, has evolved from, first, the Preparatory Certificate or Prep. Cert, then the later Royal Society of Arts Certificate in Teaching English as a Foreign Language to Adults (the RSA CTEFLA).

- The two largest validating organizations in the United Kingdom are Cambridge ESOL, which offers a Certificate in English Language Teaching to Adults, also known as CELTA; and Trinity College London, which offers a Certificate in TESOL, or CertTESOL. Both of these certificates have good reputations and are well known internationally.

- A validated course such as the CELTA or the CertTESOL will offer at least 100 hours and will include at least 6 hours of guided observation as well as 6 hours of supervised teaching practice and feedback, spread throughout the course.

- A number of other good courses are similar to the CELTA/CertTESOL approach and should not be dismissed. Look for the features that are offered by these courses, and consider your future employers. Do they recognize the certificate you are considering? Do the centre and its certificate have a good reputation?

- Full-time courses may be stressful and may leave you with little time in which to reflect upon the day. But many people respond well to such pressure and are able to give their best. Think carefully before you sign up.

- Part-time courses may give you more time in which to reflect upon your experience. But you could find that the work of the course expands to fill the available time. Pay particular attention on such a course to how you are using your time.

www Check your understanding of Chapter 3 by completing the quiz available on the companion website at: www.sagepub.co.uk/brandt

Chapter 4

Knowing your certificate course

In this chapter you can learn about:

- why certificate courses are designed as they are
- the advantages of taking a standardized course
- the broad areas covered by a good certificate course
- how to recognize syllabus statements and exploit them to your advantage
- some similarities and differences between Cambridge ESOL CELTA and Trinity College London CertTESOL courses
- the six main course components: input, teaching practice, lesson planning, feedback, observation and written assignments
- how you will be assessed.

▶ WHY CERTIFICATE COURSES ARE AS THEY ARE

In Chapter 3, I described the role of validating organizations, such as Cambridge ESOL and Trinity College London, in initial certificate courses in English Language Teaching, and I mentioned that these two organizations currently validate two of the most widely accepted and recognized certificates, the CELTA and the CertTESOL respectively. These organizations do not themselves, however, run certificate courses. Instead, they both provide training centres with a detailed set of intentions in the form of course guidelines, with information about the syllabus, course length, entry requirements, assessment procedures and criteria, the qualifications of training staff and centre resources. Both organizations validate course providers, and they monitor the quality of every course they run. It is left to course providers to design and implement actual courses, based upon the guidelines supplied by the validating organization. As some flexi-

> The relationship between validating organizations and course providers can be compared to that between architects and builders: architects prepare plans, which builders then implement.

bility of design is possible, they are able to do this to some extent with local market conditions in mind. A similarly centralized approach to the certificate syllabus is taken by the School for International Training in the United States. However, unlike Cambridge ESOL and Trinity College London, this organization itself runs courses in its headquarters in the United States, as well as evaluating other courses run under its name in several other locations in the United States and overseas.

There is therefore a clear-cut division between the roles and responsibilities of Cambridge ESOL and Trinity College London, and their course providers. This may be seen as a determined effort to standardize a course that is held all over the world in a number of modes and in several different types of organization. It is an attempt to secure the academic integrity of these courses. Such a move towards standardization offers a number of advantages for everyone involved in the process.

Standardization

From your perspective, standardization means that you can be reasonably confident that you are taking a course that meets comprehensive standards and requirements that have been identified and agreed upon by a professionally qualified body, a process that is monitored by visiting validators. You can also be certain that your fellow participants have had to undergo the same rigorous selection process, and that both your own performances and theirs will be measured against the same criteria. Standardization can therefore help to ensure greater equality and fairness. Having a certificate from a standardized course can also improve your employment opportunities, as employers will be more likely to understand exactly what is meant by a pass on a CertTESOL or a Pass 'B' on a CELTA, because these organizations publish their award criteria.

However, if you take a moment to consider the enormous diversity of certificate courses around the world in terms of institutions (private schools, state colleges, universities, and so forth), language learners (age, first language, education, and so forth), course participants (age, background, reasons for taking a certificate course, for example), and tutors (experience, interests, qualifications, and so forth), you will quickly realize that standardization can only ever be an approximation, and that absolute standardization is an unattainable and unrealistic goal. This is because at the heart of the processes needed to create the product (that is, a person with an ELT/TESOL certificate) are people; and people essentially resist standardization, each having their own unique combinations of preferences, histories and interests (one participant described her tutors as all having 'their own individual peccadilloes'). The product in this case is not something like soap powder, computers, or cars, which readily lend themselves to standardization.

> While standardization offers stakeholders several advantages, it can also bring a number of problems, because the processes involved in training teachers involve people. And people, with all their various foibles, defy standardization.

People, with all their various foibles, defy standardization

Syllabus statements

First, I shall consider the standards that validating organizations, such as Trinity College London and Cambridge ESOL , have developed, showing later how these standards are applied by centres when they run certificate courses. In order to cover a range of available courses, I will consider here the syllabus supplied by three different organizations: the United Kingdom-based Cambridge ESOL and Trinity College London, and the United States-based School for International Training. I do not want to repeat information that is well articulated and readily available elsewhere (in each case, details of the complete syllabus can be found by following the links on the individual organization's website: see **www**). Instead, I hope to provide an overview, showing some of the similarities among, and differences between, the three courses.

The syllabus for all three courses includes the development of teaching skills (expressed as two components – teaching and classroom practices – by the School for International Training) and explicit knowledge (often called awareness) of English language and second language acquisition. These areas are expressed in terms of broad **aims** (the term used by Cambridge ESOL and Trinity College London) or 'goals' (used by the School for International Training). Two examples of these are shown below:

The course enables candidates to:

- acquire essential subject knowledge and familiarity with the principles of effective teaching

- acquire a range of practical skills for teaching English to adult learners

- demonstrate their ability to apply their learning in a real teaching context

Cambridge ESOL, 2005a

The overall goal of the course is for participants to be able to successfully *plan, teach,* and *evaluate* an ESOL lesson.

School for International Training, 2005c

These broad intentions are further broken down into 5 units (for both CELTA and CertTESOL), and 29 discrete **objectives** (for the SIT TESOL Certificate), arranged into the three broader areas of 'plan', 'teach' and 'evaluate'. Examples of the 29 objectives include:

- Write clear learning objectives appropriate for students.

- Develop rapport with students and create a respectful, secure, motivating, learner-centered environment.

- Discuss how student learning objectives were met with supporting evidence from individual students and from large group behaviour.

School for International Training, 2005c

Both CELTA and CertTESOL are described in greater detail, with Cambridge ESOL providing most detail in terms of units, content, and **learning outcomes** as well as information about assessment processes and criteria. However, both validating organizations eventually arrive at a list of **statements** along similar lines to the 29 objectives supplied by the School for International Training. These are called 'learning outcomes' by Cambridge ESOL and 'learning objectives and components' by Trinity College London, but their purpose is essentially the same: to provide a clear statement of what is expected of you as a participant on one of these courses. To avoid confusion, when referring to 'outcomes', 'objectives', and 'components', I shall use the broader term 'statement'. You should be able to read a set of statements for the course you are considering before you commit yourself. If they are not available, look for another course. Example statements, arranged according to units, for each of the five units of CELTA courses are as follows:

> It does not matter whether the course you are considering is described in terms of 'learning outcomes', 'components' or 'objectives', providing you are given, or can locate, a set of clear statements which tells you what is expected of you. If such statements are not available, consider taking another course.

Unit 1: Learners and teachers and the teaching and learning context

Successful candidates can:

1.1 demonstrate an understanding of the range of backgrounds and experiences that adult learners bring to their classes

Unit 2: Language analysis and awareness

Successful candidates can:

2.1 understand key terminology in ELT to talk about language and apply this terminology to planning and teaching

Unit 3: Language skills: reading, listening, speaking and writing

Successful candidates can:

3.1.1 Demonstrate an awareness of basic concepts and terminology used for describing reading skills, and apply this to planning and teaching

Unit 4: Planning and resources for different teaching contexts

Successful candidates can:

4.1a understand the purpose and principles for effective teaching of adult learners

Unit 5: Developing teaching skills and professionalism

Successful candidates can:

5.1a arrange the physical features of the classroom to suit the learners and the type of lesson, and ensure safety regulations are taken into account

Cambridge ESOL, 2005a

Example statements for each of the CertTESOL's five units are as follows:

Unit 1: Teaching skills

Trainees develop:

- an understanding and ability to put into practice basic TESOL methodologies, in a manner appropriate to course and lesson aims, and the learners' background and learning objectives

Unit 2: Language awareness

- Trainees develop:

  an understanding of the basic relationship between linguistic form (phonological, lexical and syntactic), **function** and meaning in standard English and the principal concepts and terminology used to describe the structure and use of English

Unit 3: The learner profile

Trainees address the needs of an individual learner through the preparation of a linguistic profile and needs analysis for one learner of English and the preparation of a one-to-one lesson.

Unit 4: The materials assignment

Trainees plan, produce, use and evaluate a selection of classroom teaching materials of principally their own design and prepare a written rationale and evaluation describing the following: the materials and the learners for which they are intended, the ways in which they are to be used, ways in which they might be adapted for other learners and the ways in which they were and were not successful when used in teaching practice.

Unit 5: The unknown language

Trainees receive four hours' tuition with an oral/**aural** bias in an unknown foreign language through the medium of that language only, to gain first-hand experience of a learner's difficulties and to see in practice some of the methods and approaches introduced to them elsewhere.

Trinity College London, 2005a

While you should study carefully all course information supplied by the validating organization, these statements are a particularly valuable resource to you both before the course is underway and once it has started, because they provide you with a vital source of information about what you need to do in order to pass or excel.

However, participants in the past have sometimes dismissed them. They have felt that they were 'too technical', or 'too much to take in'. Others have said things like 'The outcomes? Yes, but they're for the tutors, aren't they? They're not really for us.'

> Don't ignore the set of statements provided by the organization that validates your course. See them instead as a valuable resource that can help you succeed. Study them before your course and refer to them during it. Ask your tutor about them if anything is unclear.

Of course, tutors find them essential, but they are there for you as well. No one expects you take them in – instead, use them for guidance, as an unequivocal indication of what validating organizations intend to happen and what you will be expected to do.

The CELTA, CertTESOL and TESOL Certificate: some similarities

There is considerable similarity in terms of overall course content and approach between the syllabuses for the CELTA, CertTESOL and TESOL Certificate, and this is the main reason why it is suggested that there is a commonly found approach which is worth knowing about if you are considering an alternative to one of these courses. Although the list above includes only the very first statement that appears in the documentation for each area, it is easy to see from this limited and random sample that there are several common threads. All three address the following broad areas:

- classroom practice
- planning lessons and using resources
- acquiring basic ELT/TESOL terminology
- language awareness
- understanding language learners and what it is like to be in their position.

All three emphasize development of the following:

- an ability to apply knowledge in practice
- skills of evaluation, self-evaluation and reflection
- an awareness of professional development and the part played by a certificate course.

The CELTA and CertTESOL: some differences

Courses leading to a CELTA or a CertTESOL in particular are frequently assumed to be broadly identical. This may be because of the number of features that they have in common, some of which were described above. However, some of the differences between these two courses are significant, and these are explained below.

One difference relates specifically to the external validation process. One of the features and strengths of a validated course is that the centre offering the course will be regularly subject to a visit by a validator:

> The crucial factor for both exam boards is that each of their courses, wherever in the world they are run, is visited by an external assessor (Cambridge) or moderator (Trinity). Their job is to check that tutors are following the strict syllabus, that trainees' coursework and teaching is up to scratch and that the grades being awarded are appropriate.
>
> *Education Guardian, 27 September 2004b*

CertTESOL courses are moderated (by a Trinity College London-appointed moderator) while CELTA courses are assessed (by a Cambridge ESOL-appointed assessor). In both cases an independent person (that is, someone who is not involved with courses at the centre in question) is required to visit each course that takes place. There are differences in how someone is selected to perform this function. In the case of Trinity College London, a moderator is assigned to a course by the central organization, while Cambridge ESOL allows CELTA centre staff to select an assessor from a list. From your perspective as a participant, however, the notion of moderation rather than assessment means that on a CertTESOL course you will find that the moderator interviews you and your colleagues individually and as a group, and he or she will also assess one of your written assignments; while on a CELTA course you could find (as not all participants are selected) that the assessor observes you doing your teaching practice, at the same time as your tutor does.

On a CertTESOL course, you will spend some time learning an (ideally) new language to help you to appreciate the problems faced by your language learners. While this component is required by Trinity College London, it is not required by Cambridge ESOL. Nevertheless, many CELTA courses do include a foreign language lesson, and where this is the case, on both courses you will be encouraged to reflect upon and analyse your reactions to the experience afterwards, although you will not be tested on your proficiency in the new language (see Chapter 6, 'The foreign language lesson', for a broader discussion of this topic).

If you successfully complete a CELTA course, you may be awarded a Pass, a Pass 'B' or a Pass 'A'. Everyone who successfully completes a Trinity College London CertTESOL course is awarded a Pass.

Graduates of CELTA courses will find that their certificate is graded as a Pass, a Pass 'B' or a Pass 'A', while CertTESOL graduates will receive an ungraded certificate, though some centres may in practice choose to endorse this with a covering letter which allows for differentiation.

The Trinity College London website provides this summary of the similarities and differences between CELTA and CertTESOL:

> CELTA is a similar teacher training qualification to the CertTESOL and is offered by Cambridge ESOL. Although similar in its content, mode of delivery and assessment, the two courses differ in terms of more specific components and types of moderation and assessment. Trinity lays great emphasis on reflective journal writing, professional development and self-evaluation for trainees. Both courses are accepted by the British Council as initial TESOL qualifications for teachers in its accredited institutions in the UK and in its own teaching operations overseas.
>
> *Trinity College London, 2005c*

The differences that exist between the two courses, however, are far outweighed by the similarities and on the whole are more to do with the prominence assigned to each area rather than to the presence or absence of an entire area. This is because there is broad agreement in the profession over what the beginning teacher needs to learn. So if you are considering a course that is not one of those described here, you might find it useful to compare its syllabus with that of one of the above, to be certain that the course you are considering covers all the main areas (comparing your course with more than one of the three considered here could be confusing, as I am sure will be clear from this discussion, given the various differences in terminology and level of detail available for each).

Course components

The main areas described above (the 'what' of learning to teach ESOL, if you like) are realized in practice through established course components which you will encounter on any good course. Although slightly different terms may be used for each, and different arrangements may be made, essentially these are:

- input
- supervised teaching practice
- lesson planning
- feedback
- guided observation of experienced teachers
- written assignments.

It is also likely that you will be asked to maintain an assessment portfolio, including copies of your lesson plans and materials you used, attend one-to-one tutorials, and possibly be involved during the validator's visit.

These areas are concerned both with the 'what' and with the 'how' of learning to teach ESOL, and are all considered in greater depth below.

A three-way learning opportunity

I suggested above that it is a good idea to study the syllabus of your certificate course, in particular the set of statements or objectives, and to view these as a resource. However, such study can bring you other – perhaps less obvious – benefits, besides an understanding of what you will be required to do on your course.

Your certificate syllabus may well be the first syllabus you have encountered as a teacher. It does not matter that it is aimed at beginning teachers rather than language learners. Those who developed it faced similar problems: how to express a body of knowledge as a set of intentions or statements in such a way that it can be of maximum assistance to its users. If you take the time to study your certificate syllabus, you are beginning to immerse yourself in your new field: current educational practice in ELT/TESOL. And in immersing yourself in this way, you will start to acquire the necessary vocabulary and concepts; for example, the discussion above included terms such as 'aims', 'objectives' and 'learning outcomes'. These are all terms that you will encounter not only as a practising, qualified teacher of ESOL, but also during your own training.

> Use the syllabus to your advantage. Immerse yourself in it and you will begin to acquire some essential ELT/TESOL vocabulary and concepts. You will also start to develop the skills you need to put theory into practice.

Immersing yourself in your syllabus will also help you to begin to think about applying the statements in the classroom. For example, Unit 1 of the syllabus for both the CELTA and the CertTESOL courses includes a reference to language learners and their backgrounds. Here is an opportunity for you to start thinking about language learners in your context. You can ask yourself questions such as: Who are they? Do I know any? Why does he or she want or need to learn English? What is the experience like? In this way, you are beginning to relate a theoretical syllabus to your very practical ELT/TESOL classroom, and doing just that is what it is all about.

> You have a three-way learning opportunity as a certificate course participant: the opportunity to learn from what you are being taught; from how it's being taught; and from applying your learning to your own learners.

In learning how to teach you are also being taught, and you are in turn using what you learn in order to teach your own learners. You have a three-way opportunity to learn from:

- what you are being taught
- how you are being taught
- applying your learning to your own learners in your own classroom.

You can develop this idea further if you recognize that every aspect of the training process is significant to your current learning and your future career; so you can learn from studying your certificate syllabus, as outlined here; but you can also learn from:

> 'I had no idea before the course how a class might run. Now I have observed a class, am being taught in the format, have received instruction on the methods and am now starting to practise and try out some bits of it. By being totally absorbed in the teaching it will hopefully gradually become second nature to me.'
>
> Participant, Hong Kong

- your fellow course participants
- the techniques, methods and materials which your tutors use to teach you
- the interview and pre-course task
- how experienced teachers interact with each other in the staffroom
- the language experienced teachers use to talk about teaching
- how language learners interact with each other, both in class and out of class.

Some of these may seem surprising, and in any case, more important perhaps than any individual suggestion above is your attitude: try to see yourself as being surrounded by learning opportunities. In Chapter 6, 'Learning opportunity or learning support?' this idea is developed further.

❯ THE SYLLABUS IN ACTION

Above, I described the broad aims of courses training new teachers to teach ESOL, and suggested that syllabus statements were of particular value to you both before your course and once your course is underway. I indicated that these statements are realized in practice through well-established course components, with names such as 'input' and 'teaching practice'.

Local centres are expected to design their own timetables to fulfill the specific objectives supplied in the syllabus by validating organizations, allocating time to course components as they see fit to ensure that the aims and objectives of the syllabus are met. As a result you will find some variety in interpretation from one course to another. Each decision represents a compromise: more time allocated to one area is less time available for another. This can be

> 'It's a horrible set of compromises that more or less works in a commercial reality.'
>
> Tutor, New Zealand

difficult if you find you would like to know more about a particular area, but you see that there is no more time on the timetable allocated to it. For this reason, some courses offer sessions, particularly towards the end of the course, where participants are able to suggest the topic or topics that they would like to know more about.

Exactly what each of these components means for you as a course participant is explored below.

Input

Input (which may be referred to as workshops or seminars; my preference is for 'workshop', for reasons described below) is one of the principal means on certificate courses of conveying the content or the 'what' of the course. You will find that at least half of your course time will be allocated to workshops. They cover various aspects of teaching, and you can expect to find workshops with names such as 'Language awareness 1', 'Phonology 1', 'Lesson planning', 'The learner', 'Receptive skills 1', and 'Error correction'.

It is recommended that you prepare for each workshop as much as you can, even if this means simply being aware of the topic to come and mulling it over in your mind before the workshop. However, workshop titles such as 'Language awareness 1' can be less than helpful when it comes to preparation. You might well ask: which broad area of language? Grammar, **lexis** (another word for vocabulary), phonology, discourse (this means extended text, such as speech or writing) ...? And having identified which area – grammar, for example – you might ask: but which aspect of grammar? Past **tenses**? **Modal auxiliary verbs**? Or – which aspect of phonology? Sounds in isolation? **Intonation**, **word stress**, or **sentence stress**, perhaps?

If you do find yourself faced with a timetable which is expressed in general terms, ask for more information (some tutors admitted to writing broad topics into their timetables to allow for a little flexibility: a more general title allows a tutor to change what he or she plans to teach on any one day). Finding out before a session precisely what it will be about allows you to arrive at that session with a good idea of what is going to be discussed. In other words, you have already oriented yourself towards the topic: you arrive with an idea of what is meant by a 'modal auxiliary verb', you are not daunted

> You don't have to accept your course timetable at face value.
>
> If anything is not detailed enough to guide your preparation for a forthcoming workshop, ask your tutor to tell you exactly what it's going to be about. You need this information to prepare properly.

by the first mention of that rather formidable label, and so you do not have to spend the first 15 minutes settling into the topic, because you have already done that work at home. (As a matter of interest, 'modal' means **mood**.) It is not being suggested that, by way of preparation for workshops, you read through the entire section on this group of verbs in (for example) Downing and Locke's (1992) *University Course in English Grammar* (because the 14 pages on this area would need several hours of study to do them justice, and you would need to understand some linguistic terminology such as 'epistemic' and 'adjunct'). But it is suggested that you simply scan the area in a grammar book that has been recommended to you. (Aitken's (2002) *Teaching Tenses* would be a good place to start, as this book not only includes information about the form and use of each area, but also presents a wealth of teaching suggestions with legally photocopiable worksheets.) It would be enough to discover that you are going to learn more about verbs like 'must', 'need to', 'can', 'can't', 'would', and so forth, and that it is a complex and interesting area.

Above, I suggested that the term 'workshop' may be preferable to the widely used 'input'. This is because 'input' is suggestive of information moving in one direction, while in practice you will experience a great deal of interaction with fellow participants and with your tutors, through pairwork, group work, whole class discussion and brainstorming. You may also be called upon to lead a session, or a part of a session, yourself or with a fellow participant. These sessions, then, are quite different to the lectures that you might have experienced while an undergraduate, for example. This is because of the nature of the course: it is experiential and practical, and in many cases tutors will make use, while teaching you, of techniques that are standard practice when teaching language learners (pairwork is a good example of this). This is one of the reasons for the advice given above, when it was suggested that you take a conscious and proactive interest in all aspects of the experience.

Supervised teaching practice

Supervised teaching practice, often referred to as **TP**, is another major certificate course component. On all three of the courses discussed above (CELTA, the CertTESOL and the SIT TESOL Certificate), course participants are required to teach for at least six hours, and teaching practice must be arranged to allow each participant to teach two different levels for at least two hours at each level. Centres are expected to timetable this component to occur on a 'continuous basis'. This means that it would not be acceptable if your teaching practice was arranged in three periods of two hours each, all on the last three days of the course, for example. Instead, it should be spread throughout the entire course length, taking place at more or less regular intervals.

You will be asked to teach two different levels of learners, one at **elementary** level and one at **intermediate** level or above. It is highly unlikely that you will be asked to teach complete **beginners** or **advanced** learners, as these are considered to be specialist areas requiring more sophisticated approaches. (For more information about levels and their labels, see Chapter 8, 'Working with language learners'.)

There are various approaches to finding learners for teaching practice purposes. Many centres advertise 'free lessons' internally. In a large centre this will generally attract enough learners from the enrolled population. However, you may find that language learners are brought in from outside the school.

On many courses, especially those with more than five or six participants, it will be arranged so that you work as part of a teaching practice group. It is often designed so that each group will teach one level of language learners for half the course and then

> 'I worried a lot about which TP group I would get landed with, as I could see that this was going to be an integral part of the course.'
>
> Participant, Hong Kong

another level for the other half. Tutors will also change groups, so that your teaching practice group will have one tutor for the first half and another tutor for the second half.

On a CELTA course, you will probably find that teaching will be divided up among the participants in your group, with each of you sharing the teaching of a lesson at the beginning of the course (perhaps five of you will teach for 20 minutes each) progressively building up to teaching a complete one hour lesson by the end. (On a CertTESOL course, you may find that there is less emphasis on team teaching and **peer observation**.) On courses where you are expected to observe your peers, anyone not teaching while other members of the teaching practice group are teaching will normally be set a task to complete while observing. When one lesson is shared by several participants, extensive cooperation and collaboration is required of the members of your group in order to create a single cohesive, coherent lesson from the learners' point of view: it would be exhausting for them to receive five unrelated lessons in a single two-hour class, even with a short break. Former participants have reported that when it works well, such collaboration can be 'liberating and exhilarating'; but others have reported problems in this area, because they found themselves expected to collaborate with people with whom they did not get along. Not getting on with the other members of your group, or having one member who does not get along with the rest, can be particularly difficult because a great deal rests on your teaching practice. However, by staying alert to possible difficulties in this area when you are being assigned to your teaching practice group, you may be able to avoid future problems, either by approaching a tutor and requesting a move from one group to another or by arranging to exchange places with a fellow participant. This may not be possible, though, or the decision may be made too early on in the course for you to have formed an opinion of someone which enables you to decide whether or not you can work together. For this reason, various strategies for dealing with such interpersonal issues in this particular context are suggested in Chapter 8, 'Collaboration matters'.

I mentioned above that a great deal rests on your teaching practice. In fact, it is one of the main components used for assessment, and you should obtain a set of criteria that will be used to judge your teaching practice performance, and study them in much the same way as was suggested above in relation to syllabus statements. In the CELTA syllabus, for example, it is described as one of the two assessment components, under 'Course requirements and components of assessment' (Cambridge ESOL,

> The term 'teaching practice' is a bit misleading. It might be better to call it 'Assessment of Teaching Skills' or something similar, because so long as a tutor is present, he or she is making judgements that will be used to arrive at a final decision about your progress.

2005a); the other assessment component is 'Classroom-related written assignments', and to this extent the term 'teaching practice' may be a misnomer. In fact, there may be no opportunity for you to practise without a tutor being present. If you would like to read more about the teaching practice/assessment dilemma from an academic perspective, see Brandt (2006).

Teaching practice is always followed by an oral feedback session, and this component is discussed below.

Lesson planning

You can expect course time to be allocated to lesson planning, but you should also expect to spend a great deal of your own 'free' time on this aspect. Many former participants have reported that they spent more time on preparing lesson plans than on any other single course component; for example, participants have reported spending from five to eight hours preparing for a one hour lesson. As a result, you may feel that the time you devote to planning is out of proportion to the actual lesson itself. If you experience this, try not to worry. First of all, it is normal to spend a long time planning at this stage, when so much is new; and secondly, you will find that as you learn and progress through the course and through your first months in a teaching job, certain things will become 'second nature' to you, and so less time and effort will be required in preparation.

Tutors, particularly in the early stages of your course, will set lesson aims (which may be known as **teaching practice points**; see Chapter 7, 'Teaching practice') and they will provide you with material to use. Tutors will also help you to plan your lesson and identify relevant material when it is not being supplied. The support provided by your tutors early on in your course is likely to be gradually reduced as you are observed demonstrating the necessary skills.

Feedback

Feedback usually takes place immediately after teaching practice, because giving immediate feedback is considered to be 'best practice'. The session will be attended by your tutor and the other members of your teaching practice group, who are all invited to contribute their views on the lesson. You will probably be asked to evaluate your lesson, possibly before receiving feedback from your peers or tutor. You will also receive written feedback from your tutor, and you may be asked to complete a written self-evaluation task after each lesson you give.

A feedback pattern that occurs frequently (though you may well encounter variations on this procedure) is as follows:

- The first participant who has taught is invited to express his or her views of his or her part of the lesson.
- Fellow participants are invited to comment on their teaching peer's performance, one by one.

- The tutor provides his or her comments.
- Any other teaching participants receive their oral feedback following the same approach.
- The tutor hands out written feedback, which has been prepared while the tutor is observing, to each person who has taught.

Tutors frequently employ a positive–negative–positive 'sandwich' approach to giving oral and written feedback, and will normally be expected to make use of a centre-specific template with headings such as 'Stage of the lesson' and 'Comments'. You should ask for a copy of this template if you are not automatically provided with one at the start of your course. See Chapter 7, 'Giving and receiving feedback' for more guidance in this area.

You can expect feedback for a two-hour lesson to last about an hour. If three participants teach for 40 minutes each, they can each therefore expect to receive around 20 minutes of feedback. If, on the other hand, two participants teach for an hour each, as might occur later on in a course, then each would receive approximately 30 minutes of feedback.

One of the issues that has arisen with such arrangements for former participants is that whether or not you yourself are teaching, attending your group's teaching practice and feedback sessions may not be optional. While many former participants appreciated enormously the opportunity to observe each other's teaching practice and listen to each other's feedback, this changed as the course progressed and participants' priorities shifted, particularly as the pressure increased.

You will also find of course that your tutors have different views about teaching (just think how boring it would be if they all held the same view), to the extent that what one tutor considers excellent practice, another may think is a waste of time. There are a number of topics that occur in certificate courses that can cause heated debate among experienced teachers: examples include how to teach pronunciation, the value of **drills** (asking learners to listen to a model and repeat it in different patterns), and the use of a learner's first language. This can cause some difficulty, particularly when tutors become insistent or even dogmatic about something (yes, it can happen!).

Definitions of what counts as an experienced teacher may vary. When I completed a certificate course at International House in Hastings, United Kingdom, in 1982, I was offered a job which started on the Monday after the course had ended. Two weeks later, I found I was being observed by some of the new certificate course participants. Fortunately for them, I was not the only teacher they observed!

Guided observation

Experienced teachers, being individuals with unique sets of skills, experiences and interests, tend to have different views about what constitutes good practice in ELT/TESOL, as suggested above. This is one of the reasons why some six hours of your time on a certificate course will be devoted to observing experienced teachers and their learners. This component may begin with an opportunity to observe your tutor or tutors teaching language learners, and be followed by opportunities to observe a range of other experienced teachers. When you are observing other teachers, you may observe with a fellow participant, but course tutors will not normally be present.

Observing such variety at work will give you an idea of possibilities in terms of teaching and learning styles that are extremely difficult, if not impossible, to convey by any other means. Another reason why this component is considered useful is that it is recognized that learning can take place through observing a 'model' or 'demonstration' of good practice. However, former participants have sometimes thought that they were expected to try to copy this model. They have also sometimes felt that they were being shown a standard 'quite impossible to emulate', as one participant described it. It is better to view this component not as providing you with a model to replicate, but as providing you with exposure to a range of alternative approaches and classroom cultures, of which the teacher is one part, the learners another. You can observe both with a critical eye, adopting a technique or approach when you see a teacher do something that works for his or her learners and that strikes a chord with you.

The idea of looking for practice that strikes a chord is an important one, because the best teachers are those who believe in what they are doing: they have integrity with regard to their classroom practice. Part of your training, from your perspective at least, involves identifying what feels right in your classroom, and allowing a personalized teaching style to emerge.

> When observing another teacher, look for things that he or she does – or doesn't! do – that 'strike a chord' with you. This will help you to develop your own teaching style.

Guided observation is called 'guided' because you will be supplied with a task to do while observing. This task will help to focus your attention on the things that matter, and should relate to the stage of the course you are at and to what is happening in other components. For example, if you have just had a workshop on 'drilling', it makes sense for you to complete an observation task that focuses your attention on this area. However, former participants have found that it is not always possible to see what they have been told to look for. If the task relates to drilling, for example, but the class you are observing that day is doing a reading lesson, then it is unlikely that you will see much drilling, unless the experienced teacher you are observing knows about the task you have been set and so contrives to show you some drilling – a less than ideal situation.

If you find yourself observing a class to which the task you have been set does not apply, do not despair. There are plenty of other useful things that you can study in any lesson, including:

- how much time the learners spend speaking English – to the teacher, to each other
- how much time the teacher spends talking (bear in mind that it is the learners, and not the teacher, who need the practice!)

- how much time the learners spend 'off-task'
- how the classroom is arranged and rearranged as the lesson progresses
- what use is made of visual aids, including a whiteboard
- what kind of notes learners are making (these may be their only record of the lesson)
- what the teacher does to try to motivate his or her learners
- the range of activities that the learners engage in
- learners' different learning styles and approaches
- one particular learner, for the whole lesson
- how the teacher handles any discipline or control issues that may arise
- the teacher's body language – use of gesture, eye contact and so forth
- what errors the learners make, and how the teachers handles them
- how the teacher draws out a quiet learner or calms an excitable one
- how the teacher manages the various transition stages of the lesson, for example, from taking the register, to collecting homework, to setting up an activity, closing it down, and moving on to the next one
- factual elements of a lesson such as the amount of time spent on aspects of it, the language point(s), the number of learners, their breakdown in terms of approximate age, gender, first language.

This list is meant to be suggestive. It is not complete by any means and you will be able to think of your own, particularly as the course progresses. The list may also be useful if you are reading this book before starting your course and you have taken the initiative to observe a class at a welcoming centre beforehand. People have often said, before starting a course, 'but I don't know what to look for'. The list above will give you some ideas.

It may be the case that the teachers you are observing are not, technically, part of the certificate course team but are employed by other departments to teach general English, for example. This may mean that they receive no extra remuneration for the potential work involved in accepting you into their classroom, nor are they given time off in lieu. They may in fact receive very little recognition for the part they play in your training; and moreover they may be extremely busy and have a heavy teaching load in excess of 18 or 20 hours per week. For these reasons, being observed can be unpopular, and it is sometimes difficult, especially in smaller centres, to find teachers willing to be observed. To conserve resources, therefore, you may find that you are observing with a fellow participant or participants. Former trainees have found that such issues can make the relationship with

> The role of the teachers you observe as part of 'guided observation' is ambiguous. They are at once part of your course, yet not part of it. This means that you can't take for granted anything that they might be willing to do for you.

the experienced teacher a little awkward. For example, when observing it is often helpful to be able to discuss the lesson with the teacher before and after it takes place. It is also useful to be able to examine a lesson plan. Unfortunately, however, you may find that none of this can be taken for granted on your certificate course, because of a lack of clarity around the status of these teachers.

As with feedback, guided observation is not an optional component, and former participants have reported experiencing a similar shift in attitude towards it: while they found it vitally important in the early stages, observations were reported by some to become less useful as the course developed. This was often because participants' attention was focused elsewhere, such as on their next teaching practice class (which, because you teach for longer periods as the course progresses, and because you are expected to have learned more, becomes worth more in assessment terms) or their next written assignment. Ways of staying focused on a class that you are observing, and ensuring that time spent observing remains beneficial, are considered in Chapter 6, 'Observing'.

> It's important to stay focused on the benefits of observing a class. Observation gives you access to another classroom culture, and they are all different. You will also have relatively few opportunities to observe another class once you have graduated. from your course.

Written Assignments

You will be expected to complete at least four written assignments. While this may sound like a heavy load, particularly on a four-week full-time course, in fact for CELTA courses the combined word count for these four assignments is no more than 3,000 words. On CELTA courses, assignments focus on:

- adult learning
- the language system of English
- language skills
- classroom teaching.

Other courses may include topics such as:

- keeping a journal, for example recording the experience of learning a foreign language
- reflections on classroom practice
- an aspect of classroom management
- a learner profile or case study
- a materials project

- a survival kit
- an article review.

The purpose of these written assignments is to show that you are able to relate ELT/TESOL theory to practice and that you are familiar with and can use correctly key ELT/TESOL terminology, concepts, and methodology. You are also required to be able to identify your own strengths and weaknesses, and identify steps you would take to address your weaknesses to develop as a teacher once the course is over. You should in all cases be given feedback on your written work, and, depending on the course that you are taking, you will find that some or all of your written assignments are internally assessed by tutors and externally by the visiting validator. If you are taking a CELTA course, and you fail one assignment, you cannot pass the course. However, you should be given the opportunity to re-submit it. Likewise, on a CertTESOL course, you can be referred on one or two units, being given the opportunity to re-submit your work, provided you have demonstrated some potential for progress during the training period (Pugsley, 2005c).

Some courses may require far more of you in terms of written assignments, so, as with other aspects of the course, it is worth checking this one out to make sure that you are getting both what you want and what you are capable of doing. See Chapter 6, 'Written assignments' for more information about these.

Assessment: what to expect

If you take a CELTA, CertTESOL or a TESOL certificate course, you will not have any formal, written examinations of the kind you might recognize from previous education experiences. Instead, you will find that you are more or less continually assessed, and that the specific focus of this assessment is teaching practice and written assignments. On a CertTESOL course, the visiting validator will read the written work you have produced for Unit 4 (The Materials Assignment) and will interview you on the basis of it. The validator can pass or refer you, but not fail you – that is, he or she cannot make you do the whole course again simply because of your performance in this one unit (Pugsley, 2005a).

As you make progress through the course, you will receive frequent feedback on your progress in the form of feedback sessions after teaching practice, one-to-one tutorials and possibly a written mid-course evaluation. You may also be required to keep a portfolio of your work which might be shown to the validating organization or its representative.

Cambridge ESOL describes CELTA assessment as follows:

> You will be assessed throughout the course, with no final examination. [...] There are two components of assessment:

> **Teaching practice**
> You will teach for a total of six hours, working with classes at two levels of ability. Assessment is based on your overall performance at the end of the six hours.

Written assignments

You will complete four written assignments: one focusing on adult learning; one on the language system of English; one on language skills; and one on classroom teaching.

To be awarded the certificate you must pass both components. There are three grades – Pass, Pass 'B' and Pass 'A'.

Cambridge ESOL, 2005c

From this it appears that only teaching practice and written work are assessed but it is important to remember that you are in fact more or less under constant scrutiny.

By now you should have a very clear idea of the 'shape' of ELT/TESOL certificate courses from the perspective of those who provide them. Exactly how this shape can begin to translate into your experience is the subject of the next chapters.

Knowing your certificate course: Key points to take away with you

- Trinity College London and Cambridge ESOL do not run ELT/TESOL certificate courses themselves. Instead they validate courses and provide a syllabus, with details of required course length, entry requirements, assessment procedures and criteria.

- Syllabus statements should be available to you for consideration before you commit yourself to any course. See these as a learning opportunity.

- If you are considering a course other than a Cambridge ESOL CELTA, Trinity College London CertTESOL or School for International Training TESOL Certificate, compare your syllabus with that of one of these courses to be certain that you will be taking a good course that offers value for money.

- As a participant on a certificate course, you have a three-way opportunity to learn: from what you are being taught, from how it is being taught to you, and by applying your learning to your own learners in your own classroom.

- Although different terms may be used, your course should offer: input, supervised teaching practice, lesson planning, feedback, guided observation of experienced teachers, and written assignments. If your timetable does not give you enough information about each component, ask for what you need to know.

- Assessment is mostly continuous, which means that you will be more or less under constant scrutiny.

www **Check your understanding** of Chapter 4 by completing the quiz available on the companion website at: www.sagepub.co.uk/brandt

Getting started

ON YOUR MARKS: APPLYING FOR A PLACE

According to Cambridge ESOL documentation, to apply for a place on a CELTA course you need ideally to:

- have a standard of education equivalent to that required for entry into higher education
- be aged 20 or over
- have a standard of English which will enable you to teach at a range of levels

Centres may still accept you if you do not have formal qualifications at this level but can demonstrate that you would be likely to complete the course successfully. Some centres may, at their discretion, accept applicants aged between 18 and 20.

Cambridge ESOL, 2005c

While Trinity College London documentation states that for a CertTESOL:

- Course providers set their own entry requirements but as a minimum [...] all trainees must have sufficient educational qualifications to gain entry to higher education (i.e. university or equivalent).
- Trinity requires that all trainees be at least 18 years old, but individual course providers may set a higher age limit. Trinity does not stipulate an upper age limit for the course.

Trinity College London, 2005c

Other attributes will also be taken into account. Course providers are likely to consider such matters as your potential aptitude for study and ability to respond to the pressures of teaching, your likely ability to develop rapport with your learners, and your capacity to undertake rigorous training. The School for International Training, for example, in a section entitled 'What are the entrance requirements?', lists attributes of ideal applicants together with what might normally be understood as 'entry requirements'. They write:

> You must have a high school degree and show a capacity for college-level education including a good understanding of the English language and solid writing skills. You must remain calm under pressure, be willing to accept the authority of your trainers, commit to conveying a difference of opinion in a respectful manner, and be willing to work as a positive team player. [...] Non-native speakers typically have a minimum TOEFL score of 550 on the written test or 213 on the computerized version, an IELTS Band 6.0 or higher, or a CEF B2 to C1. Non-native speakers must also have a second interview to ensure their listening/speaking skills are adequate to take the course and to teach English. All participants must show a willingness to plan and teach in groups and to work reflectively.
>
> *School for International Training, 2005a*

Assuming you meet these minimum requirements, or the similar ones that will be set by any centre offering a good certificate course, and assuming you have identified a potential course at a suitable centre, you will then need to go through their application process. This may involve some or all of the following stages:

- completing an application form
- doing a pre-interview task
- attending an interview, or being interviewed by phone
- doing an interview task
- doing a pre-course task.

At each stage of this process, remember that you are entering a competitive market. It is possible to be rejected after completing a pre-interview task or, having survived that stage, after the interview.

One way to ensure that you create for yourself the best possible opportunity for success is to approach the process as if you were applying for a coveted job.

> Approach the application process as if you were applying for a coveted job: because, in a way, you are.

Snapshot of the application stage

Alison Standring, an experienced teacher in ELT/TESOL, describes her reasons for applying for a place on a CELTA course, and her experience of the application process:

My Experience of the CELTA Course

Alison Standring

My reasons for doing a CELTA

I was in my third year of university when I decided to do a CELTA course. My fellow students were applying for jobs in the City, in fields such as marketing, advertising and insurance, none of which really appealed to me. As finals approached and pressure grew, I came up with a plan. I would do a four-week CELTA course as soon as I'd graduated, find a job somewhere exciting for a year and use the time to decide what I really wanted to do 'once I grew up'.

The application process:

The first step was choosing where to apply. After a bit of research, I selected International House in Hastings: International House because it had a good pass rate, and Hastings because it was cheaper than London. The application form included a number of language analysis tasks and I had to head to the library in an attempt to brush up my hazy knowledge of the English language. What *was* the difference between an adverb and an adjective?

After the application form came the interview where three of us tried to illustrate how we would teach an extremely uncooperative student (the interviewer) the meaning of questions such as 'Would you like a cup of coffee?' and 'Do you mind if I close the door?' Despite my questionable handling of the task, I obtained a place on the July CELTA course and, reading list in hand, was determined to prepare myself thoroughly for it. Needless to say, by July, although I'd bought several of the books from the reading list, I hadn't read nearly as many of them as I'd planned. (Given the intensive nature of the CELTA course, this is not a state of affairs I would recommend!)

(continued below)

The application form, pre-course task and the interview that Alison refers to are considered next.

Completing an application form

When you make an initial enquiry, all good centres will require you to complete an application form. As you might expect, this form will ask you for personal details, as well as details of your education and experience, including any teaching experience you may have.

You may be asked to complete a short task at this stage, as part of the application process. Questions at this stage are frequently concerned with why you want to take the course. Below, you can read how one applicant completed this part of her form:

English Language Teaching Certificate

Application form

I would like to apply for the following course : ~~part time 2006~~ / part time 2007

~~full time 2006~~ / ~~full time 2007~~

(Delete as applicable)

Contact details:

Name: Jennifer Ann Scott

Date of birth: October 18th 1980

Please state your reasons for applying for this course. Describe how you expect to benefit from it and how you will be able to contribute towards it. Write 200–300 words.

I am applying for this course because I have always been interested in language, and I enjoy working with people.

As you will have seen from the above information, I studied English Language and Literature at university. I chose English because when I left school I thought I might be a journalist or a writer. But when I graduated two years ago, I wanted to travel before I settled down. I decided to visit Spain, and while I was there I became interested in teaching and learning language, because I found that I often had to 'teach' some English to my Spanish friends, and also because I was trying to learn some Spanish myself.

I like the fact that the course is about teaching adults. I'd thought about teaching before, but I've never been very interested in working with children. I'd prefer to work with people whom I can relate to as an equal, and with whom I might have some things in common.

I think the course will bring all of these interests together for me, and I'd expect to learn more about English from a foreigner's point of view while on the course. I'd also expect to learn more about various techniques to help someone understand something – while trying to teach my Spanish friends I would sometimes get frustrated because I couldn't think of different ways to help them say or understand something.

I'm a very outgoing, sociable sort of person and I think this will help me in the classroom and when working with the other course participants. I also think that my knowledge of English language will help too. I really hope that you are able to offer me a place.

This applicant, although only 25 years old at the time, in answering this question was able to draw upon *a range of experience*, including having:

- studied at university
- learned a foreign language
- worked with speakers of other languages
- lived in a country other than her own.

She also drew upon her *knowledge of the course and her self-awareness*, mentioning how she:

- likes working with adults
- is interested in the English language
- is outgoing and sociable (and so is likely to be able to work well as part of a team).

Once you have completed and submitted an application form, it is likely that you will be asked to complete a more extensive pre-course task or tasks.

Learning from pre-course tasks

When you make an initial enquiry, all good centres will be able to give you extensive written information about the course you are interested in taking. Included in this information may well be various tasks to be completed before the course or possibly before the interview. Alternatively, these tasks may be given to you later, after you have completed an application form and paid for the course. Whichever approach is taken, it is a good idea to study all of the course information in detail. Read it with a highlighter pen to hand, so that you do not have to read through the whole document again in order to locate that key bit of information at a later stage. Note down any questions that come to mind, as well, so that you can either contact the centre to find out the answers, or, alternatively, ask about them during your interview.

Pre-course tasks vary greatly from centre to centre, in terms of number, content, length and purpose. As mentioned above, you might find you need to complete a pre-interview task, an interview task, and/or a pre-course task. If you are planning on taking one of the three courses mentioned above, you will find that, unlike other course components, this one is not standardized. Each centre takes its own approach to this component, and you may find that a task is set in order to help tutors to make judgements about your suitability for a place on their course, but not all centres do this. However, regardless of the course or centre to which you are applying and the approach they take, pre-course tasks will have some features in common. They:

- give you an opportunity to orientate yourself towards the course (one of their aims)
- do not contribute towards your final grade
- may not be marked.

The purpose of these tasks, therefore, may be twofold: to help tutors to make judgements about your suitability, and to help you to orientate yourself. However, former participants have described approaching them entirely as if they were tests, something they

> Your pre-course task will help you to orientate yourself towards the area and the course. Tutors sometimes also use them as screening devices, to help them to make a judgement about your suitability for a place. If the purpose of the task is not clear to you, you should make enquiries.

have later regretted, when they realized that they had missed out on the learning opportunity that they offered. Some came to see that at the time they had been focused more on passing the test rather than learning from doing the tasks.

The former participant who commented that she 'was three weeks into the course when [she] realized how useful the pre-course task should have been' was partially right, then. These tasks can be used for 'testing' purposes; but she had seen only one reason for doing the task. She had not understood that by recognizing and applying the other reason – the one concerned with learning from doing – she could in fact afford to ignore the idea of 'task as test', because 'testing follows learning' – you can only be 'tested' on what you have 'learned'. She had lost an opportunity to learn more effectively and more lastingly. This idea – the idea that if you concentrate on learning for yourself, you can afford not to worry too much about any testing that might be taking place – is an important one, and one that will be revisited a number of times in this book. In the meantime, I will take a look at what you might be asked to do by way of pre-course tasks, and how to set about doing them.

> 'I was three weeks into the course when I realized how useful the pre-course task should have been. I say "should" because actually I just worked to get it done and handed in. The only thing I remember about it is the panic I felt when I saw all those symbols and lines for the sounds.'
>
> Participant, Spain

You will probably also be asked to produce a piece of writing at this stage, and it is quite likely that you will be told not to word process your work but rather to write it by hand. This requirement is to enable tutors to check your literacy skills. While this may sound surprising, it simply reflects the fact that tutors want to ensure that you have the basic skills needed both to complete the course and to be an effective English language teacher. This writing task may be quite personal, allowing you to display your abilities to reflect and to express your self-awareness.

Examples of pre-course tasks

Below, you will find an example of a completed pre-course task. It is anticipated that reading through the worked examples will give you an idea of what is expected of you when you come to do it yourself. These examples should also provide you with an indication of some skills to develop, strategies to employ, and a few resources that you may find helpful at this stage. For these reasons, I have provided suggested 'answers' rather than simply the tasks alone. If you prefer, you could ignore the 'answers' supplied and do the tasks yourself, comparing your own ideas with the 'answers' when you have finished. Whichever approach you take, as you read try to identify the type of question represented. Is it a question about grammar, vocabulary, or pronunciation, for example?

English Language Teaching Certificate

Pre-course task

1. Complete this table. Use the same verb (eat) in each case. Two examples have been done for you.

	Simple	**Continuous**
Present	He eats	*He is eating*
Past	*He ate*	*He was eating*
Present Perfect	*He has eaten*	He has been eating
Past perfect	*He had eaten*	*He had been eating*
Future	*He will eat*	*He will be eating*
Future perfect	*He will have eaten*	*He will have been eating*

2. How would you describe the *differences* between these pairs of words to someone learning English? Write a brief explanation of what you would say or do in each case.

2.1 borrow and lend
2.2 take and bring

2.1 I would say that 'borrow' is like 'taking' while 'lend' is like 'giving'. I would show the difference by drawing a picture of a library full of books with a woman going in. I'd tell the students that she wanted to take a book home from the library. I'd ask them if she can do that. When they told me yes, she could, I'd then say, 'But can she keep the book?' When they told me no, she couldn't keep it, I'd then tell them that the word to use is 'borrow' – she can borrow the book from the library. I'd then turn the example around and say, 'What about the library? Do the people there give you books to keep?' When students said no, I'd tell them that the people in a library lend books to you.

2.2 I'd explain that 'bring' is usually used for movement towards the person speaking, while 'take' is used for movement in other directions. I'd demonstrate this to students by asking a student to follow this instruction, showing her what to do if necessary: 'Maria, come here and bring your book. Now take it to Johan.'

3. Identify the *function* of each of the following sentences. One has been done for you as an example.

3.1 Can I give you a hand?	Offer
3.2 You should try to be more assertive.	*Advice*
3.3 I wouldn't do that if I were you.	*Warning*
3.4 Please pass me the salt.	*Request*
3.5 Excuse me, I think you've made a mistake with my bill.	*Complaint*

4. How many *sounds* do the following words have? One has been done for you as an example.

4.1 keep – *3*	4.3 what – *3*
4.2 ships – *4*	4.4 expel – *6*

5. What are the qualities of a good teacher?

Write no more than 200 words, and please write by hand – do not type or use a word processor.

I think good teachers are people who are enthusiastic about their subject and know it inside out, but they also recognize that they don't know everything, and they are not afraid of making mistakes themselves. In other words, good teachers are still learning themselves. Being a learner yourself can help you to understand what it is like to learn, and it can make you more humble. I think a good teacher is a humble person, not at all arrogant. I also think that a good teacher has leadership skills – that is, he or she can set an example that others will want to aspire to. Good teachers will have a positive influence upon their students, and their students will respect and admire them but not be intimidated by them, because a good teacher must also be approachable, encouraging, friendly and warm.

I also think a good teacher is a creative person – you have to have ideas to teach well. However, good teachers also value their students' contributions, and they work hard to create a positive atmosphere in which students are willing to share their ideas and don't feel threatened at all. I think good teachers are more like guides who, in this supportive atmosphere, allow students to make mistakes and learn from them.

Finally, good teachers aren't at all cynical. They genuinely care – about their subjects, their students, their colleagues and their work.

Grammar in pre-course tasks

Question 1 in the pre-course task above is a grammar question. Tutors often include grammar in a pre-course task, and for a number of reasons. Firstly, it is undeniably a significant part of the course, so this can form a good introduction for you to an important area. Secondly, it is the area that people generally find most challenging and off-putting, so completing it may provide a good indication of your commitment to ELT/TESOL (both for yourself and for your tutor). Thirdly, it is easy for tutors to design a task in this area that can be done by people with no or little experience of ELT/TESOL, because there are many excellent and readily available resources to help you to approach this area more or less independently. Finally, tutors may use the area to gauge your language proficiency, particularly if English is not your first language.

In this section you might also be asked to identify parts of speech, countable and uncountable nouns, and/or concrete and abstract nouns, and you might be asked to explain the difference between various verb forms, such as, 'I've been living here for two years' and 'I've lived here for two years'. It is also likely that you would be asked to think about how you would describe the meaning of structures to a learner, such as 'to have something done', as in 'I'm having my hair done at 2pm'.

Vocabulary in pre-course tasks

Question 2 in the task above is a vocabulary question. It asks you to think about the meaning of words, and how to communicate it. You might also be asked to think about two-part verbs such as 'to give up'; **idioms** such as 'to sit on the fence'; and the difference in style between words such as 'fag' and 'cigarette', or the various meanings of one word such as 'push' in 'Push off, why don't you!', 'She's a bit pushy', 'I'm sorry, I'm pushed for time', 'She was hard pushed to give me the time of day', and so forth. As with grammatical forms, it is likely that you will be asked to say how you would go about explaining the difference in meaning between words to language learners.

Functions in pre-course tasks

Question 3 in the task above is a question about the function of language. 'Function' is the word used when we want to talk about what a person hopes to achieve by using particular language. It means the job, purpose or role of the language you have chosen to use. For example, if you say 'Can I give you a hand?', you are making an offer. If you say 'I don't agree' or 'You could be right, but ...', you are expressing disagreement. If you say 'I'm really very sorry', you are apologizing. In each case, there are a number of ways of performing the function. For example, to express disagreement, you can also say 'I'm not sure I agree with that', or 'You've got a point, but ...', or 'On the contrary ...'. Each one of these ways of expressing disagreement is called an exponent of the function – exponent simply means 'example'.

You may be asked to identify these and other functions including, for example, making a suggestion, complaining, requesting, refusing, inviting, accepting, and agreeing. You could be asked to identify several ways of expressing a function (that is, several exponents), and to think about how you would convey the meaning of each function or exponent to learners.

Pronunciation in pre-course tasks

Question 4 in the task above is a question about pronunciation. This particular question asks you to think about the relationship between the spelling of a word (sometimes known as **orthography**) and the sound of a word (its pronunciation). In English the sound–spelling relationship is not always one-to-one, in the sense that you will find the following:

- The same letter does not always represent the same sound. Think about the letter 'e', and how it is pronounced in the following words: red, we, her, English.

- The same sound is not always represented by the same letter. Think about the vowel sound in 'see'. Now look at how the same sound is spelt in these words: receive, tea, field, ski, people.

- Some letters are not pronounced at all in certain words. Think about these words: sword, mortgage, knife.

⦾ Some sounds occur where there is no corresponding letter in certain words. Think about the word 'one'. What is its first sound? It might help you to answer this if you listen to someone else saying it, and watch them as they do so. You should be able to hear (and see) that it begins with the sound /w/ (the slashes on either side of the symbol 'w' show that this is a sound, not a letter).

As well as individual sounds, you might also be asked to think about the syllables of words, in particular which syllables are stressed, that is, spoken with greater emphasis than other syllables in the word.

A **monolingual learner's dictionary** (an English–English dictionary designed for learners; the *Longman Active Study Dictionary* (2000) is a good example) can help you both with sounds and **stressed syllables**, because immediately after the **headword** the pronunciation of the word is given, in the form of **phonemic symbols**. Do not worry too much about what the symbols mean (although it is worth noting that all monolingual learner's dictionaries which use phonemic symbols also provide a key to these symbols), but note that such a dictionary can help you with questions such as question 4 in the task above, because each symbol represents one sound. Stressed syllables are indicated in the same part of the entry with the use of the symbol ' which appears immediately before the syllable that is stressed.

Teaching and learning in pre-course tasks

Question 5 in the task above is a question about teaching and learning. In questions of this type you may be asked to:

⦾ identify your likely strengths and weaknesses in teaching

⦾ think about different teaching situations

⦾ describe a successful learning experience that you have had

⦾ describe a good teacher you have known

⦾ identify the needs of a group of adult learners who have just arrived in an English-speaking country to work and live, and who know very little English.

You might also be asked to comment on statements such as:

⦾ 'Learners don't need to attend classes to learn English. They can learn from books, dictionaries, radio, television and the internet.'

⦾ 'Grammar is more important than anything else, and learners need to learn this first because it follows that learners who have a good grasp of grammar will be able to read, write, speak and listen to English.'

In each case, you may be asked to write around 200–300 words.

In relation to completing your pre-course task, two areas are considered in greater detail below. These are: identifying your strengths and weaknesses, and conveying meaning. These areas are given particular attention because they are essential skills for any teacher in ELT/TESOL, not only at this pre-course stage, but also during and after your course.

Identifying your strengths and weaknesses

Questions asking you to identify your strengths and weaknesses are common, because you are expected to refine this skill while on the course. An example of such a question that might appear in your pre-course task is 'What do you think would be your strengths and weaknesses as a language teacher?'

> 'Assignment 3 asks me to describe my strengths as well as my weaknesses – what strengths? I can't go up to my tutor and say "Hey, what am I good at?". I know what I'm bad at, but there ain't anything so far I think I'm good at. I don't even know if I'm on the right track assignment wise until I get it back. HELP!'
>
> Participant, Hong Kong

However, many former participants have found such questions very difficult to answer, particularly at this early stage of a course. It is also the case that what may be a weakness in one situation is actually an advantage in another. One of the best approaches you can take to this question is to make a list of a few words that you feel describe your personality. Ask a friend to help you if you find this stage difficult. For example, if I were to do this task, I might come up with the following:

- methodical
- organized
- shy.

If I think about each one of these points in relation to some actual situations, I quickly find out that each one may be considered to be a strength in some situations and a weakness in others. Take being 'organized', for example. The good side about this is that I can usually find what I need,

> 'I often see how strengths can create weaknesses in other areas. The line between a strength and a weakness becomes blurred and I often feel that each strength I may use to develop my teaching has a "but" attached to it.'
>
> Participant, Hong Kong (Extract from answer to Assignment 3: 'Lessons from the classroom')

when I need it. The bad side is that there are four other people in my family, and to expect them to be as organized as I am is unreasonable of me. Yet, of course, this is sometimes exactly what I do. It can be one of my weaknesses, and I sometimes have to work to counter it.

This process will help you to identify your strengths and weaknesses, something you may be asked to do before a course is underway but which you will certainly need to be able to demonstrate during your course. This skill may be required, for example, in completing one of your written assignments (see Chapter 6, 'Written assignments'). The ability to be frank and forthcoming rather than coy about your strengths and weaknesses is a skill worth developing at this very earlier stage. Try not to be the kind of person who says 'Hey, what am I good at? I know what I'm bad at, but there ain't anything so far I think I'm good at'. Rather, think in terms of your characteristics, and how each proves useful or less useful in relation to a particular set of circumstances.

Communicating meaning

Throughout your pre-course task, questions that focus on communicating meaning to learners are quite usual, whether this is the meaning of a grammatical form such as 'They have lived there for two years', or the meaning of a vocabulary item such as 'weep' or 'call off', because such tasks can start you thinking about learners, what it is like to be one, and what they need from you.

In answering such questions, and at other stages of your course, you may find that some or all of the following techniques will prove useful:

- gesture (for example, indicating tears to show sadness)
- demonstration ('to switch on' or 'to switch off' can both be illustrated by action, for example)
- speaking clearly and perhaps slowing down a little, avoiding a patronizing tone
- avoiding *complex* English and using *simple* English, rather than *reduced* English ('Could I offer you some assistance?' and 'Can I give you a hand?' are both relatively *complex*; 'Can I help you?' is *simple*; 'I help you?' is *reduced*, and to be avoided.)
- making use of diagrams or drawings (for example, a map or a picture of an object. You might use the latter to convey what the word 'luggage' meant, perhaps.)
- using the objects around you (for example, the meaning of the word 'under' can be conveyed by placing one object under another)
- rephrasing something in a different way (for example, you can ask a learner 'Have you finished your homework?' or 'Have you done your homework?' or 'Do you have your homework?' or 'Can I see your homework?')

These ideas can be used to help you answer specific questions concerned with communicating meaning. Other broader strategies to help you with this stage of your course are considered next.

Pre-course task strategies

There are a number of practical strategies that you can adopt when completing your pre-course task or tasks:

- Use whatever reference materials and books you can get hold of, such as the learner's dictionary referred to above. See **www**, where you will find some suggestions that will help you at this stage of your course and throughout. Bolitho and Tomlinson's (2002) *Discover English* is a particularly helpful resource for anyone tackling language awareness questions.
- Call or email the centre if something is not clear to you. Do not be afraid to ask!

- Speak to a teacher in ELT/TESOL and/or someone who has been through the course themselves if you can, before and/or after completing the task, or while you are doing it; and do so without feeling that you are 'cheating' in any way (a feeling reported by former participants) because your purpose in doing these tasks is to *learn*.

Pre-course tasks are only one part of the application process, however; the other parts are the application form, mentioned above, and the interview, where you have the best opportunity of all to make sure that you are making the right decision.

The interview

Interviews for places on certificate courses, like pre-course tasks and application forms, vary from centre to centre in terms of length and structure. In some centres, interviews may take 45 minutes; in others, no more than 30 minutes. You may be asked to complete a task during your interview, but not all tutors do this. You may be interviewed together with other candidates, by more than one tutor, or by phone.

As with some pre-course tasks, the purpose of the interview is twofold. Through a face to face meeting, possibly with an interview task, tutors are able to make more refined judgements about your attitude, instincts, inner resources, and potential than is possible from an application on paper. To this extent, the idea of 'interview as test' applies. Tutors are looking for applicants who arrive prepared. They look for a positive attitude towards English and towards people from other language backgrounds and cultures. They look for people who are articulate, resourceful, and who display a level of confidence likely to enable them to stand up in front of a class of strangers and address them coherently. You will need to be able to demonstrate such attributes in order to get a place on a course. However, as with pre-course tasks, there is a learning opportunity for you in the interview. But this one in particular is easily forgotten in the heat of the moment, because you are concentrating so hard on passing the test that the interview represents.

If you approach the period of time leading up to the interview as an opportunity for you to learn as much as you can about the area (whether or not you have had a pre-interview task to complete), and you maintain this desire to learn during your interview, taking an active stance and asking good questions, listening, and making notes – then your behaviour will have two positive effects: one, you will learn more about ELT/TESOL and the course than you might otherwise have done; and two, you will be behaving in a way that shows your interviewer that you can prepare, and that you are willing and able to learn. All good news if you are going to be a teacher.

The people who have failed at the interview stage, therefore, are often those who have not prepared by studying a suitable introduction to ELT/TESOL (including language awareness), who are passive rather than active in the interview, or who fail to express a positive attitude towards the profession and its people.

However, of the very many people who do get places on courses, a number have later regretted not fully exploiting the interview as an opportunity to learn about the course. They have said things like 'Why didn't they tell me there was so much homework?' and 'Why did no one tell me we would be assessed in TP from day one?'

Much of the responsibility lies with tutors for providing the answers to such questions without applicants having to ask. Indeed, a colleague of mine sees his role in an interview as being 'To check out if they've got what it takes', and 'To tell them about what they are letting themselves in for'.

But tutors are far from infallible, and so to prevent information that you need slipping through the net, you need to prepare. Only through careful preparation will you be able to ask the right questions at the interview, so that you are as well informed as possible by the start of the course.

My colleagues and I developed various questions and prompts which we would choose from when interviewing applicants for places on our certificate courses. They include:

- Tell us about yourself.
- What sort of person are you?
- What is your preferred learning style?
- Name one strength that you think would help you in the language classroom.
- Why do you want to take a certificate course?
- Why you want to become an English language teacher?
- What did you learn from your experience of learning a foreign language?
- How might you get students talking in class?
- How would you help someone who did not understand something you had said?
- What do you think are the benefits to a learner of attending a class that is (a) one-to-one; and (b) in a group?
- Describe a positive or negative learning experience you have had. What features made it so?
- Describe a teacher you liked at school. Why did you like him or her?

We also developed a set of 'frequently asked questions', questions that we were often asked by applicants. These included:

- Does everyone pass the course?
- What is the grading system? What written assignments will I be asked to complete?
- Do the written assignments contribute towards the final grade?
- Is all of teaching practice assessed?
- How is teaching practice arranged?
- How large are classes for teaching practice?
- Will we have to do any peer teaching?
- Will I be told if I'm not doing well?

- How much homework is there?
- How much time will I need to allow for homework?
- What computer facilities for participants do you have?
- Will I be able to teach children after completing the course?
- Will I be given a study space?
- Where do the language learners come from?
- Does your school help with job guidance and placement?
- Do you offer jobs to people who pass the certificate at your centre?
- Will I be able to word process my assignments?
- Will I have access to the internet?
- Is there a dress code?
- How many course participants are there in a group?
- What sort of people will be in my group? What sort of age range? Will some of them already have teaching experience?
- Will there be extras to pay for on the course – books, stationery, photocopying, use of internet, for example?

You may wish to ask some or all of the above yourself, at your interview; but do also think of others that you *personally* would like to ask (by doing this you will be exploiting a good learning opportunity).

Seven steps to interview success

Former participants have described various strategies that they used both during the interview and to prepare for it, from which these seven steps to a successful interview have been developed:

Seven steps to success in your certificate interview

1. *Find out a little background information about the centre.* Is it part of chain? How long has it been open? How big is it? How many teachers work there?
2. *Research ELT/TESOL.* Find out as much as you can about it! (Use the resources suggested on **www** to help you here.) Talk to teachers and observe a class, if you can.
3. *Look the part.* You are moving into a profession – so dress and carry yourself like a professional. It indicates that you take both the interview and teaching seriously.
4. *Don't dominate; but don't be too reticent either.* Remember that an interview is a dialogue, an exchange of information. It should flow freely. A good teacher is not one who dominates his or her class. And if you are too reticent, tutors will question your ability to stand up in front of a group of people and address them, not to mention organize their learning.

5. *Prepare questions to ask.* Use this book to help you to identify good questions. Make sure you leave the interview with the information you need.

6. *Prepare answers to questions you anticipate being asked.* This will help you to respond with confidence. Use positive language to convey your enthusiasm for your new area.

7. *Read this book!*

The application process described above exists in part in order to help tutors to identify people who will be likely to succeed. From your perspective, this means that once you have been accepted, you can approach the course with some confidence: you would not be there if someone (who is highly skilled at identifying suitable applicants) did not think you could succeed.

> If you are given a place on a course you can be reasonably certain that the tutors think you have every chance of passing it.
>
> Take this faith that the tutors have shown in you and turn it into confidence in yourself: start the course knowing that they believe you can pass.

❯ GET SET: PRE-COURSE PREPARATIONS

Former participants have made many suggestions to help people who are about to take a course. For full-time courses, the most frequent recommendation is for people to give up all employment, even a part-time job, for the duration and if possible for a week or two immediately before your course starts.

However, people on part-time courses have also found that having a job adds to the pressure of the experience. Many people managed to continue successfully with their full-time jobs, but others offered advice such as:

> If I were taking a course and I knew what I now know, I'd look very carefully at my work commitments. I think I might even ask my boss for 'light duties' ... if you've got a stressful day job or a heavy workload, it's almost impossible to give a certificate course your best.
>
> *Participant, part-time course, Australia*

First and foremost, former participants recommend that you should not underestimate the demands of the

> 'I particularly feel the squeeze because I'm getting very little exercise as a result of my working schedule. This leads to a "survival" state of mind where I take every day at a time.'
>
> Participant, part-time course, Hong Kong

> 'Had I not been working part-time, I believe I would have had sufficient time to learn and enjoy the course rather than endure it in my determination to pass.'
>
> Participant, Hong Kong

task you are setting yourself. They recommend that you take a number of proactive steps, before the course gets underway, which will help you to accommodate to it. These are:

- Ensure as far as possible that you are physically fit when the course starts.
- Stock up your fridge so that you do not need to spend precious time shopping for provisions in the first few days of the course.
- Warn family and friends and seek their support in terms of freedom from as many obligations or commitments as possible.

Pre-course preparations

- Cancel or postpone any other appointments or demands on time where possible.
- Buy the stationery and books that are recommended by your centre, in advance.
- Arrange for appropriate accommodation, preferably requiring the minimum amount of travel between home and the centre. Some centres will provide assistance with this, including, for example, arranging for you to be accommodated with a host family or in a hotel.
- Ensure that a comfortable study space, free of distractions, is available to you at home.
- Compile a portfolio of potentially useful resources for teaching such as newspapers, magazines, photographs, etc.

- Get ahead by doing the pre-course task as thoroughly as you can, plus any other recommended pre-course study. Familiarize yourself with basic concepts and terminology in ELT/TESOL by studying suitable methodology and language awareness books, such as the ones detailed on www. The glossary can also help you here.

- Familiarize yourself with the local environment, before the course starts, if it is new to you. Take a walk! You do not want to waste valuable time getting lost in your first few days.

With these few things in place, you are now in a good position to start to enjoy your course.

▶ GO: FIRST DAYS

You will almost certainly need to spend some time at the very beginning of your course orientating yourself towards your new environment. For example, you will need to find your way around the centre, learn new norms of behaviour, start to acquire a new vocabulary, find out who is who, who does and does not do what, and where the things are that you need: from the lavatory to the photocopier to the coffee machine. Much of your time in the first few days will be spent orientating yourself towards your new environment, and it will help you greatly if you recognize this and allow for it by setting time aside in which to do it.

> Don't forget that you will need time to orientate yourself to your new environment. Set time aside for this in the first few days.

> At one centre where I was assessing a course, participants had to complete a form in order to be given a key to the lavatory for the duration of their course, as well as pay a deposit!

Former participants have also observed that there can be an inordinate and unanticipated amount of paperwork to manage in the first few days. You will probably find that your centre has a form for practically everything: for teaching practice feedback, lesson plans, the written assessment, course evaluation (often carried out at the end of the first week, and/or halfway through a course, as well as at the end) and for borrowing equipment. This can be a rather daunting start to the experience, but if you expect it you can be prepared, by setting aside time for it and by ensuring that you have at least two binders and sets of dividers to hand. Try to complete forms and file

> 'I remember that the tutor quite put the wind up me with all those forms to fill in for TP – lesson plans, TP feedback, etc., etc. I felt totally overwhelmed and wondered if I was going to make it.'
>
> Participant, Hong Kong

everything away as soon as you can. Procrastination is not a good idea on an intense course such as this, regardless of whether you are taking a full-time or a part-time course.

There are of course a number of ways in which you could organize your material as you receive it, but former participants have pointed out that it can be very difficult to see clearly how to organize your material at the beginning of the course because you do not know what to expect. By the end of his course, one participant had developed a system of two files, one for his own personal notes and one for his portfolio, which had to be submitted at the end of his course, and which can be seen more in terms of providing an assessment record. He organized his portfolio as follows:

1. Assignments and feedback from his tutor
2. Teaching practice: (a) lesson plans, (b) handouts for learners, (c) tutor's written feedback, (d) self-evaluations, (e) peers' feedback (it is a good idea to arrange this section so that the materials for each teaching practice lesson you give are filed together in one plastic pocket)
3. Feedback from tutorials
4. Course evaluations.

In his personal file, he placed the following:

1. Administration
2. Language work: (a) grammar, (b) vocabulary, (c) phonology, (d) reading, (e) writing, (f) speaking, (g) listening
3. Methodology
4. Classroom management and teaching skills
5. Observations
6. Copies of anything he wished to keep from his portfolio (on this subject, many former participants noted that it is much easier to do this as the course progresses, rather than trying to photocopy everything at the end).

Some tutors may make their own recommendations for file organization at the start of their courses, but if they do not then the approach above would be a very good start. Adopting it from day one could save you time and reduce anxiety during a demanding stage of the course.

Snapshot of early days

Below, you can read more about Alison's experience of the course. Here, she describes arriving at the place she was to stay while taking the course, and her experience of the first few days. As you read, you might like to make a note of the following:

- what she appreciated about the first few days of the course
- the things that concerned her.

My Experience of the CELTA Course
(continued from above)

Alison Standring

Penultimate moments

The night before the course began, I arrived in Hastings and located the house I was going to live in for the next four weeks. I was sharing the house with five other people: two were doing the CELTA course with me; two were teachers on the summer programme at International House; and one was an aging full-time teacher with a very young Japanese girlfriend. We were all so different; would we get along?

That first night, I went to the pub with the other two CELTA trainees and we swapped stories about our reasons for doing the course (one wanted a career change after 10 years of working with computers; the other had been teaching in Japan for 5 years and was now looking for a formal teaching qualification), our expectations of what the course would involve (no-one was very sure) and our general hopes and fears (our hopes were of travelling to exciting destinations and escaping dreary routine-filled lives; our fears were of not being able to handle the CELTA workload or of making idiots of ourselves in front of the students).

Day One:

On Day One, we located the building where the course was going to take place. It had once been a large house and was surrounded by beautiful gardens. The day started with 'getting to know you' activities. We wrote our names on sticky labels and walked around asking our fellow trainees about their likes, dislikes, hobbies and interests. So far, so good. Next we had a 'foreign language lesson' in which we learnt how to count to ten and tell the time in Japanese (I can still remember). The idea was to experience what language learning was like for EFL students. Finally, after a short break, we were divided into three teaching groups. Each group consisted of six trainees and one course tutor. Again, I hoped we would all get along, because I could see that it would be helpful if we did.

It was at this stage that the mood of the day changed. We were told that, after lunch, we would have to 'teach'. My task was to conduct a 20-minute general knowledge quiz. I panicked. It was too soon! I hadn't had enough preparation! I'm useless at quizzes! What if I froze? What if the students wouldn't do what I asked them to? Fortunately, there wasn't enough time for me to have a nervous breakdown. Before I knew it, I was standing in front of 15 very pleasant Polish teenagers making a stab at some sort of quiz. Then, it was all over. In hindsight, it was the best way to do it. Once, I'd 'taught' my first lesson, I'd crossed a major hurdle. Having to do it on Day One meant I hadn't had the opportunity to get overly stressed.

▶

Week One:

For the rest of Week One, my main concern remained being able to get through a lesson without a major disaster. (I wasn't too worried about details like whether I was actually teaching anyone anything or not!) In the mornings, we received input on issues like classroom management and lesson planning and, in the afternoons, we had teaching practice (TP). At the end of each afternoon, we would have TP feedback where trainees would comment on each other's strengths and weaknesses and the course tutor would proffer advice. This was very supportive but fairly basic at this stage and so not difficult to act upon e.g. most of us had to be reminded that it is a good idea to face students when you talk to them. A personal realization was that I would have to rethink my wardrobe. Wide-necked tops are not ideal when you have to bend over and wraparound skirts have the potential for coming undone!

(to be continued)

What Alison appreciated about the first few days:

- the thought of the exciting opportunities that would present themselves once the course was over
- being 'thrown in at the deep end' and so having no time in which to worry too much
- getting over the hurdle of teaching that first lesson
- supportive feedback from her tutor, which was easy to take account of.

What Alison was concerned about in the first few days:

- getting on with the people she was sharing a house with
- not knowing what the course would involve
- the workload
- making a fool of herself in front of the learners
- getting on with the other people in her group, including the tutor
- performance nerves
- teaching without any major disasters
- dress code – what is suitable in teaching situations.

Alison's main concerns are addressed in the next three chapters: 'Learning', 'Teaching', and 'Working together'.

Getting started: Key points to take away with you

- When you complete an application form, draw on your experience, your knowledge of the course (having read this book will help) and your self-awareness.

- Study all of the course information that you are given in detail. Highlight key points for your future reference.

- See any pre-course tasks as an opportunity to learn and orientate yourself before the course starts. Don't just do them to get them done, then forget all about them.

- Try to put yourself into the shoes of your learners. This will help you to understand the challenges they face.

- If you find it difficult to identify your strengths and weaknesses, think instead in terms of your characteristics and the situations you find yourself in. In some situation, a characteristic will be a strength, in others, a weakness.

- In the interview, tutors look for people who are prepared, articulate, resourceful, and confident; and who have a positive attitude towards English and towards people from other language backgrounds and cultures. Think carefully beforehand about the questions you need to ask to get the information you want. Make a list to take with you.

- Having passed the application process, you can afford to have some confidence: tutors accept people they believe can pass.

- The paperwork in the first few days can be quite demanding: stay in control of it from the beginning.

- It is recommended that you do not try to work part-time while taking a full-time course.

- If you are planning to continue in full-time work while taking a part-time course, look very carefully at your commitments. Try to reduce them if you can.

- Remember that the first few days will probably be tough but enjoyable.

www **Check your understanding** of Chapter 5 by completing the quiz available on the companion website at: www.sagepub.co.uk/brandt

Chapter 6

Learning

In this chapter, you can learn about:

- the topics you can expect to cover in workshops
- the foreign language lesson, and how you can make the most of it
- guided observation, and how to make the most of the opportunity to observe experienced teachers
- written assignments and how to tackle them
- how to manage your time to ensure you make the most of the experience.

▶ WORKSHOPS

Workshops are one of the main ways that tutors will use to pass on the content of your certificate course, that is, information about areas such as phonology and lesson planning.

Below, you will find an example workshop schedule. This shows the kind of topics that you can expect to cover. Participants are expected to attend all the workshops on the schedule below, as well as teaching practice and lesson preparation, which would take place in the afternoons on this course. Note the helpful level of detail that is provided: rather than simply writing 'Language awareness 1', the course organizers inform participants that this workshop will be about form, function, meaning and use, and that it will also cover some basic terminology. This level of detail is useful for you, because it aids your preparation; in relation to form, function, meaning and use, for example, you might like to look up the meaning of these words in an ELT/TESOL context (Bolitho and Tomlinson's (2002) *Discover English* would help you here). If this level of detail is not provided, you should ask for it.

An example workshop schedule

The example workshop schedule below is for a four-week full-time course. Note that this is one example and that every centre will have its own schedule. While many of the areas covered will be in practice very similar, different workshop titles may be used. For example, one centre might call 'Language skills 2: developing reading skills' by the name 'Receptive skills 1: introducing reading'. This does not matter at all: what matters is that you have a level of detail that enables you to begin to consider the topic beforehand and do a little research if you have the time.

English Language Teaching Certificate Workshop schedule			
Wk	**Day**	**9am–10.30am**	**10.45am–12.15pm**
1	M	1. Introduction; course overview 2. Overview of language learning (please bring your completed pre-course task)	1. The foreign language lesson 2. Feedback
	T	The EFL classroom: Learning & Teaching a language	Language awareness, grammar 1: form, function, meaning and use; basic terminology
	W	Lesson planning 1	Presenting language 1: presenting new structures
	T	Language skills 1: introduction	Language awareness, grammar 2: present tenses
	F	Language awareness, vocabulary 1: the word	Language awareness, phonology 1: **phonemes**
2	M	Classroom management: ways of working	Understanding your learner 1: motivations and needs
	T	Lesson planning 2	Language awareness, vocabulary 2: **denotation**, **connotation**, and **collocation**
	W	Practising language 1: drilling	Language awareness, grammar 3: talking about the past; using timelines
	T	Language awareness, phonology 2: word stress and **weak forms**	Language skills 2: developing reading skills
	F	Practising language 2: less controlled activities	Conveying meaning: techniques for conveying meaning and checking understanding – concept checking
3	M	Language awareness, phonology 3: sentence stress	Language skills 3: developing writing skills
	T	Language awareness, grammar 4: talking about the future	Understanding your learner 2: L1 interference

Wk	Day	9am–10.30am	10.45am–12.15pm
	W	Language skills 4: developing speaking skills	Language awareness, phonology 4: intonation
	T	Language skills 5: developing listening skills	Practising language 3: communicative practice
	F	Language awareness, grammar 5: mood	The Communicative Approach
4	M	Language awareness, vocabulary 3: two and three part verbs; idioms	Identifying and correcting spoken errors
	T	Identifying and correcting written errors	Language awareness, grammar 6: conditionals
	W	Evaluating teaching materials	**Authentic materials**
	T	**Supplementary materials**	Using games in the ELT/TESOL classroom
	F	Technology in ELT/TESOL	A career in ELT/TESOL

You can view most of your workshops as three-way learning opportunities, because you can learn from:

- what you are being taught
- how it is being taught to you
- applying your learning in your own classroom.

However, one workshop offers a rather different experience. In this workshop, unlike the others, you are not expected to learn what you are being taught, though you are expected to learn from how you are being taught and then to take this learning and apply it later. The difference between this and other workshops, however, may not at first be apparent. How to recognize the difference and maximize the learning opportunity the workshop provides is described in greater detail below. The workshop concerned is the foreign language lesson.

The foreign language lesson

Many certificate courses will provide you with an opportunity to 'learn' a hitherto unknown foreign language, usually in the very early stages of the course, possibly on the first day. Former participants have described this component as being of enormous value:

'The most effective feature was the first class where we were all put into a room and not told what the lesson was. Then the tutor began to speak in a foreign language and we had to participate and figure out what was going on. This was brilliant to me because it gave you a first hand look and feel as to what the students were going to be feeling AND there is no lesson or tutor who could convey that feeling in a regular classroom lecture.'

Participant, Hong Kong

Different courses will allocate different amounts of time to this feature. In all cases, however, where this session is offered, its purpose is the same: to give you the experience of *being in the shoes of a language learner*, and in all cases some time will be spent in 'debriefing' or 'feedback', in which you will be expected to reflect upon and analyse your experience. You will not be tested on how much you have learned of the new language, because actually learning the language is not the main purpose of the experience, as will be shown below.

Being in a learner's shoes in this context means two things: firstly, you are on the receiving end of various techniques that you will encounter later on in your course, and, secondly, it means being in a classroom where *the new language alone is being used*. The new language is two things at once: the *medium* of instruction, and the *content*, or focus, of that instruction.

As with a few other areas of these courses, such as the pre-course tasks, the languages selected for this component are not standardized within the courses run by one validating organization. Instead, languages to be taught are chosen with two points in mind. Firstly, a language is selected in order to reduce the likelihood of participants having any prior knowledge of it (this cannot be guaranteed, of course, but tutors will make every effort to ensure that no participant is familiar with the language); and secondly, the language offered will depend on the skills of the existing staff (because teachers in ELT/TESOL fre-

> Over the years as a visiting validator, I have observed several different languages being taught as part of the 'Foreign Language Lesson', including: Greek, Turkish, Maori, Swahili, Tamil, Swedish, Basque, Khmer and Xhosa.

quently take jobs in other countries to gain more experience, it is often conveniently the case that a member of staff will have sufficient knowledge of a language that is not well known locally).

Whichever language you are presented with, however, it is important to understand why you are spending time on your course in this way. Remember that the idea is for you to be in your learner's shoes, so that you have first-hand experience of what it is like to be in a class where no one is speaking your language, and where the teacher is speaking a language that is completely foreign to you. You are expected to 'learn' some of this language and then perform in front of complete strangers.

One participant expressed her reactions to this experience: 'I was very confused and experienced embarrassment, nervousness, then tiredness and even frustration at not being able to converse.' Another wrote, 'I remember feeling horrified and not wanting to be picked to translate or speak', but she added that 'it allows you to go in to your own class later and be much more sensitive and patient with the students.' For reasons such as these it is a useful experience and one which participants, particularly in retrospect, find very beneficial. As well as providing a 'first hand look and feel as to what the students were going to be feeling', participants have said that the foreign language lesson:

'is a great way to start the course because not only do you learn about learning but you learn about each other and the tutor too'

Participant, Australia

'was terrifying at the time but really useful later. It made me realize just how hard learning a language is'

Participant, Spain

'was absolutely wonderful because it put me right into their shoes. I thought I knew what it was like to be a language student, but actually I had no idea, probably because it's so long since I studied another language'

Participant, Hong Kong

While these participants all recognized the benefits in retrospect, several also pointed out that these benefits were sometimes hard to discern at the time. This may be because the foreign language lesson experience is an intense one, requiring complete concentration, and it can be particularly difficult to reflect upon such an experience while it is taking place. It may also be something to do with your expectations.

Some former participants have arrived in their classrooms for the workshop called 'The Foreign Language Lesson' on their timetables, expecting the session to be an overview of learning foreign languages. It did not occur to them that they would be expected to learn a foreign language themselves. Nor did they expect their tutor simply to walk into the classroom and start talking in Xhosa, for example, without explaining what was happening, or why. This may well be the approach you experience, because some tutors feel that part of your learning comes from working out what is going on and why you have been placed in this position, and surviving in a way in which we sometimes expect our learners to survive. Not surprisingly, perhaps, many former participants have experienced confusion, disorientation, and frustration at finding themselves on the very first day in a language class in which they are expected to learn enough Xhosa to take part in a brief conversation.

This is a good example of a workshop for which you may need to seek more information. If you see 'Foreign Language Lesson' on your timetable, therefore, ask your tutor to tell you which language you will be learning. This is because it is unrealistic to be asked to learn a language you do not know you are going to be learning, at the very least; let alone a language that you do not want or need to learn. However, you may need to summon up all of your powers of persuasion here, because you might find that your tutor resists telling you which language you will be learning, in order to maximize its impact on the day.

It is also the case that you will be attending a class where the main purpose appears to be one thing but is in fact another. There is, if you like, a 'hidden agenda'. On the surface the purpose is for you to 'learn' a foreign language, and former participants have sometimes spent most of the lesson in a state of some anxiety, believing that they had to learn the material that was being presented and which they were practising. In fact, you are not expected to retain the content of the lesson (that is, the language) much beyond the end of the lesson. What is expected instead is that you will leave the session with a better understanding of some of the processes involved in learning another language, including the *difficulties* faced by learners in your classes, and some of the *techniques* that you can use in order to assist them.

It is also worth remembering that you are being placed in the uncommon position of being a true beginner, while in practice, classes of true beginners are quite rare; and you yourself should not be asked to teach such a class while taking a certificate course because this is considered to be a specialist area which requires slightly different skills and techniques.

> 'Do the trainees understand why we do those games with them in the foreign language lesson, and should it be made clear at the beginning, so that they feel easier about it? Last time they didn't know why they had had a foreign language lesson until long after it – do we need to make it a mystery?'
>
> Tutor, Hong Kong

Armed with these understandings, you can lessen any possible confusion or disorientation and ensure that the experience is of maximum *immediate* benefit. Approach the session or sessions, therefore, with their real purpose in mind: to help you to become aware of the processes involved in learning another language, rather than learning the language itself. This can take some of the pressure off you at a delicate stage of the course.

OBSERVING

Time spent observing classes, whether they are being taught by your tutors, experienced teachers, or your fellow course participants, usually accounts for a significant proportion of certificate courses. It is essentially an opportunity for you to gain experience of, and learn about, different learning environments, interactions, approaches and processes.

A glance at your certificate course timetable or course outline may tell you that six hours of your time will be spent observing others on a certificate course. In fact, these six hours will be spent observing experienced teachers; depending on which course you are taking, a much larger proportion of your course time could be spent observing your peers. If you are taking a CELTA course, for example, you could find that you spend some 24 hours observing your fellow participants' teaching practice (how this occurs will be shown below); while on a CertTESOL course, observing your peers will be an option rather than a requirement. Time allocated to observing peers can be quite easily overlooked or misunderstood. This is because such observation can be less visible, because it may be included as part of the teaching practice arrangements and will therefore lack the status of a distinct course component.

Peer observation

If you are taking a CELTA course and you are part of a teaching practice group of five, then a quick calculation reveals that you will spend 24 hours observing your fellow participants' teaching practice, because everyone teaches for six hours on this course and there are four others in your group. However, this 'component' might not appear on your course timetable with a label like **peer observation** or something similar, because it is included under teaching practice, and so some former participants have found that they have failed to realize until quite late that a significant part of their course was being spent in this way. If, however, you are aware of the amount of time that you will spend observing your peers at the beginning of your course, then you will be better able to ensure that you use this time effectively from your first peer observation.

Former participants have found peer observations very useful for a number of reasons. They made comments such as the following:

'You could see your peers doing things wrong and right more easily than when you were up there doing it yourself because the pressure was off.'

Participant, Hong Kong

'There is less pressure on you so you can relax and enjoy the teaching.'

Participant, United Kingdom

'It's easier to see the flaws when another person is doing them.'

Participant, Spain

'It was always exciting to sit back and watch others commit blunders. It was like watching yourself, so you tried not to repeat the same mistakes.'

Participant, United Kingdom

'This was, for me, undoubtedly the strength of the course. It exposed me to alternate ways of doing things. Seeing other participants implement suggestions, noting how they taught using a particular technique, and seeing the learners' response helped me to develop a repertoire of tools to try.'

Participant, Hong Kong

'Observation was where I learned. Observations of fellow trainees, as well as other qualified teachers solidified what was taught in input.'

Participant, Hong Kong

'The best thing about observation for me was seeing that what they did, I could do, too. This applied equally to watching my peers and the most experienced of teachers and tutors.'

Participant, Australia

'Observing the other trainees, and being observed by them, is an excellent learning process and impetus – and the analysis of the lesson that follows the lesson itself is an excellent thing. You see everything under a microscope, so to speak. You see all your own and others' weak points in the lesson, and the strengths. It's very educative.'

Participant, Hong Kong

Key points for participants with this aspect of the course were therefore the opportunity to see what works well and, in particular, less well; to relax a little and enjoy watching teaching and learning taking place (this applied particularly to those who were not waiting for their turn to teach); to be able to relate the content that was presented in workshops to the practice of teaching; and the opportunity to see that they, too, were capable of doing what they were observing. It is, essentially, both experience-building and confidence-building.

However, as mentioned above, not all courses offer as many hours of peer observation as CELTA courses. You should not worry too much about this. On courses with fewer hours of peer observation, you will find that the available time will be used productively, in other ways. What is important, however, is making sure that you make the best use of your time, no matter what aspect of the course you are engaged in.

Observing experienced teachers

Several of the benefits described above applied equally to observing experienced teachers, although not surprisingly perhaps there were fewer instances of 'blunders' reported (nevertheless, they still occurred from time to time, of course, and participants described finding these interesting). In relation to observing experienced teachers, participants made comments such as:

'I am observing our course tutor on Tuesday morning – an intermediate lesson – wish we could have more of these observations – they are the most valuable part of the course. There is no better learning than learning by watching followed by trying to do what you have seen.'

Participant, Hong Kong

'I could learn from the more experienced teachers and also understood that even for the communicative approach to teaching, teachers could have different styles and all of them could be effective.'

Participant, Bahrain

> Experienced teachers sometimes slip up:
>
> 'Actually I feel trainees rather like the idea of mistakes made by us trainers! It makes us look human! My tape got mangled in the machine – so I was able to get them laughing at my predicament.'
>
> Tutor, Hong Kong
>
> 'Our tutor was hesitant and made some mistakes which I was very pleased about – not because she made mistakes (!) but because I can see that I am capable of doing what she did, given practice.'
>
> Participant, Hong Kong

'Observation helped and I would have liked more opportunity to observe: it gave me a feeling for how a class can be run and insight as to the many different teaching styles and "tools" there are to draw upon when preparing a lesson. It helped me see the difference between elementary and more advanced students and the pace a class moves at – it was really useful.'

Participant, Australia

Many former participants have expressed a desire to be able to observe more than six hours of experienced teachers, particularly in the early stages of the course, and some take the initiative to arrange this. There is nothing preventing you from doing the same. If you find that you have the time therefore (this may be more likely if you are attending a part-time course) and you have the inclination, do not hesitate to ask your tutor to arrange extra observations for you. While this may not always be feasible, your tutor will almost certainly make every effort to respond to your initiative.

'Observation consistently gets very good feedback from trainees on the final feedback form, many even asking for more than the set hours.'

Tutor, Singapore

Observation tasks

I have mentioned that while observing experienced teachers, you will usually be set a task. These tasks vary from centre to centre and from course to course. You may, for example, be asked to focus on one learner. You could be asked to study how the teacher uses resources, or what pronunciation or vocabulary work he or she does with the learners. These are just a few examples to give you an idea of some possibilities here.

There can sometimes be a problem seeing the aspect of a lesson that you have been asked to watch for. In Chapter 4, 'Guided observation', I suggested a number of ways in which you can make sure that this time is being spent to your advantage. Those questions or pointers apply equally well when you are observing your peers and so you may find it useful to copy these pointers down and carry them with you. They can help to guide you when it comes time to give feedback to the fellow participant that you have observed, especially in the early stages of the course, when you are less sure about what you need to be looking for.

To return to the time that you will spend observing experienced teachers, below is an example of the kind of task that you might be set, completed by Jan, a participant. This is followed by her learning record for the same lesson, a sheet she was asked to complete on her course, after every observed lesson. Note that at this centre, guided observation is called **directed observation**, but both terms refer to the same course component.

As you read these two documents, try to develop a picture of the class in your mind. This is how it was: the class took place in a large room, bright and airy, with floor to ceiling windows at one end, through which you have a view of the kind of luxuriant and deep green foliage that grows in a subtropical country. The kind of carpet that you find in offices is on the floor (good for reducing noise). There is a large magnetic whiteboard on one wall (a magnetic one doubles it value, allowing you to attach **flashcards** to it with magnets, for example), and a notice board on another, which is covered in learners' work. There is a large wall clock. There is also a map of the world on another wall, and the learners have marked their home towns on it with Blu-Tack and small flags with their names. A framed **phonemic chart** showing all 44 phonemic symbols (symbols for sounds, or phonemes) of English hangs in the corner, near the whiteboard. Sixteen learners sit in a semi-circle on chairs that have tablets attached, the kind that fold away down the right-hand side (and are always awkward for left-handed students). The teacher, a man in his thirties, stands in the middle of the room, near the whiteboard. Our observer, Jan, sits demurely at the back, behind the semi-circle of learners (a good place to sit? Not really. It is difficult to see what the learners are doing; and you cannot see their faces, so you cannot take advantage of that feedback either. But you may be expected to sit here. Try suggesting a different seating arrangement – it would be to your advantage). As you read, fill in the gaps: add the people, and build up a picture of the activities that took place.

English Language Teaching Certificate

Directed Observation Task 4

Date: *10th July*   **Level:** *Intermediate*
Type of class: *General English*   **Time:** *10.50–12.30*

As you observe, make notes on the following:

1. Students: Age, nationality, sex

All sts are mid 30s–mid 50s.

4 Hong Kong Chinese, 4 mainland Chinese, 3 Taiwanese, 3 Japanese, 2 French.

2 males, 14 females.

2. The lesson aims:

Speaking and reading skills development.

3. Was there any focus on reading/listening skills during the lesson? How was this integrated into the overall lesson?

First half – focus on speaking – stress and fluency

Second half – focus on reading and speaking – letters to Sherlock Holmes, sts have to figure out – who did it?

4. Was a text used with the class? How much time was spent using the textbook compared to supplementary materials? Was the text book adapted in any way?

No text book. This lesson is the first one I've seen that is run on the same lines as our TP – no text book, games, mingling – with presentation, practice and production.

English Language Teaching Certificate

Directed Observation – Learning Record

Observation number: *4*

Summary of lesson

1. T. checks homework

2. Game/introduction. T. tells sts 'I'm thinking of a famous person' and gets sts to ask him 20 questions – T. gives clues, e.g. not alive now, was a character in a novel etc – elicits 'Sherlock Holmes'. Then T. elicits as much information about S.H. as possible. He asks sts:

– Who was he?

– What was he?

– What do you know about him?

– Did he have a friend?

– Where did he live?

– When did he live?

– Was he a good detective?

– What does a detective do?

T. writes answers up on w/b as they are given. Plenty of language comes up and is discussed: to smoke a pipe; Dr Watson; violin; London; fog; to investigate a crime; criminal; a 'whodunnit'; to commit a crime/murder; jail; prison. T. often concept checks.

3. Then T. arranges class into 4 groups and hands out letters – a different one for each group. Letters all give different angles on same story. Sts read, discuss their letters and surmise about what must have happened. Then T. creates 4 new groups, each one with one member of the old groups. Tells sts – 'don't pass the letters around, instead tell each other about what you read'. Sts have to work out what happened based on all of the information.

What techniques/activities would you like to remember and make use of in your own teaching?

– T. uses a game to introduce some of the vocabulary and lead in to the topic – it encourages speaking and stimulates interest in following activity, and T. used opportunity to help sts with pronunciation and stress

– when introducing vocabulary, T. always clicks the stress and gets sts to repeat both chorally and individually

– T. uses phonemic symbols on w/b for pronunciation of new vocabulary (I must learn how to do that – it's really useful)

– T. gives them plenty of practice speaking. This was a very lively class.

As you read the above in order to build up a picture in your mind of the lesson that Jan observed, you will have encountered some of the conventions used in outlining a lesson. Note in particular Jan's use of abbreviations such as 'T.' for teacher; and 'sts' for students (you might also find 's/s' or 'ss'). Such abbreviations are commonly used in lesson plans as well, as mentioned earlier. On other occasions you may want to make use of diagrams and drawings too – to show, for example, the seating arrangements, or how a teacher divided up the whiteboard. You can see also that a considerable amount of detail is necessary if you are to be able to reconstruct the lesson again later. Providing such detail can help you to avoid being frustrated at a later stage of your course by finding such cryptic notes as '½ stresses on w/b' or 'change underlined words alphabetically in pairs' – both examples are taken from my own CELTA notes, and I have no idea what they mean!

It is also helpful if you can attach a copy of any handouts used in the lesson you have observed. However, as I have discussed elsewhere, you may find that the teachers you are observing have an ambiguous status in relation to your course. This may mean that, because they have full teaching loads, they are not so able to take your needs into account in terms of providing you with copies of handouts or the course book that is being used in the lesson, let alone a lesson plan. If you find yourself in this situation (you may well not: many teachers being observed will be more than willing to give you some time both before and after their lesson, as well as ensure that you have copies of all of the necessary materials) then you can always ask a learner at the end of the lesson to lend you his or her handouts for a few minutes, to allow you to make your own copy.

Observing a lesson and spending your time making notes such as those above will serve you well, without a doubt, as tasks like this can help to focus your attention on key features of a lesson. But you might also want to spend at least one lesson just sitting, thinking and absorbing the atmosphere. To accommodate this you may recall that I suggested above that you could arrange for additional observations, because former participants have found this component extremely valuable. Such additional observations provide an excellent opportunity for you to spend time in another teacher's classroom without

> 'The course has brought across to me more clearly than anything ever before the myriad facets of teaching.'
>
> Participant, Hong Kong

feeling obliged to complete a task or lesson record. Though you might have nothing concrete to show for time spent in this way, you will nevertheless leave with a deeper appreciation of the 'myriad facets' of teaching and learning.

▶ WRITTEN ASSIGNMENTS

You will certainly have a few written assignments to complete on your certificate course. The number of assignments, the choice of topic and the approach taken will vary from centre to centre, and from course to course, and may include reflecting upon a teaching practice lesson.

In this section, you will find the four assignments set by tutors on a certificate course. The criteria that tutors used to assess the four assignments are also supplied (remember that, depending on your course, you may find that not all of your assignments are assessed). The following five criteria applied to all assignments.

The participant has:

- displayed familiarity with key concepts and methodology
- shown an ability to relate theory to practice
- displayed the ability to use clear, coherent language which is essentially free of errors in spelling, punctuation, grammar and discourse
- made suitable and effective use of reference materials
- produced accurate work that is sufficiently detailed.

The criteria that are specific to each assignment follow each one, and you will also find a few recommended resources to help you to answer questions of the same type. This is followed by a suggested procedure for doing written work of this kind within the time scale of the course: your ten-point plan for tackling written assignments.

You will also be able to read one participant's complete answer to the fourth assignment.

Four assignments
Assignment 1
This was the first assignment set by a CELTA centre:

**English Language Teaching Certificate
Assignment 1: Language Analysis**

I live in Bahrain.

I've lived in Bahrain.

I lived in Bahrain for ten years.

1) What are the differences between the tenses in the sentences above in terms of their FORM, MEANING and USE?

2) What problems might students have in distinguishing between the tenses in these examples?

3) How could the differences be made clear to students?

Length: 750–1,000 words   **Due: Friday 3rd**

Recommended resources for this and similar assignments
Good resources to help you to answer questions of this type include:

- Aitken, R. (2002) *Teaching Tenses: Ideas for presenting and practising tenses in English*. United Kingdom: ELB
- Close, R. A. (1992) *A Teacher's Grammar: the central problems of English*. United Kingdom: Language Teaching Publications
- Lewis, M. (1986) *The English Verb: An exploration of structure and meaning*. United Kingdom: Language Teaching Publications
- Lewis, M. and Hill, J. (1985) *Practical Techniques for Language Teaching*. United Kingdom: Language Teaching Publications
- Swan, M. (2005) *Practical English Usage*. United Kingdom: Oxford University Press

Criteria
Besides the five criteria above, tutors used these additional points to assess this assignment:

The participant has:

- used basic terminology to describe language form, meaning and use
- identified relevant features of language to teach
- made suitable and effective use of reference materials.

Assignment 2
This was the second assignment:

English Language Teaching Certificate
Assignment 2: Materials evaluation

This assignment involves you looking critically at an EFL textbook. It is recommended that you use one of the TP textbooks: either Cunningham and *Moor's Cutting Edge Elementary*; Soars' *Headway Pre-intermediate* or Doff and Jones' *Language in Use* Intermediate classroom book. Below are headings and questions to think about. These questions are not exhaustive but cover the main areas you need to consider.

1. Approach

How is the syllabus organized? Is based on grammar, function or vocabulary? Give examples to support your answer.

(The teacher's book normally has an introduction which will help you to answer this, but don't believe what they say without actually checking the book to see if it's correct.)

▶

2. Lesson style

How does the book present language? Does it use listening, readings, dialogues? Is the presentation different in each unit or generally the same? Would you prefer to present in your own way (e.g. set the scene, elicit the language) or as the book does? Do you think you could use the practice activities as they are or do they need adapting? Is there a balance of skills activities? Are there speaking, reading, listening and writing activities?

3. Students' needs

How suitable is the material for your TP students? Consider interests, cultural background, age, etc. Can you pick out some units which are more/less suitable than others? In what ways could you adapt the material to make it more suitable?

Length: 750–1,000 words   **Due: Friday 10th**

Recommended resources for this and similar assignments
Good resources to help you to answer questions of this type include:

- Ur, P. (1999) *A Course in Language Teaching Trainee Book.* United Kingdom: Cambridge University Press (Part 4 in particular)

Criteria
Besides the five criteria above, tutors used these additional points to assess this assignment:

The participant has:

- shown an awareness of different ways of selecting and organizing the content of language teaching materials
- demonstrated the ability to evaluate materials to enable decisions to be made with regard to adapting/rejecting/replacing/supplementing published materials
- shown an understanding of the need for balance in language teaching materials
- demonstrated the ability to take the needs of a group of learners into account when selecting materials.

Assignment 3
This was the third assignment competed by the certificate participants:

English Language Teaching Certificate
Assignment 3: Case Study

This case study must be done on one of the students in your TP class.

Your assignment must cover the following four areas. The first two should be <u>brief</u> and the second two more detailed.

1. Learning background

    1.1. First language and, <u>briefly</u>, differences between it and English

    1.2. Other languages and proficiency in speaking and writing them

    1.3. Education (formal and informal)

    1.4. Previous language learning experience, including self-image as a good/bad learner

2. Motivation

    2.1. Reasons for learning English (social/profession/migration)

    2.2. Future plans

    2.3. Anything particular they want to learn

3. Problems with English

    3.1. Pronunciation problems

    3.2. Grammar problems

    3.3. Other problems

    3.4. What they find difficult about learning English

4. Learning style

    4.1. Do they speak/read/write/listen to English outside class?

    4.2. What do they expect and like about classes?

    4.3. What do they dislike about classes?

    4.4. How do they study outside class time?

    4.5. What can you say about their learning style, and in relation to this, how suitable is the methodology we use for them?

    4.6. Outline how you think the student could best be helped to improve their English.

Length: 750–1,000 words   **Due: Friday 17th**

Recommended resources for this and similar assignments
Good resources to help you to answer questions of this type include:

- Scrivener, J. (2005) *Learning Teaching*. United Kingdom: Macmillan ELT
- Swan, M. and Smith, B. (2001) *Learner English: A Teacher's Guide to Interference and Other Problems*. UK: Cambridge University Press
- Ur, P. (1999) *A Course in Language Teaching Trainee Book*. United Kingdom: Cambridge University Press

Criteria

Besides the five criteria above, tutors used these additional points to assess this assignment:

In relation to one learner, the participant has:

- shown an awareness of some of the factors that influence the learner, in particular his/her first language
- shown an understanding of the learner's motivation and language needs
- identified a number of specific problems and difficulties that the learner has in relation to learning English
- identified some features of the learner's learning style and related these to the methodology in use
- in the light of the above, made a number of relevant and practical suggestions with regard to developing the learner's language skills.

Assignment 4

This was the fourth assignment which participants completed:

English Language Teaching Certificate
Assignment 4: Lessons from the classroom

This assignment is intended to assess your ability to identify the strengths and weaknesses of your own teaching and to draw implications for your development from observing others.

Please answer **all** of the questions in a total of 750–1,000 words.

1. What do you feel are (or will be) the strengths of your own teaching? Give examples from your own teaching to show why you think you have (or will have) these strengths.

2. What do you feel are your weaknesses at the moment and how do you think they can be overcome? Again, give examples to show why you feel you have these weaknesses.

3. What strengths have you noticed in your peers' teaching that you would like to emulate?

4. What things do you remember from your observations of experienced teachers that you would like to incorporate into your own teaching?

With all of the above points, relate them to your approach to teaching, saying why you think these strengths are important and why any weaknesses need to be overcome.

Length: 750–1,000 words   **Due: Friday 24th**

Recommended resources for this and similar assignments

Good resources to help you to answer questions of this type include:

- Scrivener, J. (2005) *Learning Teaching*. United Kingdom: Macmillan ELT
- Ur, P. (1999) *A Course in Language Teaching Trainee Book*. United Kingdom: Cambridge University Press
- The section on 'Identifying your strengths and weaknesses' in Chapter 5

Criteria

Besides the five criteria above, tutors used these additional points to assess this assignment:

The participant has:

- shown an ability to reflect upon his or her own teaching and that of others, and identified strengths and weaknesses
- demonstrated the ability to respond actively to weaknesses identified
- shown the ability to learn from observing others.

'Lessons from the classroom': an example of a completed assignment

Below you will find an example of a completed assignment (assignment 4, as above) written by a participant who was awarded a Pass 'B' on her course.

As you read, you will see that this participant chose to highlight her insights (with the use of underlining). It was insights such as these which helped her to achieve a Pass 'B'.

ELT certificate: Assignment 4

<u>Lessons from the classroom</u>
C Jones, June 2006

<u>Introduction</u>

My background on joining the ELTA course did not include any formal teaching experience. I have found it very useful and relevant to reflect on the stages I have been going through in this process of being a learner teacher.

Insights on my development have come from: feedback sheets from my teaching practice; peer observations of my teaching; my mid-course evaluation; my own reflections and also those kept in a course diary which I chose to keep, as well as some reading I have done.

<u>What do you feel are (or will be) the strengths of your teaching?</u>

I feel my lessons are always <u>well prepared</u> and <u>well organized</u> and this is supported by tutor and peer feedback. I have been careful to ensure that I have prepared material

---

sufficiently to practise things first, to try and anticipate possible problems. In TP Point 3, I had anticipated the student problem with the pronunciation of 'third' and researched a method to assist students. This worked very well in class.

I am pleased with the <u>materials</u> that I use; overheads are clear and my handouts for various activities generally work very well. At the start of a lesson I have been able to use good materials to <u>set a relevant and interesting context</u>. I have also found my <u>instructions have been clear</u> so that students understand what they are required to do.

Teaching techniques such as <u>eliciting, drilling, stress marking, concept checking and monitoring</u> all seem to be progressing well. In TP Point 4, the drilling of the months of the year worked well and the random drilling I did on the board was fast and effective at reinforcing the pronunciations and checking the students' abilities. It would also appear that my lessons are <u>fun</u> and <u>interesting</u> and especially so when I am enjoying myself and presenting confidently.

Feedback from my tutor has highlighted that a key strength is my <u>awareness of my own strengths and weaknesses</u>, and the comments I make in feedback sessions. I think this will ultimately prove to be invaluable in my future teaching as it is enabling me to take forward my own professional development. For example, in TP Point 1, my <u>language grading</u> was a problem but I asked for assistance from a member of my group; then I managed to <u>address this point successfully</u> in TP Point 2. Problems with my <u>whiteboard being untidy</u> have been improved through my <u>preparing a whiteboard plan</u> in advance of the lesson. In TP Point 4, I became aware of the importance of being <u>student-focused</u> in order to actually help the students to learn and achieve. This shift in focus meant that in TP Point 7 I paid good attention to students and I was able to pick up some of their problems and to adapt my plan to deal with the language difficulty. I had developed a nice <u>rapport</u> with the students.

<u>What do you feel are your weaknesses at the moment and how do you think you can overcome them?</u>

There are a number of areas in my teaching where I need to develop my skills further.

Although I have addressed my problem with <u>language grading</u> I know I need to be constantly vigilant to avoid lapses into more complex sentences than are required. Now that I am <u>making the shift to a more student-focused</u> style of teaching I need to practise and pay attention to picking up on inaccuracies and <u>making effective corrections</u> but without destroying the communication that develops in the classroom. I plan to <u>get closer to the students</u> in my last TP session in order to identify errors and will attempt <u>to apply some of the techniques covered in our input sessions</u> on error correction. I have started to introduce <u>flexibility</u> in the way that I deal with materials and to be <u>adaptable</u> in the way that I present and set up practice activities.

Another weakness in my teaching relates to some aspects of my class management: specifically my ability to <u>organize my students</u> into groups to do activities. In nearly all my lessons so far comment has been made about my not being effective in getting the students into groups and in TP Point 5 some hesitancy on my part resulted in students not getting up when they should and not working together. Whilst this issue has not seriously hampered my teaching I have <u>developed a specific strategy</u> to deal with it. My plan is to:

— pay particular attention to the class management methods of teachers I observe

— build class management cues into my teaching points

— review this aspect critically at the end of each lesson

— read reference books on the subjects e.g. Effective Class Management by M. Underwood

What strengths have you noticed in your peers' teaching that you would like to emulate?

<u>Trainee A</u> is a teacher already and has been helpful as a <u>role model</u>. He demonstrates a relaxed manner, fluent style, excellent eliciting, often with fun realia e.g. a real birthday cake to elicit 'when's your birthday?'! He has a clear loud voice with key phrases to prompt drilling e.g. 'repeat' or 'again'.

<u>Trainee B</u> always has a clear and neat whiteboard, which is an excellent <u>model</u> for me; and her materials are always clear, colourful and beautifully presented. Her class management skills are also good; she is able to get students to stand up, to work in pairs, etc. very efficiently and with minimum fuss.

<u>Trainee C</u> always presents <u>fun</u> and <u>enjoyable</u> lessons. He makes good use of the OHP and has also developed his own effective method of <u>clarifying pronunciation</u> with the catch phrase 'watch my lips'. The lesson that I take from this is that <u>one can develop an individual approach</u> to dealing with various aspects of teaching. He also <u>focuses well on the students.</u>

What things do you remember from your observations of experienced teachers that you would like to incorporate into your own teaching?

I have found formal observations very valuable in providing me with a role model. In particular I have found it useful to see:

— teachers' <u>relaxed manner</u> creating a <u>convivial atmosphere</u> in which students are <u>encouraged to participate</u>

— <u>clear instructions and presentation</u> of new material

— one teacher who demonstrated excellent <u>adaptation</u> of part of a course book

— teachers <u>tackling exercises</u> I would have thought were <u>too difficult</u> for students

— <u>tactful and timely error correction</u>

— how <u>students perform better</u> when they are dealing with material that is <u>relevant</u> to them

(1,088 words)

Several of the insights and skills that this participant has described were identified by tutors and other participants as strategies that are likely to lead to success on a certificate course, and they are discussed more fully in Chapter 9, 'Succeeding'.

In the meantime, you can read about how to tackle written assignments, such as those above, effectively and efficiently in the time available.

Tackling written assignments

If you have recent experience of writing essays or assignments, as will be the case if you are a university or college graduate, then you might prefer to skim this section rather than read it in detail, as it is likely that much of the advice that follows will be familiar to you.

Ideally, you will be given all of your written assignments at or near the start of your course, with their respective deadlines. If you find that this is not going to be the case, ask your tutor to give you all your assignments and deadline information as soon as possible. There is no good reason for a tutor to refuse this request, and having the assignments early on can be very beneficial for you, because it allows you time in which to reflect upon the topic in relation to what you are learning on your course.

At this point, you might also want to make sure you have the following information:

● Will your course provider give you an opportunity to re-submit the work before the end of the course?

● Does the validating body have a referrals system which allows you to re-submit an assignment after the end of the course?

To complete written assignments and ensure that you maximize your chances of doing well, the first step is to study the question and its *criteria* so that you have a good idea about what you are required to do in order to answer it. If you have not been given any criteria, which could happen, you should ask your tutor for a set in relation to each question.

Armed therefore with all of your written assignments and their criteria, you can now start to work your way through each one. First, spend some time just *thinking generally about the question and its criteria.* Mull it over; have it in the back of your mind for a while. Try to relate each topic to what you are learning. Time spent in this way is useful for two reasons. It will help you to:

● clarify the question and criteria in your mind

● plan your reading so that spend your time effectively.

Next, you need to *allocate time in which to do the work.* Having thought about the question, you should be able to decide approximately how much time you will need to do this. You can build this time into your schedule – see the section below called 'Organize yourself: the personal planner'. This will help you to:

- see how much time you are able to allocate
- plan how best to use that time.

Once you have thought about the question and its criteria, and you have set aside some time for the assignment, you now should think about the *specifics* of the question. To help you to do this, underline the key words. This will help you to:

- analyse the question
- identify the points that your assignment should cover.

A good way to focus your ideas is to prepare a table, with one side showing the things you need to do and the other side showing what you should not, or need not, do. For example, in relation to Assignment 1 above, I might prepare the following table:

Assignment 1, with key words underlined:

> I live in Bahrain.
>
> I've lived in Bahrain.
>
> I lived in Bahrain for ten years.

1) What are the <u>differences</u> between the <u>tenses</u> in the sentences above in terms of their <u>FORM, MEANING</u> and <u>USE</u>?

2) What <u>problems</u> might students have in <u>distinguishing between the tenses</u> in these examples?

3) <u>How</u> could the <u>differences be made clear to students</u>?

What I need to do	**What I don't need to do**
Identify and describe the difference between the tenses in terms of their forms, meanings and uses.	Describe each tense in full – I do not need to write about all aspects of the form, meaning, and use of each form.
Identify and describe problems students might have in distinguishing these forms (focus on meaning and use in particular).	Describe problems that students might have with the individual forms – I must keep my focus on difficulties distinguishing one from the other.
Describe how I would teach the differences between these forms – how I would set up situations and activities in class to compare and contrast their meaning and use. To think about – level of proficiency of students? Could refer to a particular group in answering this question. Also – my assumptions – I would be assuming that these three forms are not new to students.	Describe how I would teach each form in isolation.

The left-hand column of this table provides guidelines that can help to keep me focused on the question.

Having focused your thoughts in this way, you can now begin to *collect material* to help you. This could be in various forms, including:

- your course notes (these are particularly valuable to you because your tutors will certainly have covered the key points through workshops and other course components)
- textbooks such as those in the 'recommended resources' sections that follow each of the four assignments given above; you will also find the resources suggested on www helpful
- course books in use in your centre
- lesson plans that have been prepared by former participants and by experienced teachers (does your centre keep a file of these in its resource room?)
- examples of former participants' assignments (ask your tutor if you can look at examples of these)
- journal articles (look at the *ELT Journal*, published by Oxford University)

  Press, in particular; your centre should subscribe to this. See www for a link to this journal.)

Once you have collected materials you think can help you, use them to *make some notes*, then start to *organize your notes* under headings. For example, for the language analysis assignment above, I might prepare the following headings:

Assignment 1: Outline

1. Introduction

2. What do we mean by 'form', 'meaning' and 'use'?

3. The three forms
   3.1. How they differ from each other in terms of:
      3.1.1. Form
      3.1.2. Meaning
      3.1.3. Use

4. Learners' problems
   4.1. Form
   4.2. Meaning
   4.3. Use

5. Teaching the differences
   5.1. Assumptions
   5.2. Target learners: intermediate students
   5.3. Teaching techniques and materials

6. Conclusion

7. References

These headings effectively provide you with an outline of your work. You are now in a good position to *write a first draft*. Having done this, *review your work* in relation to the assignment question and criteria, and proofread it for small errors, before you *prepare a final draft*.

To summarize, here is your ten-point plan for tackling written assignments:

Your ten-point plan for tackling written assignments

1. *Think generally* about the question and its criteria.

2. *Allocate time* in which to do the work.

3. *Think about* the specifics of the question; prepare a 'to do/not to do' table.

4. *Collect material* to help you do the assignment.

5. *Note* down some ideas on paper.

6. *Organize* your ideas.

7. *Write a first draft*.

8. *Review* your work in the light of the essay title and proofread it for small errors.

9. *Write a final draft*.

10. *Submit* your work on time!

As you will have noted from this and previous chapters, managing your time is of vital importance in helping you to learn on certificate courses.

▶ A TIME FOR ALL THINGS

Regardless of whether you are taking a part-time course or a full-time one, you may feel under pressure. This could be due to a number of factors: being under continuous assessment is one of the reasons frequently mentioned by participants. Another reason often given is connected to the course design: it is arranged so that participants cover as much ground as possible in the shortest time. This is a deliberate decision, because if you were to cover the same amount of information over a longer period, the course would have to be more expensive, and would require more time away from the workplace – time when you could be earning. A 150-hour course (for example) with the same syllabus as at present could have some 'white space', or periods of course time where nothing was scheduled, and while this would be of great benefit to you (time for reflection, for a start), some consumers might feel that they were getting poor value for money, and so providers may try to avoid this.

As a result of such factors, you could find that your course is an unusually intense experience, particularly if you have opted for a four-week course. Because of this intensity, it may be that four-week certificate course designs do not provide optimal conditions for learning, and this is something that you could think about –

and learn from – as you progress through the course. The extent to which this might be true becomes clearer if you think for a moment about the implications for language learners, if we were to design courses to help them learn English along the same lines as our four-week intensive certificate courses. Under these conditions, language learners would be expected to study for an average of 8–10 hours per day (which would include preparation for class, recommended reading, homework and assignments, etc.), possibly including weekends, if they felt they were falling behind. Our learners would also be required to give six hours of presentations to people who may already know the content of each presentation. They would be assessed continually on their performance throughout the course, and at the end they may fail, having paid a significant amount of money to join.

In fact language learning courses are usually arranged quite differently, even those that prepare learners for significant public examinations, and as you move through the course you might like to reflect upon the differences. Intensive language learning experiences do exist, of course, but they often exist in a context of choice: the consumer may find that he or she has a wide range of alternative course designs open to him or her.

> 'I'm wondering how I'm going to juggle time back home with two young and active and very busy "rules-of-their-own" kids (8 years and 5 years); will need to put in some time and effort and thought, definitely.'
>
> Participant, Hong Kong

You are likely to find, therefore, that there is a great deal to take in and do, and only a short time in which to do it. This kind of pressure may affect both your enjoyment of the experience and your learning while on the course. This participant described her experience:

> 'Although I did enjoy the course I felt as if we rushed from one thing to the next with hardly any time to absorb what we had just learnt. The Input Day being a prime example. All these subjects completely new and we just whizzed through them. I just can't imagine what the 4 week course is like. I suppose that is the whole thing with an intensive course. But it does make me question just how much people actually retain afterwards, obviously you need to carry on studying to really take on board everything you cover on the course.'
>
> *Participant, United Kingdom*

This participant had arrived at a key understanding: the course is a springboard, and you are absolutely not expected to absorb everything while on it.

The course as springboard

In fact, a great deal of your learning *should* occur after the course has ended, when you return to or take up a teaching position. During this period, you will be full of ideas presented on the course and possibly keen to try them out and experiment, free of the 'burden of continuous assessment', as a participant once described it. You will reinforce what you learned on the course and continue to develop as a teacher, because ideally, you will continue to read, study, observe and learn from your learners, observe your colleagues and exchange ideas, and become involved in other aspects of ELT/TESOL, in order to continue the development that you have set in motion by taking a certificate course (the various ways in which you can do this are discussed in Chapter 10, 'Continuing to learn'). The understanding that the course is best seen as a springboard is the reason why it will later be recommended that you start to teach *as soon as possible* after graduating from your certificate course.

A certificate course is a springboard

Former participants have also found that the amount of work involved means that it is absolutely essential to stay 'on top of the huge amount of stuff that comes at you', as one participant described it. Two skills in particular can help you to manage this workload. The first is the ability to distinguish tasks that represent *learning opportunities* from those that *support learning,* while the second skill is the ability to *organize yourself.*

Learning opportunity or learning support?

On a certificate course, you will be assigned various tasks (such as teaching practice, or completing an assignment, or filling in a form to get a number enabling you to use the photocopier). You will also set yourself your own personal tasks (such as highlighting key points from yesterday's feedback, or filing feedback, or collecting magazines to use as a source of ideas and images at a later stage). People who stay in control of the workload are those who identify such tasks, note them down as they are assigned or thought of, and set aside time in which to attend to them, having considered their priority. However, former participants have sometimes found prioritizing difficult to do, because it can seem that everything is important and urgent. But some things are much more important than others.

In previous chapters, I have emphasized the need to identify, and use, 'learning opportunities'. I have said that some learning opportunities are more obvious than others: feedback, for example, is a very obvious opportunity, while studying your syllabus statements is perhaps less obvious. Indeed, one of the aims of this book is to help you to identify learning opportunities that may be difficult to recognize.

Some of the tasks presented to you on your certificate course will represent learning opportunities. Some, however, will not, because they function not as opportunities for you to learn but rather as supports to learning. Think about the examples provided above. Teaching practice, completing an assignment, and highlighting key points from yesterday's feedback are all examples of learning opportunities: you can learn through doing them. Filling in a form to get a number for the photocopier, filing your feedback notes, and collecting magazines are all examples of tasks that *support* your learning. They are good to do, and will help your learning to go more smoothly, but clearly if you are under pressure then it would be a better idea to prioritize learning opportunities rather than the tasks that support your learning. Understanding this distinction will help you to begin to prioritize your tasks and organize yourself, which in turn can help to alleviate any pressure.

Organize yourself: the personal planner

In Chapter 5, I suggested that one way of organizing yourself is by having practical systems in place at the start of the course to help you deal with the paperwork, such as sets of binders, dividers and filing categories. Organizing yourself, however, also means managing your time effectively.

> 'TP 2, and the first assignment, are keeping the pressure on. And, this pressure hasn't let up since the start of the course.
>
> It is all a matter of "time management", but – a day has only 24 hours!'
>
> Participant, Hong Kong

One of the most effective time management strategies that I have seen in operation on certificate courses involved creating a 'personal planner'. The participant who developed this started with his course timetable. As soon as he received it he transferred all of the information *that related to him* from this timetable to a planner that he had designed. He included information from his course handbook about assignment deadlines, tutorial dates, and so forth. This planner was for all of the hours he felt he could devote to the course, and he had printed a fresh one for each week, because this gave him a complete overview of the course.

He then allocated time on his plan for the various tasks as he received them, and he set aside time for the other things that he needed to do. To his plan, therefore, he added tasks such as:

> 'The only way I survived was by meticulously planning such that every last minute was put to good use.'
>
> Participant, United Kingdom

- course reading
- written assignment research and writing
- lesson preparation
- meetings with TP team members
- 'housekeeping', that is, administration (filing, forms to be completed, etc.).

You can improve upon this participant's idea by doing the following:

- Reflect upon the kind of person you are. Perhaps you are a morning person, at your best between 6 am and 9 am? If so, set this time aside for tasks that are learning opportunities: course reading, perhaps, or for giving some thought to your next lesson. Plan to do this kind of work when you are at your best.

- Set aside 'time for all things': all the tasks suggested above, and any others that you have identified. Assign time to new tasks as they come in. Mark each one 'LO' (learning opportunity) or 'LS' (learning support) so that you can give priority to the former if you need to.

- Plan time for 'R & R': not rest and recreation but *relaxation and reflection*. In Chapter 3 I suggested that reflection could assist with learning, but that on courses such as these, particularly full-time ones, it could be 'squeezed out'. By planning for it in this way, you help to prevent such squeezing out.

- Plan 'contingency time', to use when things have not worked out as you anticipated.

- Plan free time.

- See your planner as a flexible friend. Write in pencil, to allow you to amend it and update it as the course proceeds.

Above, you have one person's idea for managing the pressure that such courses can bring. Even with the improvements suggested above, it may not suit you. If this is the case, you may want to think about developing another approach to surviving the pressure that former participants have experienced. As you do so, bear in mind in particular the need to recognize learning opportunities and prioritize them; and the need to stay in control of the workload.

> 'The course is very intensive with little free time in which to muse, so you have to create it yourself: by working late, for example, or giving up that dinner out with your boyfriend that you'd planned.'
>
> Participant, United Kingdom

Participants who have excelled on their certificate courses are those who have taken account of many of the points made and strategies suggested in this chapter. Other strategies to help you to reach your personal best both while on your course and afterwards are discussed fully in Chapter 9, 'Succeeding'.

Learning: Key points to take away with you

- Remember that while you will observe experienced teachers for 6 hours, you could spend up to 24 hours observing your peers teaching. Make sure you gain maximum benefit from time spent in this way. Use the questions/pointers provided in Chapter 4, 'Guided observation', to focus your observation during this part of the course.

- Keep a good record of every class you observe, whether it is being taught by experienced teachers or your fellow participants. Include copies of all handouts or materials used in the lesson. These notes will prove useful as you progress through the course and also once you have graduated and are in your first post-certificate teaching job.

- Former participants have found guided observation of experienced teachers so valuable that it is worth trying to arrange for more observations than the scheduled hours.

- Ideally you will be given all of your written assignments at or near the start of your course, with their respective assessment criteria and deadlines. If this does not happen, ask your tutor to supply all of this information at the earliest possible opportunity.

- Remember that you are not expected to absorb everything presented on the course. Rather, you are expected to show a growing appreciation of the practice of ELT/TESOL and some of its underlying principles. Demonstrating a 'growing appreciation' means demonstrating 'progress' – and it is this that your tutors want to see.

- Prioritize tasks by distinguishing those that are learning opportunities from those that support learning; concentrate on the former if the pressure becomes too great.

www Check your understanding of Chapter 6 by completing the quiz available on the companion website at: www.sagepub.co.uk/brandt

Chapter 7

Teaching

In this chapter you can learn about:

- teaching practice points: what they are and how they can help you
- lesson planning, including an example lesson plan
- some essentials for teaching practice survival, including how to deal with teaching practice nerves
- your guiding principles for effective feedback, including how to give effective feedback, and why it is important to ensure that you receive effective feedback too.

▶ TEACHING PRACTICE

Teaching practice gives you opportunities to apply what you have learned during your course, and it gives tutors opportunities to monitor your progress and provide you with feedback on it.

Particularly at the beginning of the course tutors will provide you with substantial guidance and support, which will be slowly reduced as you become increasingly independent. Part of the guidance that you will receive will be carried out through scheduled lesson planning and preparation sessions. For example, you will have a workshop or workshops on the topic of lesson planning, and you will probably have scheduled time in which you can prepare your lesson, with a tutor available for advice, should you need it. As well as this kind of tutorial support, you will also be provided with guidance in the form of 'teaching practice points'. These points are your guide: they may tell you what your lesson aims should be, and what materials to use, for example.

You may be asked to work as part of a team for teaching practice purposes, though this is not the only way in which teaching practice may be structured. Common features, however, are likely to include the use of teaching practice points – particularly in the early stages of your course – which you will use to plan your lesson, followed by feedback.

Assuming that you have been assigned to a teaching practice team, you will be likely to experience a procedure along the following lines. Tutors provide your teaching practice team with a set of teaching practice points. There will be one point for each member of the team who is teaching on that day (it may be the case that not everyone teaches on every teaching practice lesson; a rota will be prepared by your tutors to make sure that everyone is able to teach for a minimum of six hours). You then work with the other members of your team to design a coherent and cohesive lesson for your learners. After this, you will probably work largely alone to plan and prepare your own lesson section.

On the day, each member of the teaching practice team who is teaching gives their lesson; anyone not teaching will observe. After the lesson, you all meet with your tutor for feedback; at the end of feedback you may be given your teaching practice points for your next lesson. The process that occurred at one centre is illustrated in Figure 7.1 'From teaching practice point to feedback: a possible approach'.

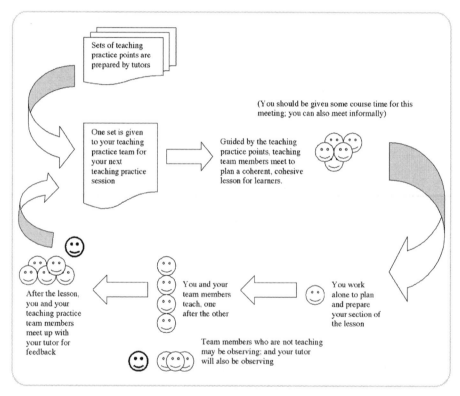

Figure 7.1 From teaching practice point to feedback: a possible approach

Teaching practice points

Below, you will find three examples of teaching practice points given to participants at the beginning, middle and end of their course. I have selected points given to participants working at different levels in order to provide an idea of what these can look like. Note how tutors have provided several suggestions to support the participants in their first teaching practice, and how, in teaching practice points designed for participants in the later stages of the course, progressively less detail is provided, such that participants are expected to write their own aims for their last lesson. Note also the language and abbreviations used (for example, the use of the word **elicit** and the abbreviation 'vocab' for 'vocabulary', both of which are commonly found in lesson plans as well as teaching practice points). As you read, you might also like to start thinking about the lesson that you would produce if you had been given these points.

This set of teaching practice points provides examples of the kind of points that you might be given if you are taking a CELTA course. It has been designed for four participants' first teaching practice session:

English Language Teaching Certificate
Teaching Practice Points

Elementary – TP Point 1

4 × 30 minutes

Date _____

Reference: Cunningham and Moor's *Cutting Edge Elementary*, Unit 4 'Loves and Hates'

Aims: By the end of the lesson, students will be able to:
- Speak and write about their own and others' likes and dislikes, using a range of activity verbs

Students will also revise present simple forms

Trainee	Description of teaching	Comments/suggestions
1	**Language focus**	P 31 Ex 1 – could use pictures of your own first, as a warm up. Then do exercise Ex 2 – as in the book Ex 3 – you might want sts to check their work with each other before you do a whole class check Grammar box – think about how you will use this. You could prepare a table of all forms for sts to complete perhaps. Draw sts' attention to 'verb + -ing' after 'like', 'hate', 'love'
2	**Practice**	P 32–33 Ex 1–4. Follow the teacher's book

▶

Trainee	Description of teaching	Comments/suggestions
3	**Reading and listening**	P33–34 Ex 1 – sts could discuss in pairs, then ask one or two to report to whole class. e.g. 'Stefan would like to live in …' Ex 2 – Sts can also check their answers to the qus in pairs, before whole group check Ex 3 – listening. Follow procedure for Ex 2
4	**Writing**	P 34 Grammar box – You could elicit all possible forms and write up on w/board. Ex 1–4 Follow teacher's book Collect writing in to correct and make sure this is returned next lesson Set homework – ask sts to write down 5 questions they might ask about Rita

These points are for four participants' fourth teaching practice session:

English Language Teaching Certificate
Teaching Practice Points

Pre-intermediate – TP Point 4

4 × 30 minutes

Date _____

Reference: Soars' *Headway Pre-intermediate,* Unit 3, 'It All Went Wrong'

Aims: Make your own aims for this lesson. Use the teacher's book to help you.

Trainee	Description of teaching	Comments/suggestions
1	Divide the unit into manageable 30 minute sections. It is not necessary to cover the whole unit, but you should think about overall aims for the lesson and providing your class with a balance of activities.	Use the course book, and add or adapt any material. You'll find some suggestions to help you in the teacher's book. You may also want to set some homework from the workbook.
2		
3		
4		

The third set of points is for one participant's last teaching practice (note how the participant has written in her own aims):

English Language Teaching Certificate
Teaching Practice Points

Intermediate – TP Point 7

I × 60 minutes

Date _____

Reference: Doff and Jones' *Language in Use Intermediate* classroom book, Unit I I

Aims: Make your own aims for this lesson. Use the teacher's book to help you.

Aims	*The students should be aware of the form, meaning and use of the future continuous tense:*
	will be + present participle

1. From this unit choose the grammar point that you want to teach. There may be more than one grammar point in the unit.
2. Decide exactly what and how much you want to teach. Remember you only have one hour.
3. Write your aims for the lesson in the space above.
4. Once you have selected the grammar point from the unit you may use the book or develop your own materials. The lesson should lead towards production of the target language. You may include any presentation technique, and any practice activities or any skills work that you choose.

Using such points, you will be expected to work with the members of your team to prepare a coherent lesson for your learners. Before you are asked to do this, though, you will be given a very good idea of what a lesson plan should look like, through workshops and teaching practice preparation sessions.

Lesson planning

Below, you will find the lesson prepared by a participant for the last teaching practice point above. Note the format of the plan – you may wish to use the same format, or follow the one recommended by your tutor. You will also find a blank lesson plan form on www which you can print out and photocopy as needed. Alternatively, you may prefer to prepare your own.

English Language Teaching Certificate
Lesson Plan

(NB: Give a copy to your tutor and to each person in your TP group before your lesson)

Name: ——————————————— **Date:** ———————————————

Level: ———————————————— **Lesson length:** ——————————

Lesson stage: ——————————— **Number of students:** ——————

Aims:
By the end of the lesson, the student will be able to:
Use the future continuous tense to explain unavailability, analyse the form and use it in context.

Contexts:
Explaining unavailability in the future

Grammar and vocabulary:
Will + be + present participle (-ing form) of verb

Anticipated problems for students:
Confusion between this form and other ways of talking about the future, e.g. 'going to'. This will be addressed by focusing on its use to explain unavailability; pronunciation – sts may find 'll' difficult, as in 'you'll be . . .', 'I'll be . . .' etc.

Points you want to work on in your teaching:
Giving clear instructions
Not making the lesson too teacher-centred
Asking concept questions and focusing on form, meaning and use

Materials needed:
Worksheet 1: photocopy of diary pages from Aitken's 'Teaching Tenses', p 179
Worksheet 2: own gap-filling exercise
30 sentences written on separate cards
Whiteboard and OHT pens

English Language Teaching Certificate
Lesson Plan (continued)

Time	Step	Comments/materials
2.00pm	Introduce target language Tell sts – I'm flying to England on Monday Ask them – Will I be able to teach you next week? Why/not? Then – What will I be doing this time next week? Elicit several answers and write up on w/board.	Example answers: You'll be visiting your friends
2.10pm	Focus on meaning Concept check by asking: Am I in Hong Kong now? (yes) Have I left Hong Kong already? (no) Am I planning to leave soon? (yes) Do I have some plans for next week? (yes) Can I teach you next week? (no) Draw a timeline on w/b next to sentences: PRESENT FUTURE ----------XXXX-------XXXX--- 2.15pm today 6pm Mon 2.15pm Weds teaching fly to UK visit friends Focus on form: Ask sts – what do you notice about all the sentences? What is the name of this form? Write name above timeline and sentences Focus on use Ask sts – When is it used?	 Expect to elicit: They are all made using: will + be + pres. part. Elicit – future continuous. It's used to talk about an action expected to cross a point or take up a period of time in the future. Often used to explain someone's unavailability

Time	Step	Comments/materials
2.25pm	Practice 1 – speaking – Guess what's written. Sentences written on cards. Demonstrate – I pick up card, tell sts they have to guess what's written on it from my sentences. Example: on card – 'I'll be watching "Star Wars" at 8pm tomorrow night. I tell sts – 'I'll be sitting in the dark'; 'I'll be eating popcorn', etc. Sts have to guess my sentence. Then hand out cards; sts play the game themselves.	Cards with 'will be' sentences
2.40pm	Practice 2. Sts work in pairs. One worksheet per pair. Three diaries on worksheet – Anne's, Sally's and Mike's. Anne is ill. Sts have to work out how Sally and Mike can cover Anne's timetable between them. Whole class feedback.	Worksheet 1
2.55pm	Home work	Worksheet 2

Abbreviations in lesson plans are widely used. Common ones include:

h/o = handout (as a verb or noun)
w/b or w/board = whiteboard
st = student; sts = students
t = teacher
OHP = overhead projector
OHT = overhead transparency
h/wk = homework
w/sheet = worksheet

You can make up your own!

This lesson went very well, and perhaps you can see why. The participant had thought carefully about the grammar point – its form, meaning and use – and she used a realistic example to introduce the grammar point. She elicited well, checked her students' understanding of the concept and gave them opportunities to speak using the new language. The only thing missing, perhaps, was the opportunity for writing and for personalization – the chance for students to use the language in a way that was personally meaningful for them. Both of these might have been possible if her lesson had been longer.

Making steady progress

This extract from a participant's journal describes his first teaching practice class and his preparations for it:

'Had our first TP on Friday. We met at 11am for a run-through. I was laden with realia, Sam with clocks, pictures, flashcards, Joan seemed very calm armed with her handouts, Nuria arrived late and flustered and disappeared to prepare. Our fifth group member, Jim – lucky Jim! – was observing us today! The run-through went smoothly but Sam panicked and decided to revise her whole section. We persuaded her not to go home but to work upstairs.

Suddenly it was two o'clock and we were on.

Sifting back through the haze, I was pleased I remembered so many names. They grasped the vocabulary well but I felt quite inadequate during drilling and when they paid no attention to my instructions I broke out in a cold sweat. Joan looked most encouraging throughout and I appreciated it!'

Participant, Hong Kong

As the extract from the participant's journal above suggests, there are many aspects to teaching besides teamwork: preparation, planning, materials selection or design, rehearsing, conveying meaning, giving instructions, checking understanding and providing practice opportunities for learners, for example.

Perhaps because teaching brings so much together, and because it is the most critical component of the course for assessment purposes, former participants have said that it is one of the best aspects of the course. Many used words such as 'real buzz', 'terrific high' and 'adrenalin rush' when referring to this component.

Some former participants have mistakenly felt that, in order to succeed on the course, they have to demonstrate excellent planning and teaching skills from the first day of

> 'TP was by far the most valuable component for me because I got a chance to combine all the skills learned and presented and I got lots of valuable feedback.'
>
> Participant, United Kingdom

teaching practice. This is not the case. Instead, tutors are looking for evidence of *steady progress* which reflects a growing appreciation, understanding and learning of the facts, concepts, ideas, techniques, methods, approaches and underlying principles which have been presented to you through workshops and which you have observed during guided observation. Your progress will be measured against criteria, which you should obtain and study.

However, you will become aware very early on in your course that you have only a short time in which to demonstrate your learning. At around the same time, you will be becoming aware of all of the various aspects and complexities of teaching and, therefore, just how much you need to demonstrate in this limited time. Such issues can increase stress and exacerbate performance nerves. People who do well on certificate courses are often those who have learned to manage performance nerves very early on, and there are steps you can take to help you to do this.

Managing performance nerves

Varying degrees of nervousness play a large part in participants' experiences of certificate courses. Nervousness relates particularly to teaching practice, whether this is being carried out with language learners or with fellow participants, and is therefore a form of performance nerves, or 'stage fright'. Participants have described experiencing insomnia, blurred vision, weeping, nausea, irritability, weakness, lethargy, near-hysteria, headaches, migraines, a racing pulse, profuse perspiration, and trembling. For example, participants have made comments such as:

'I remember that I didn't dare attempt to drill because my hand was shaking too much.'
Participant, United Kingdom

'All I remember of my first lesson is my heart pounding so loudly in my chest I thought the whole world must be able to hear it.'
Participant, Australia

I have described above how teaching practice may be shared among the participants in your group. This feature of the course design means that over the course you will spend a significant amount of time watching your fellow participants teach while awaiting your turn, something that can increase nervousness, for at least two reasons: it allows longer for tension to build up; and you may see your fellow participant doing something that you wish you had thought of, or that you had planned to do but now can see is not such a good idea. These participants describe their experience:

'I felt calm and collected for my TP. I had prepared well and felt confident that I would get it done. Then – TP. I had to sit through 1½ hours of lesson before it came to me so I got really nervous. By the time it came to me I was at committal stage – where is the asylum?'
Participant, Hong Kong

'Trainees who teach first have a better time of it. You can see the others getting progressively more nervous as they wait for their turn.'
Tutor, Spain

It may help you to know that you will almost certainly find that teaching practice times are rotated, so that everyone has a chance to teach first, second, third and so forth. This will be arranged fairly, because tutors are aware that sitting waiting for your turn can increase anxiety. However, as with other aspects of these courses, you can turn this waiting time to your advantage, by using it to study your learners, the benefits of which will be discussed in more detail in Chapter 9.

In the meantime it may also help if you can remind yourself that performance nerves are quite normal, and that people experience such nerves in a variety of other situations: for example, when taking a driving test, being interviewed for a job, or any kind of public speaking such as giving a speech at a wedding. There is a considerable amount of advice available in books and on the internet to help deal with nervousness in such situations, and you may wish to take a look at some of this before your course. If you do so, you will be likely to read about the importance of:

- planning and preparation (in good time, so that you are not making any last minute changes)
- practising (as much as you can)
- breathing deeply (just before you start to teach)
- calling upon the support of your friends and family (do plenty of 'positive chatting')

> 'In class 15 minutes before time, people were really nice to me and my nerves ebbed.'
>
> Participant, Hong Kong

- thinking positively (you know you can do it)
- believing that your audience is on your side (they believe you can do it).

In relation to certificate courses, however, four points in particular can help you deal with performance nerves. These are the understandings that:

- The more involved you are, the less nervous you will be.
- Performance nerves tend to diminish with time: both as an individual lesson progresses, and as the course progresses.
- Your learners should know that you are learning how to teach. They are very likely to be on your side and will almost certainly be supportive, considerate, and tactful.
- Knowing your audience reduces nerves, so: learn your learners!

These four points are considered in greater detail below.

The more involved you are, the less nervous you will be

Former participants have found that the more involved they are in what they are doing, the less nervous they are. They say things such as, 'It was terrible at first, and I remember thinking "I can't do this, I can't go on." But I did and as the lesson went on I forgot all about feeling nervous because I became absorbed in it.' Former participants have also found that they become more deeply involved if they believe in what they are trying to do. This means doing something not because it is expected of you, but because you have considered your learners and prepared a lesson which you personally believe will be to their benefit.

Performance nerves diminish with time

Participants have observed that they were far more nervous in the early teaching practice lessons than in the later ones. This is of course partly because of the skills they are acquiring, which give them greater confidence; but it is also because they have learned about involvement. They have had first-hand experience of *losing themselves in a lesson,* knowledge of which helps to make them less nervous at the start of their next lesson.

It will help you enormously if you can keep in the back of your mind the knowledge that you too will probably lose yourself in your lesson and experience the same *learning to be less nervous.*

Your learners should know that you are learning how to teach and will be on your side.
Former participants have found that their learners are usually supportive and sympathetic, because they are aware that you are learning how to teach and that your teaching is being assessed. Remember too that your learners are volunteers and that they are there because they want more exposure to English, something that you can provide easily.

Know your audience

> 'On a high after the last TP practice. It went extremely well – was described as excellent and I felt and presented myself with so much more confidence. I feel as though I have now got over the barrier of being self-conscious about my teaching and now feel able to concentrate on working with the students and developing techniques to communicate learning to them.'
>
> Participant, Hong Kong

I have observed that nothing helps people in teaching practice more than focusing on their audience. However, I have also seen many former participants assuming – mistakenly – that their audience is, as a participant once put it, 'the row of faces looking expectantly at me from the back of the room.' The first step therefore is to try to avoid the temptation to concentrate on your observers' expectations of you, because they are not the reason why you are standing up there in front of them. The reason is, of course, your learners, and getting to know them, and being able to focus on them, can help you to excel on your course.

Practising, not performing

People who do well in teaching practice are also those who, as well as learning to manage performance nerves, have realized that they will benefit more if they approach teaching practice as an opportunity to *practise for themselves* rather than *perform, or demonstrate, for others.* In other words, they have decided to use teaching

> 'Cathy described feeling that she had to perform and demonstrate techniques rather than help her students. She told me that if I hadn't been observing her, she might have been able to put more emphasis on helping them rather than "ploughing on regardless", as she put it!'
>
> Tutor (reflecting upon a participant's observations), Australia

practice for their own benefit, rather than 'ploughing on regardless' and being more focused on what their tutors want to see than either the learners or their own development. This is a subtle distinction, and not one that participants have found particularly easy to put into practice – because the course structure, with only six hours of teaching practice, provides tutors with limited assessment opportunities, which in turn puts pressure on participants to perform what they know tutors want to see. However, if you remind yourself that tutors are looking for evidence of progress, then this can help you to focus on practice, because progress should be a natural consequence of practice.

Your essentials for teaching practice survival

A former colleague of mine, Kate, is a certificate tutor (running back-to-back certificate courses in the United Kingdom for much of the year), a teacher of tutors (this position is sometimes called a 'trainer of trainers'), and a visiting validator. She is particularly interested in the teaching practice component of certificate courses, and she decided to carry out some research with a view to helping participants to address the kind of issues described above, including the 'performance nerves' and 'practice versus performance' ones.

> 'In feedback she said that this was the first lesson she'd actually been able to stop and reflect in – "three times in the lesson and for about two seconds each time". She said that in previous lessons she had been too caught up in managing the process to be able even to stop and think.'
>
> Tutor (reflecting upon a participant), Australia

First, Kate gathered some data from participants. At the end of several courses, as well as asking her participants to complete the standard course evaluation, she asked an additional question: 'If, at the start of your teaching practice, you'd known everything that you now know, what "mantra" would you have used to get you through and help you to enjoy the experience more?'

Below are some of the responses Kate collected.

> 'I've estimated times for each of my activities – have to now rehearse ("talk to the walls", as one co-trainee put it!) my lesson at least once from beginning to end.'
>
> Participant, Hong Kong

TP Mantras

1. For sure mine would have to be 'breathe deep, keep calm' because I had real trouble, especially at the start of the course, staying in control. The buzz caused by the adrenalin rush used to get the better of me and I'd break out in the shakes and a cold sweat!

2. I'd say to myself, 'It's OK to do it my way'. For example, I found it really helped me to transfer my lesson plan onto small cards which I then used as a reminder of what I should be doing in TP. Such personal strategies can really help.

3. Definitely, it would be 'listen to your feedback and select just one or two of your worst "TEFL crimes" to concentrate on. Choose ones that you feel most able to do something about, most easily. Set your own personal targets. Don't try to take it all on board at once.'

4. I think I'd remind myself to stay involved with the other members of my group. As the course marches on, you can sometimes forget about them because there's so much to do. This means you switch off in lesson preparation, if you're not teaching that day; you switch off during feedback, when it's not your feedback. So I'd 'say, stay switched on to others, because you can learn from them.'

5. Just before going in to teach, I'd tell myself – over and over again –'Teaching is fun! So enjoy it!'

6. I had my own mantra! It was 'slow down, stop, think'. I got through TP on those words! It applied as much to my planning as to my teaching.

7. For me it would definitely be 'slow and steady does it'. Slow, steady progress would be what I'd want. But it's not easy to see at the time. You tend to rush things and want it to be all right all at once, which just isn't possible.

8. I'd try to remind myself not to put on a performance. There were times when I was aware of playing to the audience at the back of the room. My focus instead should have been on my own teaching. So I'd tell myself something like 'do it for yourself, not for them'. This can help you to ignore the assessment that's going on all the time.

9. Without a doubt it would be 'pay close attention in input sessions, because what goes on there should inform your practice.'

10. Oh, that's easy, I'd say 'remember the learners – get them right and TP'll be right!'

11. 'Learn from reflecting, from looking back at what you've done, what you've been told, and what you've seen.'

12. For me it would be the value of rehearsing. When I'd rehearsed I was more in control. But I didn't do enough of it and it made me wobbly at times.

13. I tend to go overboard with material and planning details, so my mantra would be 'keep it simple'.

14. At the start of each TP, I'd remind myself about what I had done well. I'd remind myself of my strengths.

Kate decided to use such 'mantras' to help future participants. She began by captur-
ing the *essence* of each in a few words, and she made a list which she called 'Essentials
for teaching practice survival':

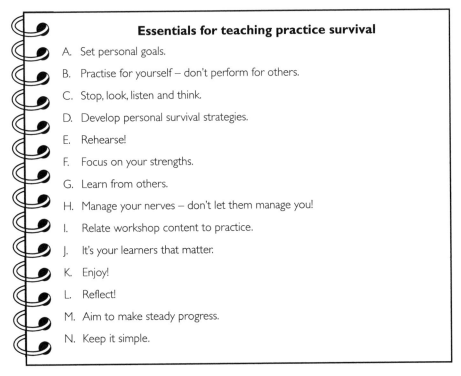

Essentials for teaching practice survival

A. Set personal goals.

B. Practise for yourself – don't perform for others.

C. Stop, look, listen and think.

D. Develop personal survival strategies.

E. Rehearse!

F. Focus on your strengths.

G. Learn from others.

H. Manage your nerves – don't let them manage you!

I. Relate workshop content to practice.

J. It's your learners that matter.

K. Enjoy!

L. Reflect!

M. Aim to make steady progress.

N. Keep it simple.

Kate uses these 'mantras' and 'essentials' as the basis for a workshop for certificate
participants. In one activity, she asks participants to match the essentials, which are
all mixed up above, to the mantras. You might like to do this activity yourself. You
can check your ideas with Kate's answer key, which you will find in the 'takeaway'
section at the end of this chapter. There, the essentials have been numbered and
arranged in the order that corresponds to the order of the mantras, above.

Having done this, you might also like to rearrange these essentials into your own
personal order of priority, and add any other that you think of as you progress
through your course.

A number of these essentials were identified by tutors and participants as strategies likely to lead to overall success on the course, and are discussed in more detail
in Chapter 9, 'Succeeding'. You may wish to turn to this chapter now and follow up
on one or two of the strategies that are particularly relevant for you at the stage you
are at in relation to your course.

Teaching practice, however, is of little value without feedback. Perhaps because
of this, many participants also consider feedback to be one of the most fruitful
aspects of these courses. This component is considered below. First, read Alison's
description of teaching and feedback during the rest of her course. In particular,
note what she says about feedback.

My Experience of the CELTA Course
(continued)

Alison Standring

Week Two:

In Week Two, we started teaching from course books. By now, I was ready to think more about lesson content and delivery. I benefited from the feedback I received after TP and also from observing teachers at International House. Generally I enjoyed the week and was starting to feel more relaxed. For my two housemates, it was a different experience: one seemed to have antagonized the new course tutor and could do no right in her eyes, the other (already an experienced teacher) had consistently received tougher criticism than the rest of us. This was partly because she was far better and it was thought she could handle it, and partly because she didn't have a very 'TEFLY' teaching style.

Weeks Three and Four:

During this period, I was fortunate enough to have my favourite course tutor. One of the reasons I liked him was that he condensed feedback to one or two main points. Another reason I liked him was that, instead of focusing on mistakes I already knew I'd made, he usually pointed out things I hadn't realised.

Alison raises a number of issues here:

- what can happen when a participant does not get on well with a tutor
- how a tutor gave more critical feedback to an experienced participant
- the existence of a 'TEFL' teaching style
- the value of receiving focused feedback
- the value of having her attention drawn to things that she had not noticed herself.

Issues such as these, and others, are considered below.

▶ GIVING AND RECEIVING FEEDBACK

We give and receive feedback from others all the time, from family and friends, colleagues, acquaintances and strangers, and we receive it in a variety of ways: through the spoken and written word (brief exchanges, conversations, emails, letters …) and through body language (gestures, posture, proximity, eye contact …). The feedback that you will give and receive after teaching practice and through other elements of the course is simply an extension of this day-to-day feedback, one which is focused on teaching performance, and which takes place in a context rich with other sources of feedback: language learners, experienced teachers that you are observing as well as those you meet casually in the staffroom, and so forth.

Former participants have described finding feedback after teaching practice to be of particular value, for a number of reasons. Such feedback can:

- be very motivating, as you hear an experienced, authoritative tutor describe or comment upon what you did well, particularly as you know that your performance is being compared to the expected certificate standard

- help you to identify areas you need to work on, which can guide your practice and therefore lead to more progress

- encourage reflection, and develop the skills required for reflection

- help you to develop the skills you need in order to give constructive feedback

- allow you to hear different people's views of your lesson, or aspects of it

- give you an opportunity to clarify anything you are not sure about

- allow the free flow of ideas, between and among tutors and participants.

> 'I found this to be the richest source of learning. I was really very fortunate to be part of a group that gave feedback well – we were all very open and frank, which we needed to be.'
>
> Participant, Australia

> 'Having someone else tell you that your drilling was getting a lot better, or that your reading activity went really well, was very good for morale.'
>
> Participant, Spain

Below, you will find an extract from a report written by the validator after visiting a certificate course. Her visit took place in week 9 of a 12-week part-time course. She had made notes about each participant, from which you will be able to see the significance that tutors attach to the development of the ability to give and receive feedback. This is followed by a description of a feedback session she attended, for two participants who had taught for an hour each. Note that the 14 learners and their participant-teacher would have had 7 observers.

This extract will give you a good overview of the processes involved in a post-teaching practice feedback session, in the context of a certificate course.

From these comments, it will be evident that giving and receiving feedback is, as a course component, considered to be as important as teaching practice. It follows that your performance in feedback is just as important as your performance in teaching practice. This makes good sense because:

- an effective teacher is a reflective teacher (he or she can look back and learn)

- an effective colleague is a constructive colleague (he or she can listen and help).

But, just as with teaching practice, it is important not to fall into the trap of believing that you need to *perform* in feedback, just because your behaviour here is being monitored. Some former participants have done just this, describing feeling a need to 'play the game' in feedback.

Section 7: Grades

Trainee E

Trainee E has grasped the basic principles, but generally he struggles to adapt his teaching according to feedback, and he can be defensive. His assignments are average. Overall – potential pass

Trainee G

Trainee G is very creative and produces original, student-centred lessons. She has excellent eliciting and concept checking skills, and is very supportive in feedback, with many constructive ideas. She implements suggestions very effectively. A strong pass.

Trainee L

Trainee L is a trained school teacher but this seems to interfere with his teaching rather than assist. He tends to expect too much from his students and he overloads them as a result. Not very open to suggestions/ideas in feedback, and can be quite critical of his peers at times. Weak pass, may fail.

Section 8: Feedback

I observed two trainees teaching an elementary-level class for an hour each. Besides myself and the two teaching trainees, present in the classroom were three trainees who were part of the TP group (not teaching); their trainer; the trainer-in-training; and 14 students.

The tutor began by asking Trainee A to comment on her performance. She was very aware of her strengths and weaknesses, noting that a particular strength of her lesson had been good student–student interaction. She felt she had to work on 'teacher talking time' and 'student talking time'.

The tutor then invited the other members of the group to contribute. They had plenty of ideas and a good discussion ensued. The tutor then drew everyone's attention to the need for students to have enough time to read before attempting to complete a related task. Trainee A had assumed that students needed the same length of time to read as she did.

The tutor then concentrated on Trainee A's strengths, which in this lesson were: excellent materials; classroom management; and rapport.

Trainee B began his feedback by commenting on his problems with language analysis – he felt that he had not anticipated some of the problems that the students had. He felt that the strength of his lesson had been the production activity, which worked well.

This was followed by the other trainees offering constructive comments such as the need for Trainee B to smile more – he could sometimes appear to be overly serious which some students might find intimidating. The tutor pointed out several things which had gone well, such as his excellent pronunciation work and flashcards.

The tutor then summed up the complete lesson by focusing on the following points:

— anticipating students' language difficulties when planning

— using a range of correction techniques for oral work

— allowing enough time for students to do activities such as reading

— the importance of rapport

The tutor focused on several strengths of the lesson — the quality of the materials overall, Trainee A's ability to give feedback on her students' performance, and Trainee B's excellent production activity.

Figure 7.2 Extract from a visiting validator's course report

If these participants were *receiving* feedback, this meant listening to feedback and appearing to accept it, even though they may have had a different view of what had happened or disagreed with the comments made. Participants have described doing this sometimes in order not to 'rock the boat' or 'upset the tutor'. The participant who made the last comment had added, 'I want to pass, after all.'

For former participants who are *giving* feedback, 'playing the game' has sometimes meant being less than forthcoming in order to avoid giving negative feedback, because it was felt that this could offend and so upset group dynamics, and that it would reflect poorly on the person giving it, in the eyes of the tutor. So they 'fell into a pattern of civility', as one participant described it.

However, if you pretend to listen to and accept feedback, fearing the consequences of challenging it, you are doing yourself out a personal learning opportunity (the opportunity to express and explain yourself, to question, to seek clarification, to gather more information ...).

And if you give less than honest feedback to a fellow participant then you are diminishing any trust that the team may be in the process of building.

> 'Flashcard' is the term used in teaching to refer to symbols or pictures, sometimes a manageable A4 size or smaller, which a teacher uses in the classroom to introduce or check language or ideas. You should find that your centre has a bank of these in its resource room; but it's worthwhile making your own collection

> 'Verbal feedback was always sensitive – often too much so. There needed to be a more robust interaction. Strengths were always identified, weaknesses were gently skirted. This did not help to build confidence – I prefer a much more direct approach.'
>
> Participant, Hong Kong

What use are your team members to you if they cannot be relied upon to tell you the truth about your work? And what use are you to them if you cannot be frank, for fear of hurting feelings? You can see that lack of candour threatens the very foundations of a successful team. A good teacher has integrity, and believes in what he or she is doing, and giving feedback is an excellent opportunity to develop that integrity.

Participants talk about feedback:

'I would appreciate feedback from all tutors and other TP groups because my group fell into a pattern of civility!'

'It's difficult to be critical of peers so as not to hurt feelings!'

'Everyone had to say something positive about everyone in the group. Sometimes it felt as if a lot of time was being wasted with waffle. I'd have been happier for other members of the group only to have commented if they had something they actually wanted to say.'

'Sometimes in feedback I felt we were just going through the motions. People weren't really saying what they thought.'

'The other members were too kind. I wish they'd told me the truth, as I feel like no matter how bad I get they will say something positive and I'll never learn.'

'Feedback again seemed very generous but perhaps we are all too myopic to see what we do well.'

Participants speak in feedback:

'I was so nervous today. I never really settled into the lesson.'

'I just didn't drill enough. I'd planned to, but I don't know why, I just didn't do it.'

'Miming is a hit. They loved it. We loved it.'

'I had two strategies up my sleeve in case the game didn't work.'

'It worked well, it was a good steady pace. I enjoyed it.'

'I think most of my instructions were OK. I was really trying.'

'At the end they were too interested in writing down the flipping words to be able to do the mingle activity.'

To the list above, therefore, can be added a note on the need for candour (sensitive candour, of course):

- an effective teacher is a *reflective* teacher

- an effective colleague is a *constructive* colleague; and

- an effective team member is a *sensitively candid* team member (he or she can be relied upon to be forthcoming and frank).

But being sensitively candid is a skill, and you may find that you receive little or no help on your course in developing this skill. To make matters worse, because it is linked to trust, it is far better (for you and your fellow participants) if you have this skill more or less in place from day one of your course. So what's involved?

> Tutors speak in feedback:
>
> 'You're all so hard on yourselves!'
>
> 'There was lots of student participation. They had a lot of fun.'
>
> 'I thought you used your materials very well. Basically you were using the same transparency but you used it in three different ways.'
>
> 'You were brave to try the miming, in case it didn't work.'
>
> 'You gave a fun lesson and it's just a pity you didn't have time to do the selling activity.'
>
> 'Next time, try to make sure you get as much as you can from the students, and give as little as possible.'

Your guiding principles for effective feedback

Below are some guiding principles which can help you and your fellow participants in feedback. These principles can also help you to prevent some of the problems that former participants describe in Chapter 8, 'Working with fellow participants'.

Guiding Principles for Giving and Receiving Effective Teaching Practice Feedback

Effective feedback …

… is focused, related to criteria, and contains relevant, meaningful information, based upon accurate and specific data (in particular, the impact that teaching has had upon the language learners).

If you are observing a fellow participant, this means that you need to make careful notes about what has actually happened in class, and draw upon this information when giving feedback. Do not talk about your impressions, or what you think happened; talk instead about what actually happened, particularly in relation to the language learners.

... focuses on observable behaviour rather than a person's characteristics.

It is vitally important that you comment upon a person's observable behaviour rather than his or her personality. For example, as a certificate participant, I was told (rather frequently!) that I was 'too serious'. I was also told that I did not praise a student whose perform-ance was felt to be praiseworthy, and that I had appeared to be a little 'cold' because I had simply acknowledged what he had said, and for the rest of the lesson I did not pay him a great deal of attention. The first comment is an observation about my personality (and about which I can do little on a four-week course) while the second one (now that I know about it) describes very specific behaviour and is something I can – and did – change, in the very next lesson. When you are called upon to give feedback to a fellow participant, remem-ber to focus on his or her behaviour.

> 'The suggestions and comments after were very worthwhile – I especially appreciate the tutor's tact, encourage-ment and challenge – there's always something specific to work on, and enthusiasm over what went well.'
>
> Participant, Hong Kong

... tends more towards description than evaluation.

Drawing on the example from my own certificate course above, a fellow participant could have said to me:

> 'I wondered about Javier today. He was making a real effort. I noticed that he immedi-ately used the words you had introduced, and he had checked their pronunciation in his dictionary too. He's the kind of guy that needs a lot of praise for this, and I don't think he got it.'

Alternatively, she could have said:

> 'I felt that you didn't pay enough attention to Javier. You didn't notice that he was using the words you had introduced or that he had checked the pronunciation in his dictionary.'

The first comment could prompt me to reflect on Javier and his work today: why hadn't I noticed this? Had I ignored him? What made me do so? How could I avoid this next time? The second comment, however, might make me defensive: 'Oh, really? Well, I think I did pay him enough attention. And I did notice that he used the words we were working on, what makes you think I didn't?' Tutors frequently identify defensiveness in feedback as a barrier to participant learning; so when giving feedback, try to describe rather than evaluate, in order to avoid making your fellow participant unnecessarily defensive. And likewise, try not to become defen-sive yourself.

... relates to goals that you, the recipient, have defined.

When asked to provide your analysis of a lesson you have just given, your personal goals for that lesson are a very good place to begin. My goals for the next lesson I gave, after receiving the feedback described above, included 'ensuring that I paid equal attention to and involved all members of the class, and that I gave praise where praise was due.' Effective feedback, after this lesson, would focus on this goal, and any others that I had defined. If asked to give feedback, it will help you if you first establish what your fellow participant's personal goals were.

> 'Making people do what you think they ought to do does not lead towards clarity and consciousness. While they may do what you tell them to do at any time, they will cringe inwardly, grow confused, and plot revenge.'
>
> Polster & Polster (1974)

... includes feedback from reflecting on your own performance as well as feedback from others (your tutor, peers, and any other observer).

Setting personal goals and then reflecting upon and evaluating your performance in the light of those goals is a powerful source of feedback, because such feedback is often closely related to your personal development and, and as a result, may be very readily assimilated.

Feedback from others, however, gives you invaluable information that you cannot find out alone: it can tell you how your behaviour appears to others. Such feedback is vital because understanding the impact that people have upon each other is fundamental to teaching and learning.

.... is supportive and constructive, and encourages dialogue and discussion.

Effective primary feedback supports and develops a person's own ideas. It acts like a signpost. It shows a person where to go. It looks forward, rather than back. So

> 'One problem I find with feedback is that it comes when trainees are exhausted and perhaps a bit emotional after planning for ages and doing their lessons. Often they switch off and are only interested in the grade – especially when they need it to pass. This is unfortunate because these are usually the trainees who could do with listening. Peer feedback can also become less useful as the trainees become worried about giving negative comments on other's lessons in case it affects the trainer's grade. Verbal feedback given by trainees to trainees also often seems to focus on minor issues (i.e: "I think you should have used a blue pen for underlining", rather than "So, why exactly did you hit Mohamed?")'
>
> Tutor, Bahrain

instead of saying, 'You didn't …', try 'Next time, why don't you …?' or 'Have you thought about trying …?' Such questions can be a very supportive approach to giving feedback.

Effective feedback also creates opportunities for discussion, involving all members of the group, not only the person who has taught and the person giving feedback. This is an important understanding, because former participants have sometimes fallen into a pattern of 'switching off' or 'going through the motions' when it is not their turn to receive feedback. It will help you greatly if you can stay active and involved in all aspects of the process: giving and receiving feedback yourself, but also by paying attention to the feedback being given to and received by your fellow participants.

> 'Trainees get bored with feedback, especially when you are not talking about THEIR TP!'
>
> Tutor, Hong Kong

… is less likely to happen if the tutor dominates or reminds participants of the power invested in him or her.

Tutors in feedback are carrying out a dual function: they are expected to make assessment decisions about your performance, and they are expected to provide you with feedback to enable you to improve. As a visiting validator, I have found

Feedback can show you where to go

that tutors are not always very good at separating these two functions. This can affect participants, because the power of the source of feedback can affect both their perception of it and their desire to respond to it.

For example, you might find on occasion that a tutor decides not to give you much feedback, because he or she wants to see how well you can identify your own strengths and weaknesses. This is perfectly reasonable because the ability to do this is one of the many skills that you are expected to develop on this course. However, tutors, being fallible, may do this before you are quite ready. If you feel you want more feedback, or assistance in any other area, for that matter, never hesitate to ask for it. And if you find that a tutor is giving more priority to assessment at the expense of feedback, tell him or her: supportively and constructively, of course!

> 'I found that one tutor I had was absolutely wonderful in her approach and I never felt criticized. She was always so supportive and kind when things didn't work out quite the way I planned in my lesson. I believe that it is all in the "delivery" of how you say it more so than what they are saying and she was always nice about her observations of a less than stellar lesson on my part.'
>
> Participant, Hong Kong

… is voluntary, meaning that it should be solicited by the person who has taught.
Effective feedback is solicited feedback, because feedback should be wanted, needed, and as mentioned above, related to something specific. If you give unsolicited feedback, you cannot be sure that the person wants it or needs it, or that he or she will be able or willing to act upon it. It could therefore be a waste of effort, and, moreover, you risk irritating your fellow participant.

> 'Until we are aware and see our weaknesses for ourselves, no amount of telling or pointing them out will help.'
>
> Tutor, Hong Kong

However, there is often an expectation on certificate courses that all members of the teaching practice group should contribute towards everyone else's feedback, meaning that you may feel obliged to say something simply because it is expected of you. If you find yourself in this position, discuss it with your tutor early on, and try to agree upon another approach with all the members of your group, which takes into account the points raised here.

... reduces uncertainty, leaving you knowing exactly what you need to do.
Good feedback will leave you with a very clear picture of what areas you need to focus on next time. It will not leave you ignorant or confused. If, at the end of your feedback time, you are still uncertain about something, then the session has failed and you should take the opportunity to clarify it before the session ends. Once again, do not hesitate to ask your tutor for clarification, even it means running over time.

Giving and receiving feedback is a complex process, and many factors influence it. You have read above a description of 'best practice' in the area, and applying these ideas will go a long way towards preventing any serious problems arising and therefore towards improving the quality and outcome of the experience for you personally.

Teaching: Key points to take away with you

- Teaching practice is one of the main components of assessment.

- Guidance will be provided by tutors during scheduled lesson planning sessions, in the form of 'teaching practice points'. These points may provide information about what to teach, with some suggestions about how to teach it and what materials to use.

- You will be given a suggested lesson plan format, but you should also consider designing your own.

- Performance nerves are normal. You will find suggestions for coping with nerves in books and on the internet – do some research before the course starts, because you may find some that appeal to you.

- The more involved you are in your lesson, the less nervous you will be.

- As the course progresses you will gain first-hand experience of nervousness diminishing during a lesson, which you can use to build your confidence.

- The 'essentials for teaching practice survival' are: 1. Manage your nerves – don't let them manage you! 2. Develop personal survival strategies; 3. Set personal goals; 4. Learn from others; 5. Enjoy! 6. Stop, look, listen and think; 7. Aim to make steady progress; 8. Practise for yourself – don't perform for others; 9. Relate workshop content to practice; 10. It's your learners that matter; 11. Reflect! 12. Rehearse! 13. Keep it simple; 14. Focus on your strengths.

- Good feedback is invaluable. It can: motivate, encourage reflection, allow you to hear different people's views of your lesson, give you an opportunity to clarify things, and encourage the free flow and exchange of ideas.

- Good feedback is focused on observable behaviour, not people's characteristics; it describes rather than evaluates; and it is supportive and constructive.

- An effective teacher is a <u>reflective</u> teacher; an effective colleague is a <u>constructive</u> colleague; and an effective team member is a <u>sensitively candid</u> team member.

www **Check your understanding** of Chapter 7 by completing the quiz available on the companion website at: <u>www.sagepub.co.uk/brandt</u>

Chapter 8

Working together

In this chapter you can learn about:

- what to expect from your language learners in terms of language proficiency
- how learners' language backgrounds and proficiency can affect class composition
- your fellow participants and the support they can provide you with
- why collaborating with fellow participants on your course is expected and how you can make the most of the opportunity
- your teaching team performance plan
- what to do if collaboration breaks down.

▌ WORKING WITH LANGUAGE LEARNERS

This participant on a part-time course had a clear idea of the variety that is possible within one class and the impact that such variety can have on her classroom management. She wrote:

'Met our TP students at last. There were 21 of them. And not one of them had an eye in the middle of their forehead. They were keen to learn ...'

Participant, Hong Kong

'The classes of adults are usually made up of very diverse people with very diverse motivations. For instance you might get a young woman who doesn't work and who has had very little social contact outside her immediate family, or a more mature housewife learning English so she can communicate with her grandchildren brought up in an English-speaking country. Then there is the young man who wants English in order to emigrate to an English-speaking country or to improve his job prospects. In those cases it's important to be aware of their personal circumstances and to organize the classroom so when they are grouped together it's done in a sensitive way, that is, not to put the eager young man with the shy young girl. Equally the housewife might feel uncomfortable with the young man.'

Participant, Hong Kong

As well as the factors which the participant above identified (age, background, personality, and motivation), other major ways in which learners can differ from one another are in terms of their first language and their proficiency in English.

> 'With Chinese students it is particularly important to be sensitive as they are generally very shy and are not so forthcoming in oral participation.'
>
> Participant, Hong Kong

Monolingual and multilingual classes

Classes which consist entirely of speakers of the same language are known as monolingual classes. For example, in Bahrain, I taught groups of around 30 Bahraini university students, all of whom spoke Arabic as their first language but needed English as it was the medium of study at their university (this is an ESL situation, as described in Chapter 2, 'The profession'). Classes of learners who speak a variety of languages, on the other hand, are known as multilingual classes. For example, in the United Kingdom, I taught a class which consisted of learners whose first languages were French, Spanish, Turkish and German (this is an EFL situation, because the students eventually left the United Kingdom to live and work in contexts where English was not the main language).

As you might imagine, there are advantages and disadvantages to such class compositions. From the learners' perspective, being in a multilingual group means that using English to communicate with each other is more realistic than using it to communicate with someone who speaks their own language, which would be the case if they were part of a monolingual class. However, an advantage of a monolingual class is that the learners, coming from the same language background, will have in common some language-related problems in learning English. An example of this would be the distinction between the sounds /p/ and /b/ (remember that the slash on either side indicates that what lies between is a *symbol for a sound* rather than a *letter*), which is problematic for those who speak Arabic as their first language, because Arabic makes no such distinction. A teacher of a monolingual group of speakers of Arabic as a first language, therefore, may well choose to spend some time helping learners first to perceive the difference between these sounds and then to produce the different sounds themselves. This is something which may not be possible to quite the same extent in a multilingual class, because, for example, the French learners in the class will not have this same problem, and you need to allocate time fairly to all of your learners.

> 'The mixed nationalities in my class meant that the few European students had quite different language and pronunciation problems to the Chinese Korean, and Japanese students.'
>
> Participant, Hong Kong

Proficiency and level

The other major way in which learners can differ is in terms of their proficiency in English. This is the reason why many institutions require language learners to take what is known as a **placement test**. The purpose of this test (which will often involve a test of grammar and vocabulary, as well as tests of all four language skills: reading, writing, speaking and listening), is to allow staff to make a judgement about a learner's level of English so that he or she can be placed in a class with learners of a similar level. Suitable course books and materials for teaching that level can then be selected. As a result, both classes and course books are often organized and labeled according to level. Levels frequently found in language schools include any or all of the following:

- beginner
- elementary
- lower intermediate
- pre-intermediate
- intermediate
- high intermediate
- upper-intermediate
- post-intermediate
- advanced.

The term **false beginner** may also be found, though this is usually used to talk about individual learners, rather than being a formal level into which a learner may be placed. A false beginner may be defined as:

> A learner who has had a limited amount of previous instruction in a language, but who because of extremely limited language proficiency is classified as at the beginning level of language instruction. A false beginner is sometimes contrasted with a true beginner, someone who has no knowledge of the language.
>
> *Richards, Platt & Weber (1985)*

You may also come across classes called **FCE, CPE**, IELTS, or TOEFL: in each case, these abbreviations refer to public international examinations (see the glossary on **www**) and the purpose of these classes is to prepare learners for these examinations.

Course books take a similar approach. According to the *EL Gazette*, November 2005, the top five best-selling ELT/TESOL students' books for September 2005 were *English File Intermediate Student's Book* (Oxenden, C., Lathan-Koenig, C. and Seligson, P., 1999); *English File Upper-Intermediate Student's Book* (Oxenden, C., Lathan-Koenig, C. and Seligson, P., 2001); *Inside Out Intermediate Student's Book* (Kay, S., Vaughan, J. and Hird, J., 2001); *New Headway English Course, Student's Book, Advanced Level* (Soars, J. and Soars, L., 2003); and *Cutting Edge: A Practical Approach to Task Based Learning, Advanced Student's Book* (Cunningham, S. and

Moore, P., 2003). *Cutting Edge*, to take one example, has six levels, called starter, elementary, pre-intermediate, intermediate, upper-intermediate and advanced.

What levels mean for you

You can get a good idea of what you can expect learners at these levels to be able to do by reading the **level descriptors** that most centres have, so ask for a set of these as they will tell you not only what levels the centre offers but also what each level means to them. Studying examples of course books such as those above will also help you here. Before your course has started, if possible ask to spend an hour or two in the resource room of the centre where you will take your course. Spend the time just browsing through various course books, or any other book that has been given a level (an example of this would be Murphy's (1997) *Essential Grammar in Use with Answers: A Self-study Reference and Practice Book for Elementary Students of English*) and you will find out what learners at each level are expected to know by the time they have completed a level. Alternatively, if you are not able to visit your centre before you start your course, you can take the same approach in any bookstore or library.

Examples of students' writing can also tell you something about what to expect. Below you will find an example of writing at each of five levels. As you read, think generally about how you would help each learner to improve his or her writing.

My country

My country is the Bahrain. Everyone are no that blace. I am like the bahrain very much because almost of desart and I am like desart. Bahrain not country big. The Bahrain small and butful. It have Butiful place, have the seef mall and the ristrint. I going with many frind to see the pipole and shobing. My famly big famly. I have many brother and 12 uncle. I am like play football but my brother he not like.

Extract from a composition by 40-year-old Bahraini engineer, attending an elementary class in general English in his free time, in a private language school in Bahrain.

I am of Paris but I live here at London since 1 year. This is the first time I am in London. I do not write very well English. It is difficult to me.

My job is with computer. I have chance to find this job. I work with the man who is married with my sister. It is many years I am knowing him. She is going with him since they are 16. Last year, they are married at Paris. He has a business with computer.

Extract from a passage written by a French man in his mid-thirties studying English in a pre-intermediate class in a small private language school in London.

Nike

Very easy to knowing Nike's advertising. Sometimes, they invite some famous footballer like David Beckham, Ronaldo to advertised for them, or some famous singer like Britney spears…. Nowaday, there is so much branches like Reebok, Adidas, and very competing in the market, so they advice to increasing development and creating new products, almost concentrated in young people who interested in sport aspect.

Extract from a composition by a 20-year-old Vietnamese learner attending an intermedi-ate class in Business English in Hong Kong.

Life of the students' with television

Students who are watch a lot of television programme will become worse in eye-sight. As the students may get lots of information through television turn them lazy so no reading habit. Homework is not done because time spent watching television. No exercise cause obesity among student. Finally television can spread some western cultural and influence student which may cause vandalism.

Extract from writing completed under examination conditions by an 18-year-old Malaysian learner attending an upper-intermediate class at university in Kuala Lumpur.

I am leaving this beautiful campus, leaving this peaceful country, with complex feeling, not knowing when or whether ever I may return. I have been hungering for this day since the day I left Beijing 9 months ago, and that is because my family, because my wife and my son are there. Today, I welcome the end of this course with hesitation. I don't know why and no one can tell me the answer, but I swear that my heart, sincerely, will be with you, and the life here will be a very important page in my career. Adieu, my friends, would I could press you all to my heart.

Extract from a speech prepared by a student attending an advanced English language programme in Brunei.

The idea of 'levels' suggests that you can expect your classes to consist of groups of learners with approximately the same level, or standard, of English proficiency. Creating such classes is a way of standardizing: we are saying that all learners at this level need to learn these aspects of the language, and that these books could be suit-able for them. In practice, of course, it is not so straightforward. In Chapter 4, 'Standardization', I suggested that people, being unique, resist standardization. I was referring then to teachers, but the same of course applies to language learners, each of whom arrives with a unique, personal, proficiency profile. This means that although learners' placement test results may put them into the same class, in fact you may find some significant differences among them in terms of what they know, how well they know it, and where the gaps in their knowledge lie. It is also the case that learners are sometimes placed together even though their placement test results indicate that they should be in different classes; this may sometimes be done by centres when, for example, there are not enough learners at one level to make it financially viable to run a class at that level.

> 'Our TP students were a very mixed bunch – their levels of English varied enormously. And it was much easier to concentrate on the strong students, as of course they were much more forthcoming, so the weaker ones were probably left out a bit.'
>
> Participant, Hong Kong

The influence of a learner's first language

I mentioned above the idea of learners in monolingual classes having in common certain difficulties in relation to learning English. As an example, I described the difficulty with /p/ and /b/ that speakers of Arabic as a first language can have. This difficulty is reflected in the first example of writing above, in the learner's use of 'blace' instead of 'place' and 'shobing' instead of 'shopping'. The idea that a learner's first language can interfere with the learning of English is not new, and is often referred to as 'first language interference' or 'L1 interference'. A number of aspects of a learner's first language may interfere with English; in particular, grammar, vocabulary, pronunciation (this one is often the most obvious, accounting for a learner's 'accent'), and orthography, or the way it is written. If you are interested in knowing more about the particular problems faced by your Dutch, German, Italian, French, Arabic, Russian, Portuguese, Swahili, or Chinese learner or learners, then Swan and Smith's (2001) *Learner English: A Teacher's Guide to Interference and Other Problems* compares aspects of several other languages to English, and is an invaluable resource, worth purchasing early on in your career.

As well as learners, the other people who will have a significant impact during your course are your fellow participants.

▶ **WORKING WITH FELLOW PARTICIPANTS**

Just as language learners can vary in terms of age, background, personality, motivation, first language and English proficiency level, your fellow course participants will offer similar diversity. As suggested by the brief biographies of several participants and course graduates that you read in Chapter 2, 'What kind of people go into English Language Teaching?', you will probably find that your colleagues vary in terms of their ages, backgrounds, teaching experience (if any), personalities, preferences, learning styles, reasons for taking the course, first language and proficiency in other languages. This diversity will affect you because most English language learning and teacher training is carried out in groups. There are often of course operational reasons for this: whether the people are teachers or language learners, it is more cost effective to run a class with 20 students, rather than 4. However, there are also sound educational reasons for teaching people in groups. As a result, you are likely to find yourself working in various ways alongside a diverse range of people, which can have advantages and disadvantages.

Ways of working

A class of 20 can be managed in a number of ways; as a teacher, you can address the whole group, possibly directing questions at individuals within the group, or you can set up what is called **open pairwork** in ELT/TESOL. This means asking two learners to engage in a dialogue, for example, while the other 18 learners listen and observe. Alternatively, you can ask a learner or learners to address the class (this happens when learners give presentations, for example); or you could break your large group up into 5 groups of four, or 4 groups of five; or you can ask your learners to work in pairs (and do what may then be referred to as **closed pairwork**, which happens when a complete class is arranged into pairs, all of which are engaged in an activity at the same time). These are just some of the ways in which a large class can be arranged, and of course deciding when and where to use them requires several factors to be taken into account, not least of which are the intended learning outcomes.

As a participant on a certificate course, it is likely that you will yourself experience all of these different ways of working, because your tutors will be making an effort to use them with you in workshops. This is because not only can these different ways of working create more effective learning conditions for you personally in your certificate course context, but tutors hope that in experiencing first hand the value of 'closed pairwork', for example, you will be more likely to use this technique with your own learners, and do it more effectively, too. This is, in other words, a specific example of the kind of three-way learning opportunity referred to in Chapter 4: you have here the opportunity to learn not only from *what* you are being taught, but also from *how* it is being taught to you, and from *applying* your learning to your own learners in your own classroom.

Collaboration matters

Former participants have found, however, that the teamwork which has the greatest impact is carried out not in workshops but in relation to teaching practice. Teams formed for teaching practice purposes have a high impact upon individual participants because, first of all, you will probably remain throughout the course in the group to which you were assigned at the start; and secondly, teaching practice is a significant component of assessment. If this is the arrangement on your course (remember that not all courses take this approach) your teaching practice group will be involved in planning lessons, in teaching (in the sense that they will teach parts of lessons which precede or follow yours) and in observing and providing feedback.

While tutors at the start of your course will usually make an effort to create groups that are likely to work well together and be productive (they may take such factors into account as age, male/female balance, and previous experience), this is of course not always possible. For every group that works well together, I have seen one that breaks down at some stage, occasionally irretrievably. However, former participants have described in such positive terms the benefits of successful teamwork that it is worth making a particular effort to maintain the well-being of your team. These participants on a course in Hong Kong commented:

> 'I like the fact that we're working in groups – you can learn more. Each one in our group has real strengths.'

> 'I'm quite taken by the group learning on this course; it's very hard to daydream when your colleagues are needling you for ideas!'

> 'The size of the course (18 students) is nice. We've got to know each other and help each other. Our ups and downs seem to occur at different times, which means that there is usually someone "up" who can help someone who is "down".'

> 'Jim and I collaborated on this teaching practice and he gave me lots of good ideas to use. I felt our group relationship has built up. It's a nice feeling.'

> 'I met up with Carol for a strong coffee an hour before class started because she was in a similar state of nerves. We did lots of positive chatting. I think we helped each other.'

> 'I really needed to talk after teaching practice in particular, to get it all off my chest. I was so glad I was in a good supportive group because I really needed them to help me vent.'

While these graduates of other courses held around the world said:

> 'I made some good friends on that course. Five years later, we're still emailing each other regularly.'

> 'I found the course workload quite heavy and peers' help and support helped a lot.'

> 'I think teamwork helps a lot – like our own students, the trainees learn from each other. If a TP group is on average strong, it tends to pull the level of the weaker trainees up. Furthermore, through having to plan and negotiate the content of lessons to ensure continuity, the trainees become aware of the student's learning process as a whole, rather than seeing their lesson as an isolated component. Once trainees have finished the course they may find themselves sharing courses in academies etc. with other teachers, so this awareness developed in TP is required. Finally, the sense of team-ship rather than rivalry seems to predominate on the courses in which I've been involved.'
>
> Tutor, Spain

> 'What mix of trainees will I have? Will they work well together – will they accept my guidance? How can we build up a trust?'
>
> Tutor, Hong Kong

'It was good to have to work with others – to bounce ideas off each other – especially when you first saw the teaching material and did not know how to approach it at all … I gained a lot of experience from explaining and discussing what we were doing.'

The benefits of teamwork in a variety of contexts have long been recognized and there is an extensive literature available on this subject, should you wish to investigate further. In relation to certificate courses, as some of the comments above indicate, teamwork can help you to:

- build your confidence
- make friends and allies
- establish a network that could be of value to you once you graduate from the course
- improve your reasoning, problem-solving and decision-making skills
- learn from, and about, others' strengths and weaknesses
- develop your ability to collaborate and communicate, giving you ideas and reinforcing your own learning as you communicate your own ideas to others
- develop the skills of identifying points of agreement and contention, empathizing and helping others to solve problems.

Above, I suggested that it is worth making a particular effort to maintain the wellbeing of your team and make group breakdown less likely. You can begin by thinking of your group as a *team with a task* (I see a team as a group with a common purpose). Imagine yourselves as chefs in a five-star restaurant, and a mission: to prepare one of the finest meals ever held for several discerning guests (think of a lesson as a feast for language learners).

See your lesson as a feast for your learners

A team of chefs who know each other well and have worked together for many years should be familiar with each other's strengths and weaknesses and be able to work together efficiently and effectively to produce the feast.

But imagine that until this morning you had no idea of who your fellow chefs were going to be. On a certificate course, this is precisely the situation you will be in. In such a situation you need to take rapid steps to get your team functioning and ready to meet the challenges to come.

Think for a moment about the kind of things that can go wrong when a team of chefs are not performing well. These are my ideas; you will be able to add to the list. (As you read, think about how this metaphor might relate to the experience of being part of a teaching practice group with five members, where your mission is to plan and teach a two-hour lesson for a multilingual class of 20 adults):

> 'Teaching practice groups are not without their problems, but then, working in such close quarters with peers, under the conditions and time factors that we've been given, I think we are all coping quite well.'
>
> Participant, Hong Kong

- The chefs in your team cannot agree upon the menu.
- Some of the food is overcooked because two members of your team squabbled and flounced off, leaving their dishes unattended.
- There is no bread because no one thought of this.
- There is nothing to drink because each chef thought that another was organizing this.
- One chef tries to take all the credit for the complete meal.
- One chef does not come to planning meetings – he is not available because he has a part-time job with another restaurant.

In order to prevent such problems arising, the chefs needed to recognize one essential fact: teams are made, they do not just happen. It is not enough be told that you are in 'Teaching Practice Group A'. Once created, a team has to be fostered, developed, maintained, and from time to time, repaired. You cannot assume that it can run itself.

However, many former participants have not realized that their teaching practice team requires nurturing, and so they have expected it to take care of itself and been disappointed when it failed, particularly when they observed other teams around them working successfully together to produce lessons which were well received by both learners and tutors.

Your teaching team performance plan

In order to help teaching teams work well together, former participants made several suggestions for new course participants, once all of the members of their teaching practice group have been identified. The 'Teaching Team Performance Plan' below encapsulates their ideas, and can help you to prevent some of the problems to do with group dynamics that former participants describe later on in this chapter. You may find that, on your course, time is allocated specifically for team building.

Teaching Team Performance Plan

1. *Meet*. Get together with the members of your team as soon as possible after the team has been formed (preferably the same day). Keep the meeting informal.

2. *Share*. Find out about each other. What kind of people are you working with? What are their backgrounds and circumstances? What are their strengths and weaknesses? What are their preferred ways of working? Recognize and welcome the diversity within your group. Build trust by being honest when giving information about yourself. Do not let this information unfold as the course progresses, but try to manage it yourselves.

3. *Plan*. Identify the best of way of working together. Knowing that you will have to work together to plan and teach cohesive lessons, and knowing what you do about each other, what will be the best way of working for your team, for the first lesson or two? You might want to consider, for example, electing a coordinator. Would this be a fixed or a rotating position? You decide.

4. *Anticipate*. Identify problems your group might face. For example, imagine you are taking a part-time course and you are in a group where four of you have no other job but one person is working full-time. What problems might this cause? How will you address them? Identify all such problems.

5. *Agree*. Identify problem-solving strategies. What will you do, for example, if two members of your team fall out with each other? Will your strategy be to let them work it out between themselves, or will it be seen perhaps as a problem that belongs to the team? How will your team handle it if one member tells you that he or she really does not like working in a team?

6. *Maintain*. Work at maintaining the well-being of your team. Arrange to meet periodically (outside of the normal course requirements), specifically in order to maintain your team. Ask yourselves: how is our team working? Are we performing as efficiently and effectively as we can? What do we need to do in order to improve our performance? Remember, this takes time – so make time for it.

7. *Record*. Make a brief handwritten summary of each meeting with action points, and copy and distribute it to everyone immediately afterwards (there's no need to word process this document, as this will just delay its distribution). This is what you have agreed. It will be unique to your team.

8. *Flex*. Try not to become fixed. Recognize that your team is *organic*. The processes that you put in place for the first lesson or two may not continue to work so well as the course progresses. Be prepared to adapt, and update your plan to reflect this.

There is one further point in relation to your teaching practice team that former participants have commented on and which you may wish to consider. You might have noticed that I referred above to teaching practice teams becoming aware of each other, particularly in relation to their performance. Former participants have observed that, perhaps because of the intensity of the course, it is possible for teams to feel quite isolated from the other teams, because there may be no component other than workshops that brings all of the teaching practice teams together.

However, former participants have pointed out that they have not realized this until it is too late to do anything about it, that is, towards the end of the course, when they have looked back and said things such as:

> You may find after some time that your teaching practice team feels quite cut off from the other teams. Because you can learn a lot from the experiences of everyone on your course, take steps to create opportunities for all of the teaching practice team members to meet.
>
> Some former participants have done this through a social event, organized after hours. Particularly if you are taking a part-time course, consider electing a 'social activities organizer' at the beginning of your course. It is also likely that you will want to arrange an end-of-course party, and/or create an 'alumni association' so that you can stay in touch once the course is over. Your social activities organizer can do this too.

'I would love to hear the problems and achievements of the other groups and discuss them. I'm beginning to feel cut off from the others – it is a shame considering they are all doing the same thing as we are.'

Participant, Hong Kong

Therefore, they recommend that participants who find themselves in this position should take matters into their own hands early on in the course. (This may not apply to you, as you may find that there are course components in place which bring everyone together, allowing teams to exchange experiences and ideas. Study your timetable carefully at the beginning of your course and check with your tutor if you need to.) They recommend arranging to meet with other teaching practice teams at a convenient time, in order to

> 'I think everyone is realizing the importance of group work – and making an effort to meet up either early or after the regular classes in their TP groups to co-ordinate the 2 hours of TP well.'
>
> Participant, Hong Kong

share experiences and exchange ideas, and to prevent the teams from becoming too insular and isolated and losing the benefits of team-to-team collaboration.

But, of course, as in other situations and despite everyone's best intentions, collaboration sometimes fails.

When teams go wrong

Above, I have described some of the benefits that participants have experienced as a result of effective teamwork, including things like exchanging ideas, providing support for one another, building confidence, and developing communication skills. These benefits are some of the reasons why *collaboration matters*. Another reason is that your tutors want to see that you can collaborate effectively, because teaching is about working with people; in fact, some would say that working with learners in a classroom is essentially a collaborative activity. This section outlines some of the things that can go wrong with collaboration, why they may happen, and what you can do to prevent them.

These are some comments made by former participants and tutors, in which they describe some of the things that have gone wrong within their teams. As you read, try to summarize the issue in a few words.

1. 'It is very hard for them to make time to collaborate with another person with such a demanding schedule.' (Tutor, Australia)

2. 'I work and I found it difficult to meet up with my TP team because none of them work. This meant that I couldn't liaise very much with the others before TP. It was a problem for both me and for them.' (Participant, United Kingdom)

3. 'While I felt the groups had a support role, the necessity for group collaboration resulted in too much support time, and too little effective work time. Collaboration was very expensive in terms of time relative to learning.' (Participant, Hong Kong)

4. 'We basically split the lesson into four parts and then did our own thing. Because I had been a math teacher before doing CELTA, I was fairly confident in teaching and didn't feel I needed the help of novice teachers. Also, it was too hard to spend time collaborating as it took a lot of time.' (Participant, Hong Kong)

5. 'Steven is an idea pincher – half his lesson was Jonathan's idea – the other half mine.' (Participant, Hong Kong)

6. 'Marina came to TP prep with no ideas. Just asked us if we had any for her lesson. But we had our own ideas and our own lessons to plan, and everyone should pull their own weight.' (Participant, Spain)

7. 'Weaker trainees can become a drain on the group and stronger trainees can worry that their lessons will be 'unsuccessful' because of bad planning on their colleague's part.' (Tutor, Bahrain)

8. 'One trainee reported that she spent so much time using her (considerable) counseling skills with a fellow trainee that there was significantly reduced time for group planning and her own tasks.' (Tutor, New Zealand)

9. 'Difficult relationships can be a drag on team progress, if for example one person has no idea about team collaboration or cannot plan adequately.' (Tutor, New Zealand)

10. 'Individuals can't necessarily pursue the kind of lesson they want to do and try out because of the need to fit in with the other trainees.' (Tutor, Hong Kong)

11. 'Not every one is naturally a team player. In fact teachers are by nature and profession highly individualistic people […]. Asking them to work as a team can be a tall order. Therefore if one is naturally individualistic in one's approach to work then working in a team could certainly hinder one's learning.' (Tutor, Portugal)

12. 'Many competent teachers are not good at teamwork (myself included) and I do not feel it fair on them.' (Tutor, Hong Kong)

13. 'There was one trainee who I dreaded being paired with, and often was. A real winger who drove me up the wall when it came to planning etc.' (Participant, Hong Kong)

14. 'The exercises were hard to create in our TP groups as we all have such different thoughts and ideas. Whose should take priority, I wondered?' (Participant, United Kingdom)

15. 'I like the group discussions but so often the flow of an idea or emerging concept gets lost or broken in the group discussions.' (Participant, Hong Kong)

16. 'The course was designed in such a way that you were dependent upon the previous teacher's presentation and skills. I don't think this is right, because if their lesson fails or doesn't go according to plan, yours can be negatively affected. And that's tough because every lesson counts towards your assessment.' (Participant, United Kingdom)

17. 'If there are any problems, rifts can become huge with breakaway groups working alone and refusing to help others.' (Tutor, Bahrain)

This is my analysis of the comments above. I have identified the issue, and related it to the comment or comments:

- collaboration takes time and effort (comments 1, 2, 3 and 4)
- people bring different experiences, preferences and skills to the situation (comments 3 and 4)
- some people feel protective of their ideas (comments 5 and 6)
- the belief that everyone should contribute equally to the work of the team (comment 6)
- stronger participants may feel hindered by weaker ones, or those less able to participate fully in the group (comments 6, 7, 8 and 9)
- feeling hampered by the need to fit in with others (comment 10)
- teamwork does not suit everyone (comments 11 and 12)
- people can have incompatible ways of working, and incompatible ideas (comments 13 and 14)
- ideas can get lost in discussion (comment 15)

- the performance of a participant teaching an earlier lesson section can have an impact on the next participant's lesson and performance (comment 16)
- groups can splinter and people can refuse to help others (comment 17).

If your team needs help …

If you find that you are part of a team that is struggling to work together, one of the most useful things you can do is to remind yourself of the tremendous benefit to be had from being part of a team that is performing well. You should also bear in mind the fact that, as the course progresses, you will be expected to become more independent of the members of your team, and so teamwork will have less impact.

Above, I suggested a strategy to help you to get your team underway: the 'Teaching Team Performance Plan'. The plan as it stands will help to address or prevent some of the issues here. However, it can be developed further to take account of some of the other points raised in this section. As you read on, you should recognize many of the values already presented so far in this book.

Learn from others

Teaching is essentially a creative act, so you need ideas: for the classroom and for your own development. You are surrounded by people with different backgrounds and experiences. What better way of finding ideas than by listening to others and sharing your own with them? Their diversity adds value to your experience; if you dismiss or fall out with a team member or team members, you may be cutting off a source of ideas, not to mention support. Be positive: assume that you *can* learn from others, not that you *cannot*, even if they are less experienced than you. Through exchanging ideas, other ideas can be created and developed. Understanding this can help you to see that …

Ideas are dynamic

It is through dialogue and discussion that ideas emerge, develop and change. An idea, kept to yourself, may remain stunted; while an idea exposed to others has the opportunity to grow and be improved upon. Picture your idea as a plant: kept in a pot in the dark, it will fail to thrive; exposed to all the elements in its natural habitat, it will grow large and bushy. An idea that has grown in this way belongs to the team and it is difficult to see how it can be 'pinched'; you only need to decide who is to put it into practice. Also, try to accept that several people can use the same idea (not all in the same lesson, of course!) and it will be different, not diminished, each time – so try not to see ideas as 'belonging' to people. Instead, see the creation of ideas as one of the many *tasks* of your team. This understanding can help you to …

Focus on the task, not the person

This is very similar to an idea that was discussed in Chapter 7, which is that in feedback you should 'focus on observable behaviour rather than a person's characteristics'. Focusing on the task can help you to put to one side the personal characteristics or behaviour that may be bothering you. It is, after all, completing the task that really matters. If you find that you cannot put someone's behaviour aside, however, at least adopt a *reflective* rather than a *reactive* approach, asking yourself what is bothering you, why it is bothering you, and what supportive and constructive steps you could take to deal with the matter, because …

An effective colleague is a supportive, constructive colleague

A supportive colleague is one who supports both individual team members and the team itself. This colleague will avoid doing anything that might undermine or threaten the team. He or she will make time to solve any problems that the team or its individuals are having, and will do so constructively, by focusing not on the past, but on the future: by asking 'How can we do things differently in future to improve our team's performance?'

However, if you find that a fellow participant is leaning too heavily on you, and taking up too much of your time, as can happen, try to work out with that person exactly how much time you are able to give. Put a plan in place, involve the other members of your team if you can, and try not to leave it open ended.

A supportive, constructive colleague will make an effort to improve his or her team's performance, and will do so partly by helping others. He or she will see this as one way to …

Find learning opportunities everywhere

Collaboration offers an excellent learning opportunity. Through collaboration, you can learn about others' ideas and learning styles, as described above, but you can also learn about your own impact upon others, which is part of knowing about yourself, the kind of person you are, and the kind of teacher you are becoming. And unless you know yourself, you cannot begin to develop the integrity you need in order to become a good teacher. So it may help if you can also …

See teamwork as an opportunity to develop integrity

Teamwork can help to shape your personal set of values and beliefs about teaching because it provides you with the opportunity to express yourself and listen to others, which reflects developing values and beliefs. You may hear yourself thinking 'That's a good idea. Doing that means that my learners will have an opportunity to …'. Alternatively, you may think 'Oh, I don't much like the sound of that. If I did that it would mean that my learners …'. Teamwork can improve your self-confidence, because it gives you an opportunity to begin to identify and define your professional values. You can, of course, also turn to those who have worked for many years on developing their own personal belief systems and ...

Seek your tutor's guidance and advice as needed

If all your attempts to resolve your group's difficulties have failed, then engage your tutor's help at the earliest possible opportunity. Your tutor will have set up your group, and you will almost certainly find that he or she is supportive and very willing to help you. Arrange to consult him or her as a group, so that no member is left out, and voice your concerns. Be supportive, constructive, forthcoming and frank. You may well find that simply talking things through with someone else is enough for you to resolve your differences. Finally ...

Bear in mind that it will all be over shortly

Keep things in proportion. You may never see your fellow team members again, once the course has ended. Having this in mind can help you to focus on the task and put to one side any interpersonal issues. What really matters, at the end of the day, is the work that needs to be done and your own personal development, into a rounded, successful, teacher.

Several of the ideas presented in this chapter have been identified by tutors and former course participants as strategies that are likely to increase your chances of succeeding, not only while taking a certificate course, but also in your future career as an English language teacher. These strategies are described in Chapter 9, 'Succeeding'.

Working together: Key points to take away with you

- Groups of adult language learners are not homogenous but vary in terms of factors such as age, experience, reasons for learning English and first language.

- Classes of speakers of the same language are known as monolingual classes, while classes of learners who speak a number of different languages are known as multilingual classes.

- Levels commonly found in institutions include: beginner, elementary, lower or pre-intermediate, intermediate, high intermediate, upper-intermediate, post-intermediate, and advanced.

- You will be expected to work in a variety of different modes while on a certificate course: independently, in pairs and as part of a team, particularly for teaching practice.

- It is a good idea to focus on the personal benefits of collaboration, which include making friends and allies, building confidence, learning from others and developing your communication skills.

- Tutors look for evidence of good collaboration skills.

- Your 'Teaching Team Performance Plan': Meet in order to share and plan. Anticipate problems and agree strategies for solving them. Flex, don't get fixed. Set aside time to maintain your team's well-being. Record and update your plan. Implement this plan as soon as you have identified your team members

- See ideas as dynamic and the product of good teamwork. Several people can use the same idea! Each person will implement it differently.

- Focus on what needs to be done, not the people doing it.

- Seek your tutor's help if you need it; and try not to leave this too late.

www **Check your understanding** of Chapter 8 by completing the quiz available on the companion website at: www.sagepub.co.uk/brandt

Chapter 9

Succeeding

In this chapter you can learn about:

- sixteen strategies that have helped former participants to succeed on certificate courses
- steps that you can use to help you to develop or implement each strategy.

The ideas in this chapter will help you to give your personal best and gain maximum satisfaction from the experience of taking a certificate course in ELT/TESOL. They can also help you throughout your career as a teacher in ELT/TESOL.

▶ INTRODUCTION

'My advice is: don't make the grade more important than the experience.'

Participant, New Zealand

Sixteen strategies to help you to succeed while on your certificate course are presented below. Each one is justified and described, and this is followed by several steps to help you to develop, or implement, the strategy in question.

As you read, remember that 'success' is a personal matter. For you, it might mean passing rather than failing, or passing your course with ease. It could also mean attaining a distinction, such as a Pass 'B' or a Pass 'A', if this is available at the end of the course you have selected.

Using the sixteen strategies for certificate success

It is not recommended that you try to develop all sixteen strategies. There is also no need to read this chapter all the way through. Rather, it is suggested that you select those strategies that relate specifically to your needs as you see them. To help you to do just this, they are listed below. This list gives you an overview of all of the strategies that are discussed, to help you to identify a few in particular that you would like to work on.

The sixteen strategies are:

1. Be open-minded
2. Put new ideas into immediate practice
3. Focus on your learners
4. Develop a personal teaching style
5. Become more self-aware and learn to reflect
6. Transfer and build upon existing skills
7. See learning as developmental and experiential
8. Seek out learning opportunities
9. Learn from and with others
10. Prioritize learning – yours and theirs
11. Manage the workload
12. Be realistic
13. Identify and use various sources of support
14. Practise as much as possible
15. Keep a personal learning journal
16. Enjoy yourself!

Here is a useful approach to these strategies and steps:

1. Read the list above, and, using a highlighter pen, select those that you would find it most beneficial to develop.
2. Turn to the short discussion that follows the strategy you have selected, which you will find below.
3. Read the steps that follow the strategy and highlight or make a note of the one(s) that you personally would find most useful and would be able to implement.
4. You will certainly have your own ideas for steps you could take, and you should use those too. There is space at the end of this chapter for your notes.
5. In some cases the strategies have been cross-referenced to relevant suggestions made in previous chapters, and you may wish to read or re-read these chapter sections.

Remember that learning is incremental and developmental, and that while some of the strategies and steps may seem small, research has shown that they can powerfully enhance learning when used consistently. Remember too that learning can be an interdependent process, such that learning in one area can support learning in another.

▶ SIXTEEN STRATEGIES FOR CERTIFICATE SUCCESS

All of the strategies and steps described in this chapter arose in the course of the research on which this book is based. This research was carried out over a 6 year period, and various training contexts around the world were represented, including for example private language schools, British Council teaching centres and universities. The strategies and sreps were suggested by course tutors, course participants and experienced teachers, in detailed descriptions of their experiences of different certificate courses. These descriptions were recorded in personal learning journals, course assignments and evaluations, in response to questionnaires, or while sharing their experiences in recorded interviews and group discussions.

> 'The course, in all its aspects, seems to suit a particular learner profile rather well. That profile is a person who learns very quickly, is willing to accept that learning by making mistakes is an acceptable way to learn, is not defensive, is a good team player, is able to switch off from the grades and concentrate on the process, can work under real pressure, and can apply theory to practice effortlessly.'
>
> Tutor, Portugal

▶ Strategy 1: Be open-minded

'An open mind is an essential characteristic of the successful trainee.'

Tutor, Spain

To be a successful trainee, it is essential that you approach the course with an open mind, even if you are already a practising teacher with a number of years of experience. This may mean putting to one side long-held beliefs, ideas, attitudes, or opinions, and being

'The best trainees are those who're open to new ideas. They don't come with fixed views about what's what, or, if they do have ideas, they're willing and able to question them, and receptive to totally new ones.'

Tutor, New Zealand

'I've been a teacher for 9 years and I have to say this course was tough for me. I thought I knew what I was doing but my old habits weren't always good ones. My advice? Welcome criticism with open arms. Welcome ideas with open arms.'

Participant, Spain

prepared to listen to, and reflect upon, ideas that are new to you and which might seem, at first, strange or counter-intuitive.

One tutor gave three examples of situations in which, in her opinion, participants were not as receptive as they might have been:

'Some of my toughest training moments have been with people who've just refused to let go of some conviction or other. I've tended to see it as people sometimes needing to "unlearn" stuff. To give an example, on my last course, I had two trainees, one who had the notion that "correct" English had no contractions whatsoever in it. I asked her about it and she told me that this had been drummed into her throughout her schooling in India, and she was convinced that contractions meant sloppy, poor-quality English. The other trainee refused to even consider it when I said that English had no future tense. Oh, and I remember when I was training having a heated debate with someone who categorically refused to believe that the word "box" has four sounds! This meant, I know it did, that he couldn't hear the actual sounds – his conviction that one letter equals one sound got in the way of his ears!'

This tutor did not expect her participants to accept everything she said, without questioning. But she did expect them to be receptive: to listen to what she had to say, and then to go away and reflect upon it; and perhaps even to do some independent research into the area.

You can see from this tutor's experience that being receptive could make your experience a more successful one. Below are some steps you can take to help you to do this.

1. Be open-minded: Steps to help you

(a) Use the first day or so of your course, in particular, in which to listen, watch and absorb.

(b) If you find yourself thinking something along the lines of 'I've been teaching for years and always found that X works best', try to remember that people usually have good reasons for what they do. Ask about the reasons – they may help you to change your mind or be more receptive to the idea.

(c) If you find that you strongly disagree with someone or something, try to suspend judgement until you have seen the idea in practice a few times.

(d) Be prepared to 'unlearn', or let go of, a way of doing something.

(e) Keep an 'Ideas' section in a 'Personal Learning Journal' (Strategy 15). Use this to note down ideas as they occur, without prejudging them. Many of the ideas will be useful to you at a later stage.

▶ Strategy 2: Put new ideas into immediate practice

> 'Those who shine on these courses tend to be those who put ideas
> recently learned into more or less immediate practice, even if they
> don't always work out that well.'
>
> *Tutor, Australia*

'One of the truly fantastic things about being a course tutor is that you learn what a wealth of ideas people have. And then you get to use them yourself!'

Tutor, United Kingdom

'You can see some of the trainees really making an effort to relate the ideas presented in input sessions to their own teaching. They're the ones likely to do well.'

Tutor, United Arab Emirates

As well as being receptive to new ideas, you also need to be willing to try them out in the classroom. As the quote above suggests, it is important to try out the idea: to put it to the test, if you like. If you do this as soon as possible, it will be fresh in your mind. If you find that it does not work out too well, the important thing is to reflect upon the reasons and see it as a learning opportunity. Why did it go wrong? Could you adapt the idea for use on another occasion? One course participant said:

'Being receptive isn't quite enough, you also need to be capable of putting new ideas or theory into practice. And I think you need to do all this – be receptive to new ideas, and able to try them out in the classroom – simply in order to pass the course, not only if you are in pursuit of that elusive "A" grade …'.

The ideas that follow can help you here.

2. Put new ideas into immediate practice: Steps to help you

(a) Refer to the 'Ideas' section of your 'Personal Learning Journal' (Strategy 15). Set out to incorporate one idea (no matter how small) into each teaching practice class that you give.

(b) Interpret 'new' ideas liberally. A new idea might be one that you have fine-tuned, or adapted from a familiar one, or one that merges two ideas, for example.

(c) You may find, particularly towards the end of the course, that you have established some comfortable teaching 'routines'. Deliberately set out at this stage to try out a new idea or two – any idea, that is, which is new for you. Again, use the 'Ideas' section in your 'Personal Learning Journal' (Strategy 15) to help you.

▶ Strategy 3: Focus on your learners

'My best lessons have been the ones in which I was so concentrated on my students that I forgot about everything else. And I mean everything else: when I finished it was as if I'd come out of a trance.'

Participant, Hong Kong

There is an enormous advantage to focusing on your learners: in losing yourself in them you can forget about yourself. This CELTA tutor said:

'For me, if a trainee's to get a "B" or an "A" I expect them to be completely absorbed by their students towards the end of their course, so much so that they ignore me. I might as well not be there and you can sense it if this is taking place, because everything they do is directed at their students and not done for me and you can see it in their students' eyes. I'd much rather they did that than tried to please me.'

This tutor suggests that participants should try to please their learners, rather than their tutors. This is excellent advice, not least because in pleasing your learners you will also please your tutors.

You can also spend time getting to know some of your learners outside class time. The more you know about your learners, the better you will be able to engage them in your classroom. A tutor said:

'I've often noticed that the trainees who do best on the course are those who understand that students are what it's all about, so they make the effort to get to know some of them outside the class. I think this helps trainees because it increases their confidence. They develop better skills in terms of communicating with people who have limited English.'

'In one TP session, my aim was to teach the present perfect to our class of intermediate students ... I spent hours reading grammar books and educating myself. Then, proud of what I'd learnt, I performed what I thought was a very good lesson ... But in feedback, my tutor said I had made no attempt to find out what my learners already knew or to treat them as individuals. Instead, I had assumed they all knew nothing and had marched them all through the same activities at the same time. Since then, I have always tried to assess learners' needs individually and allow them to work at their own pace.'

Participant, United Kingdom

'Teaching is an interactive activity and my students are kind of like a mirror. If my teaching's good, you can see them progress. They enjoy themselves and you feel satisfied. You're willing to acquire better teaching skills and go back to give them more. If you have had a bad lesson, your students are unhappy and you're disappointed. You'll go back and think about what you've done wrong. You'll try to find ways to improve on your skills so as to give your students a better lesson next time.'

Participant, Hong Kong

Here are some suggestions to help you with this:

3. Focus on your learners: Steps to help you

(a) When observing a class, watch your learners *as well* as the teacher. Try to sit where you can see your learners' faces; their expressions will provide you with feedback about their reaction to the lesson.

(b) Before class, ask yourself not 'What do I need to do in this class?' but rather, 'What do my learners need me to do for them in this class?'

(c) Choose material that is interesting for your learners – not for you, the teacher. Do everything for your learners' sake, never for its own sake.

(d) Create time to get to know some learners, possibly your own, but not necessarily. If your centre has a coffee room for learners, spend time there. You will be very likely to find learners who are willing to talk to you, because they will see this as useful speaking practice.

(e) After each class, spend a few minutes reflecting upon your learners and how you handled them. What have you learned about them?

(f) Use the start of a lesson, as learners are arriving, not to take a register as is usual practice but simply to chat to them. (It's a bad time to take the register anyway, as your learners are likely to be at the peak of their interest and receptiveness. There are better ways of spending the time – also, they may not all arrive on time so you will have to return to the task.) Do the same at the end.

(g) Devise a system to help you to learn your learners' names; and then use them, frequently. For example, you can prepare a plan of the classroom with a box representing each seat in the room. Then you can fill it in with the names of your learners, either by passing it around for everyone to fill in (this can be a bit time-consuming, though); or by asking one learner to complete it with the names of everyone in the class; or you can fill it in yourself. Likewise, make sure your learners know your full name and can pronounce it. Drill the name you want them to call you by, if they need the practice!

(h) In class, work towards engaging and involving each of your learners. Make frequent eye contact with each one. Be consciously inclusive.

(i) Welcome – rather than fear – your learners' contributions in class. See these contributions as your raw material. Their language is your data.

▶ Strategy 4: Develop a personal teaching style

'Understanding that I didn't have to do things I didn't like, providing I could find alternative ways of achieving the same result, gave me the confidence to begin to develop my own style. Then things really took off for me.'

Participant, New Zealand

Many people have referred to the course as placing participants on a 'steep learning curve'. One of the things that they mean by this is that participants change and develop significantly in a short time. A tutor said:

'I always tell my trainees that I'll expect to see signs of change, development, growth – and that I'll be expecting them to begin to develop their own style. I tell them that they'll see lots of different approaches and ways of doing things and that they mustn't panic or try to take it all on board, but that they should use the opportunities to find out more about themselves and about what works for them.'

'The course shouldn't be about copying a model. It should be about providing an example of the kind of thing that's possible, and then discussing it. I try to help trainees to critique what they've seen. By that I mean identify what worked well, what less well. I also ask them: is it for you?'

Tutor, Hong Kong

You will observe teachers teaching in a range of different styles and employing many different techniques and approaches in their classrooms. The decisions they make in relation to their teaching are partly influenced by their personalities: some people are good at employing humour in the classroom; some have high levels of empathy; others are known for their patience or ability to stay calm in a potentially stressful situation.

Some participants have thought that they would do best on their course if they tried to copy what they observed experienced teachers doing. This may work on occasion, but generally it is best to observe with a view to identifying the techniques that you like and would feel comfortable using.

A participant described her experience:

'I felt the best approach was to try to copy my tutor and the experienced teachers I observed, which was hard to do sometimes because occasionally I didn't like what I saw and also I felt that sometimes a teacher's style wasn't really me, somehow – I remember one very flamboyant teacher I observed, fantastic lesson really, lovely to watch, but I remember thinking afterwards – "I can never teach like that." I wish my tutor had told me it was OK to be myself. It makes sense now – of course the only thing to do is develop your own style! – but at the time there's so much to take on board, and you see so much that you want to try out … I guess it's a question really of being selective … and of selecting from what you've seen and learned according to what you feel will work for you.'

This means that you are not expected to accept everything unquestioningly, but that you are expected to become your own teacher.

Here are some useful steps to help you to develop your own teaching style:

4. Develop a personal teaching style: Steps to help you

(a) Actively seek feedback from your learners. Spend a few minutes with them at the end of a lesson. Ask them what they found useful; what was less useful. Use this information to influence the development of your teaching style.

(b) At the end of a lesson, simply jot down (in your 'Personal Learning Journal', perhaps; see Strategy 15) a few of the things you did in class that were successful. Reflect upon why they were particularly successful, and reinforce them by using them again in the near future.

(c) When observing, focus on identifying what you like and feel comfortable with. Integrate these ideas into your own teaching practice.

(d) Avoid being impressed, and stay focused on the consequences of different behaviours. Weigh them up and choose what you think is best for you and your learners.

▶ **Strategy 5: Become more self-aware and learn to reflect**

'The irony of life is that it is lived forward but understood backward.'

Kierkegaard

'If you didn't know yourself when you began the course, you'd certainly know yourself by the end!'

Participant, United Kingdom

'I think good teachers are constantly reflecting upon their practice. They try to see their practice from different angles and they call their assumptions into question. They do this alone, with colleagues, with anyone who'll lend an ear ... Just go into any busy staffroom and sit and listen for a while.'

Experienced teacher, British Council, Sultanate of Oman

'Trainees reflect critically when they examine the assumptions underlying what we tell them to do – when they start to think about why we ask them to do the things we do ...'

Tutor, New Zealand

Participants who succeed tend to be those who are willing to learn about themselves and the impact that they have upon people. They begin the course with an idea of the kind of person they are, and they recognize that they will learn more about themselves as the course progresses. They realize that good teachers have high levels of self-awareness and are able to reflect and act upon feedback from others.

'Reflection' means different things to different people. Some see it simply as thinking about something, while others see it more specifically, as the ability to look back and learn from problems that you have faced, and then apply that learning to future situations. As a participant on your course, you will find it most useful to see reflection as this ability to 'look back and learn'.

People reflect critically when they look back but also consider what underlies something that has been said or suggested. For example, you may be told on your course that 'pairwork' is a particularly useful technique. You may accept this view simply because an experienced tutor is promoting it in a workshop, and this is understandable. However, you would learn more if you enquired a little further. Critical questioning can engage reflection. Find out: Why is pairwork considered so useful? What are the underlying reasons for its widespread use? Answers to such questions will lead you into the 'communicative approach', and the benefits to learners of increasing their opportunities for oral practice.

These ideas – of becoming more self-aware, of looking back, thinking about underlying assumptions, learning from reflection and applying this learning to future situations – are vital for anyone involved in learning about teaching.

Here are a few steps to help you with this area:

5. Become more self-aware and learn to reflect: Steps to help you

(a) Becoming self-aware is difficult to do by yourself – so involve others. Identify and talk about your strengths and weaknesses; feedback after teaching practice provides a good opportunity for this. Develop strategies to sustain your strengths and address your weaknesses.

(b) In feedback, reflect upon your responses. If you detect signs of defensiveness when receiving less positive feedback, remind yourself of the learning opportunity that feedback presents. Try to see negative feedback in a positive light, as providing you with a unique opportunity to improve your practice.

(c) Start to notice the times during your day when you are reflecting on something. How do you go about doing it? Do you become distracted, or are you able to stay focused on the subject of your reflections?

(d) Get into the habit of looking back and reviewing your experience in terms of what worked, what did not, and why. Ask yourself: How did you feel about it at the time? Do you still feel the same way now?

(e) Set aside a little time for reflection each day; a few minutes, or more if you have it. Choose a time when you are comparatively free of course-related commitments, such as when travelling to or from the centre.

(f) Keep a 'Personal Learning Journal' (Strategy 15) in which you note down reflections upon all aspects of your experience. Such a journal can aid the development of a number of skills and strategies.

(g) Identify, question and explore assumptions, values and beliefs that underpin the practice you are learning about. For example, do not accept everything you are told at face value; ask questions and explore rationales instead. Assumptions may hold; then again, they may not. Be prepared for either.

▶ Strategy 6: Transfer and build upon existing skills

'Trainees who do well are those who are able to bring skills they have acquired elsewhere to their current situation.'

Tutor, United Kingdom

'I'd been a nurse for many years before I took my course and I found that many things I'd learned from those years were useful to me. I guess instead of a good bedside manner one needs a good classroom manner!'

Participant, New Zealand

As an adult learner you will arrive on your course with a wide range of skills of particular value to you as a course participant and as a teacher. Those who do well on certificate courses are often those who have identified their own skills at the start of the course, and are then able to exploit and build upon them later.

One tutor remarked:

'I think strong trainees are good at using their previous experience and the skills they have developed earlier, not just skills of reflection but others too such as the ability to be organized, not to procrastinate and so on …'

These ideas will help you to utilize fully your previous experience and the skills that you bring to the course:

6. Transfer and build upon existing skills: Steps to help you

(a) Think about your previous successful learning experiences. Include things like learning a foreign language, getting a school qualification, or moving around a foreign city. Make a list of some skills and knowledge that helped you to do well, and select those likely to be useful in your current context. Take or create opportunities to use them.

(b) Before you start your course, make a list of the skills and knowledge that you already have and which might be useful to you during the course. Pin your list in a prominent place and use it as a reminder from time to time. In the 'heat of the course', these skills can sometimes be overlooked or not exploited as fully as they could be.

▶ Strategy 7: See learning as developmental and experiential

'I believe I was successful primarily because I saw my learning as a question of developing and changing.'

Participant, Australia

Learning on these courses is developmental and experiential. Learning occurs when your experience shapes and informs your future behaviour and development. Tutors look for various signs of this process. They will expect to see that you are able to learn from a workshop and that you can demonstrate understanding of the concepts in an assignment or apply what you have learned in your own teaching. They will expect to see you taking account of your feedback, becoming increasingly aware of your strengths and weaknesses, and being able to build upon or address them. They will expect you make mistakes from time to time, but they will also expect you to learn from them.

'I saw the course as developmental. It helped that I was fully aware of my strengths and weaknesses and I listened to my feedback and tried to act on it; I used it to help me to develop into the teacher I wanted to be. I didn't always manage to fully change behaviours but I both saw and showed real improvements over a period of time.'

Participant, Bahrain

'I feel processed and changed from 3 months ago – can I go to back to being me now?'

A participant's last journal entry, Hong Kong

A key sign of development that tutors look for is a growing independence; that is, the ability to research, plan, and teach a lesson with less support from tutors and fellow participants than you might need at the start of your course. This is not something that you need to worry about particularly, because increasing independence should be the natural consequence of learning: as you acquire the resources yourself, you will become less dependent on others for support, information or ideas, for example. It may, however, be useful simply to stay alert to opportunities to demonstrate independence, particularly in the later stages of your course.

These steps can help you:

7. See learning as developmental and experiential: Steps to help you

(a) Accept that you will make mistakes and try to view them positively, use them to guide your learning.

(b) As you move through the course and become more skilled and confident, try to call upon tutors and fellow participants only for limited and focused assistance.

(c) Look for other sources of support, for example, your course notes, your feedback, materials in your resource centre, family and friends, and various useful websites (see www for some suggestions).

▶

Steps to help you *continued*

(d) Reflect upon why a growing independence is desirable. What are the personal benefits?

(e) Recognize that tutors will look for signs of development in a number of areas including your teaching practice skills, your emotional management, your factual knowledge, and your understanding of key concepts. Take opportunities that arise to practise some skills in each area, even if this involves putting yourself in non-preferred situations. If you feel factual knowledge of pronunciation is your weakest area, for example, then counter this by seeking out opportunities that require you to research and teach pronunciation.

(f) Set yourself personal, realistic and achievable targets. You can include some of these in your lesson plan; this will help tutors to see what you are trying to achieve in terms of your own personal development.

The evolution of the ESOL Teacher

▶ Strategy 8: Seek out learning opportunities

'A great deal of learning is incidental and idiosyncratically related to the
learner: it cannot be planned in advance.'

Tusting and Barton, 2003:36

Successful participants tend to be those who stay alert to learning opportunities. They recognize that a certificate course offers a rich and complex environment with constant opportunities to learn on a number of levels. They understand that learning is a personal matter and they do what they need to do in order to learn from every available opportunity.

'A CELTA course is a fertile learning landscape, full of opportunity and possibility for growth. But sometimes you have to guide trainees towards seeing – and grabbing! – the various opportunities.'

Tutor, United Kingdom

They are also able to remain focused on identifying and benefiting from learning opportunities for the duration of the course. This is particularly important in relation to course components which may become less interesting or appear less useful as the course progresses. Examples of such areas described by former participants include guided observation and attending to each others' feedback after teaching practice. Some participants described finding it difficult to concentrate during these components because they were anxious about their performance in some other aspect of the course; others came to feel that there was nothing more for them to learn. However, these are both valuable course components and if you find yourself lacking focus at any stage, you could miss an opportunity (in feedback, for example) to ask questions and influence the development of the session; while in observation, you may miss something significant that occurs in the class.

Remember also that teaching is creative, and that ideas are its raw material. Some former participants have described feeling hesitant with regard to sharing their ideas, because they doubted the adequacy of their ideas or, in some cases, because they worried that another participant might take the idea and use it themselves. They have also worried about asking questions, for fear of appearing too selfish, or unintelligent, or taking up too much time. But they are missing a learning opportunity, because only by actively sharing ideas can you test their adequacy and improve upon them if needed through discussion with others. You should not worry about another participant taking your idea, because it is unlikely that he or she will realize it in exactly the same way as you intended.

Ways to remain open to learning opportunities and focused upon them as they arise are suggested below.

8. Seek out learning opportunities: Steps to help you

(a) Look for learning opportunities everywhere. Learning opportunities can vary enormously: they include syllabus statements, feedback, assignments, teaching practice, lesson planning meetings and informal discussions with fellow participants and tutors. Remember also to distinguish between learning opportunities and tasks that support learning (see Chapter 6, 'Learning opportunity or learning support?' in particular).

(b) At regular intervals, and particularly in the latter half of the course, remind yourself about the need to remain alert to learning opportunities. This can help to prevent you becoming complacent, and missing something useful.

(c) Although some situations may appear similar to others, and it may seem that little or no learning is possible from it, it is worth bearing in mind that every teaching situation is unique (and by 'teaching situation' I mean every aspect of your course, from workshops to observation to feedback). It is therefore very unlikely that there will be nothing to learn. This understanding can help you to avoid becoming cynical.

(d) You can create learning opportunities for yourself, by being assertive, and by asking questions. Ask the kind of questions that will help to build your confidence by addressing your dilemmas, ambiguities or uncertainties. The kind of question that can be particularly useful is often referred to as a 'Wh- question' (although not all of them begin with 'wh'!) – that is, one beginning with 'what', 'why', 'when', 'where', 'which', 'who' or 'how'.

(e) Recognize and ignore the fact that overt signs of enthusiasm are not always very fashionable!

▶ Strategy 9: Learn from and with others

'TP groups were a good idea. We supported each other and learned from each other.'

Participant, Bahrain

'They've really helped each other – absolutely no competition involved – just an eagerness and sensitive constructive help. They all expressed how important that was …'

Tutor, Hong Kong

Those who succeed on certificate courses are often those who recognize the benefits of working closely with others and seeing others as 'learning opportunities'. However, the most successful participants define 'others' quite loosely, to include not only their teaching practice group members, but also all course tutors, all other participants, experienced teachers (those providing lessons for guided observation as well as others working in the centre), and language learners.

Successful participants are able to work with others, even when they feel they do not get on particularly well with that person. They are able to put personal likes and dislikes to one side in order to concentrate on the task in hand. They are also good at preventing any feelings of competitiveness from interfering with their performance and are not distracted by being the object of another's competitiveness.

Successful participants also tend not to dismiss apparently less competent peers, but recognize that it is possible to learn from others' weaknesses as well as their strengths. They also recognize that time spent supporting a less able colleague can help to reinforce their own teaching and interpersonal skills.

Here are some steps that could help you to learn more effectively from others involved in your course:

'I try to encourage a learning climate of dialogue and negotiation.'

Tutor, New Zealand

'I quickly realized that in order to get on, I was going to have to improve my attitude towards group work. You see I'm quite shy and working with others doesn't really come naturally, I'd always prefer to work on my own. But I made a real effort, and it helped. I became more confident in my dealings with people, including my students.'

Participant, Hong Kong

9. Learn from and with others: Steps to help you

(a) You may find that you are better at working alone rather than with others, or vice versa. If this is the case, look for opportunities to develop the skills required in your less preferred area. Try to work towards achieving a balance.

(b) Be prepared to learn from all kinds of people – those you like, as well as those whose company may be less preferred. Allow yourself to be influenced by diverse people with diverse backgrounds and views; try not to seek out only those people that reinforce your own established views and values.

(c) Prevent any feelings of competitiveness from interfering with your performance (and cope with being the object of another's competitiveness) by reminding yourself that tutors are looking for evidence of your progress, not in relation to your peers, but in relation to your own earlier performance and awareness – they want to see evidence of your own personal development.

(d) If you are called upon to support a colleague who needs help, see this as a positive opportunity to develop your own teaching and interpersonal skills.

(e) If you find that your teaching practice group does not have much contact with other groups, take steps to redress this. Arrange to meet up as a whole group, perhaps socially, whenever you can. You will then be able to exchange ideas and learn from people you may not normally be able to spend much time with.

(f) Try to give as well as take when working with your team. Set out to develop trust, mutual respect and open communication. See Chapter 8, 'Working with fellow participants'.

▶ Strategy 10: Prioritize learning – yours and theirs

'Learning about learning is the first step towards learning about teaching.'

Tutor, New Zealand

'The ability to learn depends on individuals. It's an entirely personal matter. What works for me might not work for you.'

Tutor, Australia

'There's been a lot of interest recently in ELT in learning and in learning independently. Just look at all the jargon: "learning to learn", "learner training", "self-directed learning" ,'independent learning centre"...'

Experienced teacher, Bahrain

The course is all about learning, but you may find it surprisingly easy to lose sight of this, with all that the experience demands of you. Those who succeed are able to focus on learning and give it priority at all stages: both their own and that of their learners. They recognize that the ability to learn is something that can always be improved upon, and so they frequently reflect upon their learning and try out new approaches, or adapt old ones – and they assist their learners to do the same.

A former course participant described it as follows:

'On my course I found that seeing my own work, or some of it, in terms of learning how to learn helped me to help others to do the same. I hadn't really expected to learn about learning on the course; I'd thought I was going to be learning all about language and how to teach it. But I realize now that while of course language and teaching matter enormously, really we should put learning first. And trying to understand my own learning processes and styles was the first step, followed by experimenting with different approaches to learning, thinking about and trying out all the different things I could do to help me personally to learn and also what I could do to help my students to learn.'

These steps can help you here:

10. Prioritize learning – yours and theirs: Steps to help you

(a) Think first of your learning and your learners' learning. Do this when you plan and when you teach, and when you reflect upon aspects of the course.

(b) Immerse yourself in all aspects of learning. Remember the 'Three-way learning opportunity' discussed in Chapter 4. You can learn from: what you are being taught; how it is being taught to you; and by applying your learning to your own learners in your own classroom.

(c) Focus on a process of becoming a teacher rather than on the product of the polished performance.

▶

Steps to help you *continued*

(d) Talk about learning on your course. Identify your own learning style and prefer-ences, and discuss these with your fellow participants. Try out any novel approaches to learning that you hear about and like. If they work, integrate these new approaches into your own personal repertoire of learning styles.

(e) Make learning an ongoing topic for discussion with your learners. Help them to recognize and reflect upon their own preferred ways of learning and to try out and integrate new ways.

(f) Learn by observing, researching, planning, reflecting, acting. Identify your pre-ferred way of learning, and try to ensure that you take a rounded approach by making use of others.

▶ Strategy 11: Manage the workload

'The course would have been utterly overwhelming if I weren't naturally
inclined to be organized and get ahead.'

Participant, United Kingdom

Successful participants are those who stay in control by managing the workload and the pressure. It is particularly important to:

● start the course with some systems in place to help you to get organized

● prepare for workshops, and, of course, teaching practice, if only by thinking or reflecting upon the topic or lesson.

A key part of staying in control is avoiding procrastination, because it is likely that you will have little time in which to catch up with work that should have been done earlier. This tutor believed that successful participants are those who do not procrastinate:

'The hardest part about doing a CELTA is getting everything in on time: the lesson plans and the assignments and staying on top of it all.'

Participant, Thailand

'Teaching a one hour lesson on Friday and every time I go to plan the lesson I think "oh I'll just finish off the ironing / wash the dog / read the paper" – ANYTHING rather than face up to the next TP.'

Participant, Hong Kong

'I've seen trainees really struggle with procrastination, with what I call "chronic procrastination paralysis". And yes, successful trainees either don't have that problem or find some way through it.'

To stay in control of the workload and to avoid 'procrastination paralysis', here are some steps you can take:

11. Manage the workload: Steps to help you

(a) Be proactive in checking deadlines and task requirements, and keep a schedule of what is due and when, and get ahead when you can. This will give you time in which to deal with any contingencies that may arise. (See 'A time for all things' in Chapter 6.)

(b) Learn to recognize pressure before it becomes too great, and try any or all of the following:
  ● Take each day, or demand on your time, as it comes.
  ● Do not do more than you need to in one area when under pressure in other areas.
  ● Say no when you need to (you might need to say 'no' on occasion, for example, to a fellow participant who has asked for your help).

▶

Steps to help you *continued*

- Be flexible.
- Ask for help when you need it.
- Create a little breathing space for yourself before pressing on with your commitments.
- Derive satisfaction from being organized, in control and from accomplishing a task.
- Distinguish the important from the urgent: and concentrate on the former.

(c) Allocate and take turns where possible: you do the research for a shared lesson one week, a fellow participant does it the next, for example.

(d) Be aware that things gather pace as the course progresses. This means that you should do as much as you can as soon as possible to avoid building up a backlog of work – it is essential to avoid procrastinating.

(e) If you are the kind of person who tends to procrastinate, recognizing that you have this problem is the first step. Brainstorm ideas about overcoming the problem with someone else, if you are unable to solve it alone. Do this as soon as you can, before the amount of accumulated work becomes overwhelming. Tutors are used to dealing with this issue and will be supportive. You might also want to consider why you procrastinate. Do you fear failure or even success, perhaps? Do you fear moving on, to new tasks and activities? Try to understand the underlying causes.

(f) Set yourself positive rewards for accomplishment.

Manage your workload

▶ Strategy 12: Be realistic

'You will see trainees give "all singing, all dancing" lessons each time, as they think that's what's expected.'

Tutor, United Arab Emirates

Successful participants tend to be those with realistic expectations, in particular of:

● their course

● themselves

● their learners.

Successful participants are able to keep the course, and their approach to it, in proportion to its overall aims. They understand that a short intensive certificate course can only 'kick start the process', a process that will continue for many years to come if they stay in the profession. Their expectations therefore are to learn some basic skills and techniques which they will continue to develop in the workplace. They recognize that these skills and techniques are a foundation for further learning.

However, the intensity of the course can be overwhelming, and some former participants have become submerged by it, allowing it to take over their lives. In such a situation, relatively trivial things can take on enormous importance, and this can interfere with your progress. Conflict and resentment can grow over issues that would in normal circumstances be readily and amicably resolved, such as access to materials and resources, arrangements for a teaching practice group to meet, or the division of labour in planning or researching a lesson. The result can be that a great deal of time and energy is wasted on the nagging resentment that can develop in such situations, as you try to justify or work through your reactions, or co-opt support from your fellow participants. Clearly, your time and energy could be put to far more profitable use on an intensive course of this type, so it is important to keep matters in proportion.

Perhaps because participants are presented with so much new information on these short intensive courses, they have sometimes felt inclined to try to incorporate

'I talked to them about the course, and the "pass" grade, having realistic goals. So many trainees get disappointed when they don't get a "B", like a pass is sub-standard.'

CELTA Tutor, Hong Kong

'Seeing that class yesterday was great because I now realize I don't have to cram a ton of stuff into 30 mins.'

Participant, Hong Kong

'To survive, I kept having to remind myself: "This is only TEFL." The course is so intensive and stressful that you have to keep it in perspective or you'll drown – it is a 3 month training course, that's all.'

Participant, Australia

> 'While I was training, the phrase "this is not rocket science" was always being bandied about ...'
>
> Tutor, Spain

as much as possible of their new learning into their teaching practice. Participants have felt the need to do this because they are aware that every teaching practice class counts towards their final assessment, and so they think they need to demonstrate as much of their learning as possible in the limited time available. It is also the case that one of the most important things you will learn about on your course is what is feasible and what is not within a set time, and this is something that is best learned through experience.

Whatever the reasons, you may find that you have a tendency to overestimate what is required of you and your learners, to 'overplan', and to make your lesson unnecessarily complex. While it is useful – if not essential – to have some extra material or an extra activity to hand, in case you have some spare time left at the end of a lesson, this does not mean you need to plan a complicated lesson involving all the techniques and different types of materials that you can think of. In fact, such a lesson may cause more problems than it solves, as one tutor noted:

'I watched G's lesson today. He'd put everything into it but managed to lose sight of his students and his aims in the course of its execution. It was as if they weren't there. And then at one stage he lost his place and nearly lost his rag too.'

Such a lesson may fail in part because you have made it too complex to implement easily, particularly when you may be under pressure and nervous.

Instead of worrying first and foremost about demonstrating your proficiency, refocus your attention onto your learners and let them and their needs drive your lesson (Strategy 3). Select your aims, techniques and materials with their needs in mind, rather than yours. This shift will help to ensure that your energies are appropriately directed and also that you do not prepare lessons that are so complex they are difficult to implement. And you will be likely to find that the demonstration of good teaching skills is a natural consequence of this refocus.

These steps can help you to ensure that your expectations are realistic:

12. Be realistic: Steps to help you

(a) See what you learn on your course as a foundation on which to build.

(b) When planning a lesson, remind yourself that you are likely to be nervous, and prepare with this in mind. Especially in the early stages of your course, you may wish to plan activities that are easier to implement.

(c) Getting to know your learners can help you find out what you can realistically expect from them (Strategy 3).

(d) Do not confuse complexity with quality. A simple lesson will be a better lesson if it is easy to implement smoothly and if it meets the needs of your learners.

▶

Steps to help you *continued*

(e) Consider what kind of plan is easiest for you to refer to while teaching. It may be that you prefer your plan to be written on A4 paper; or perhaps you prefer to note the key stages of your lesson onto smaller index cards. Find and use a straightforward approach that suits you.

(f) When you plan, with your learners always in mind, think first about what you want to do, then what tools and techniques you need to achieve your plan. Try not to let tools and techniques drive your plan. Make sure that everything you plan has value in relation to your learners' learning.

(g) Remember that you will have several opportunities to demonstrate your learning, besides that provided by your teaching practice. For example, you can demonstrate learning in workshops, feedback, assignments and in one-to-one tutorials.

(h) Look at any conflict you face from the point of view of the whole course and what you are trying to achieve while on it; and from the point of view of the rest of your life. Does it really justify all that anxiety it is causing? Does it justify all the energy it is taking, at a time when you do not have energy to spare?

(i) Have realistic expectations of yourself. You many not want – or need – to excel, and this is perfectly acceptable. Remember too that, having been offered a place and followed this with a positive attitude and sufficient effort, you are very likely to pass. Tutors try to avoid accepting people onto their courses who are likely to fail, and this is supported by available statistics which show that the vast majority of participants pass.

▶ Strategy 13: Identify and use various sources of support

'Good trainees take advantage of all the resources at their disposal.
They aren't shy about coming forward either!'

Tutor, Spain

'I've also realized how useful our tutor is as a resource. I can't believe how helpful she is. I emailed her at home with my intrepid lesson plan and bless her she returned it with lots of notes on at 1.45am!'

Participant, Hong Kong

'I always tell my trainees that they mustn't hesitate to ask for help when they need it. I tell them that I've seen people fail, and that I believe that if they'd sought help they'd have passed.'

Tutor, New Zealand

Of course, tutors are one of your key resources. But they are not your only source of potential help and guidance, and successful participants realize this at an early stage.

One participant described a situation she faced:

'There was someone in my TP group who really struggled to come to terms with it all. She talked to me, but I didn't feel really able to help her – she was in a pretty bad way at one point and was talking of jacking it all in. I tried to get her to talk to our TP tutor, but she refused, saying that he was too busy and that she didn't want to cause a problem. I think she made a mistake, not talking to him. In retrospect, of course there are many other people that she could have turned to, people that I'm sure would have listened and tried to help her – I'm thinking of one of our other tutors, or the teachers we observed in guided observation for example, or perhaps even just some of the more friendly people in the staff room. But she didn't see this at the time.'

It is absolutely critical that you seek help if you have a difficulty that you cannot resolve on your own, and, because it can quickly become too late, you should do this as soon as you can.

However, there is no need to wait until you have a problem before you seek others' ideas and opinions; instead, deliberately set out to learn as much as you can from all available sources of support.

These steps could help you:

13. Identify and use various sources of support: Steps to help you

(a) Sources of support on certificate courses exist in many forms. Make a list and call upon them as needed. You can ask a wide range of people for support; or use various resources and facilities. In relation to the latter, try:
- keeping and then referring back to a 'Personal Learning Journal' (Strategy 15)
- your own notes from workshops
- written feedback on past lessons
- the materials and resources in your resource centre (find out if they keep an archive of past lesson plans or assignments)

Steps to help you *continued*

- local bookstores and libraries which may have books that are not in your resource centre
- various websites (see the suggestions on www).

(b) Never allow yourself to flounder; always ask for help, even if your problem or difficulty seems trivial.

(c) Remember that if a tutor seems unapproachable, it may be because he or she is busy and preoccupied; or perhaps he or she may be shy and reticent by nature. These reasons should not stop you approaching any tutor when you need help. Do not create a situation in which, once the course is over, you look back with regret, saying to yourself 'If only I'd sought help from my tutor – I might have passed the course.'

(d) Set time aside for a problem-solving session with your teaching practice group. Every member has to bring one problem to share or issue to discuss. To gain maximum benefit from this, make sure yours is a genuine issue. Brainstorm solutions to each problem.

(e) Identify another or others with the same or similar problem as you. Meet up to brainstorm ideas to address the problem.

(f) Make sure that you take good notes throughout your course: these can be an excellent source of future support.

(g) Spend a little time in the staffroom, if you are given access to it. This can help you get to know some more experienced teachers and you might have the opportunity to seek their advice, ideas, or views.

▶ Strategy 14: Practise as much as possible

'Get in as much practice as you can, even if you have to rope in your family or friends as students!'

Participant, Bahrain

The course is experiential, and so you are expected to learn a great deal from *doing*. While very many practice opportunities are provided to help you, more practice can lead to greater confidence and improved performance. Some successful participants have created these opportunities for themselves, for example, by trying out a lesson on their teaching practice group, or by asking family or friends to stand in for learners.

However, you do not need to limit yourself to practising complete lessons. It can be very useful to practise techniques as well, and this can take up much less time. For example, giving a model, indicating word stress using your fingers, using the counter on a tape recorder, completing a worksheet that you have designed, using flashcards to elicit language and setting up and managing pairwork are all techniques that can be practised in your free time.

These steps can help you to identify and use practice opportunities:

> 'Our TP group used to get together to run through the lesson beforehand. That was really helpful, not only because we could iron out wrinkles but because it gave us each more time to practice.'
>
> Participant, Australia
>
> 'I used my flat mates as dummy students. It was a real giggle.'
>
> Participant, United Kingdom

---

14. Practise as much as possible: Steps to help you

(a) Do not see the teaching practice component of your course as your only opportunity to practise. Create more opportunities for yourself: practise with friends or family members in lieu of learners. You can also practise with no audience, in which case imagine a group of learners as you run through your plan. In all cases consider making an audio or video recording of yourself for future viewing.

(b) When new techniques are introduced in workshops, highlight those that lend themselves to practising in your free time, and set out to do so as soon as possible.

Practise as much as you can

▶ Strategy 15: Keep a personal learning journal

'Keeping a journal was, for me, an essential part of the experience. It allowed me to see my progress and to sound off in private: both vital at times!'

Participant, Hong Kong

You may be required to keep a 'learning journal' as a part of your course. If this is a course requirement, your tutor will probably provide you with completion guidelines and it is likely that he or she will want to see some, or all, of your journal during the course. Such a journal, because it is being written for a tutor and as a course requirement, may become a different kind of work to the essentially private and personal record recommended here.

There are excellent reasons for keeping a personal learning journal. In this kind of journal, you record your personal reflections upon what you are learning. The very process of organizing your thinking about your learning in order to put something down on paper encourages reflection and critical evaluation. You can, for example, relate your learning to what you already know. You can make a note of something you are uncertain about, or something you find confusing or ambiguous and which you would like to clarify.

'One strategy I adopted was to keep a diary. I did this initially as a kind of glorified note-keeping, with highlights and stuff to help me to learn and remember, but it became quite special. It's full of ideas, notes, thoughts, funnies from my classmates, even cartoons that I cut out and pasted there. 18 months down the line, I still occasionally refer to it.'

Participant, Bahrain

'I kept a journal, and by sitting down after every session and thinking through all that was said and done, I found it helped me enormously to remember, accept, reject and file away all the input that was going on.'

Participant, Australia

In your journal, you may choose to include all your course materials and notes if you prefer. However, this can become cumbersome, and many former participants have found it more important to keep their journals portable.

Keeping a journal offers a number of benefits. Two key benefits are mentioned in the quotation above: a journal provides you with a record of the progress you have made, and it can act as a good release for pent-up frustrations. A journal can also encourage and provide data for critical reflection; and this can be an excellent source of material for assignments such as one in which you are asked to identify your strengths and weaknesses. A journal can help you take control of your own learning, not only by providing you with a record of your progress, but also by helping you to identify areas that might need more attention.

Here are a number of steps to help you to keep a personal learning journal:

15: Keep a personal learning journal: Steps to help you

(a) Consider how much time you are willing or able to spend on your journal, and allocate time accordingly.

(b) If your journal ever becomes onerous, adapt your approach to it. For example, write less, or write in note form, or take a break for a few days. Do not let it become just another hurdle.

(c) Develop your own headings and write to those headings. For example, a former participant used headings such as these: 'Workshops', 'Feedback', and 'TP Group'; while another used headings that included 'Reflections', 'Ideas', and 'Queries'. Keeping such a journal is a personal matter and you will have your own preferences with regard to organizing it.

(d) Having kept a journal for a time, make it work for you. Reread it, highlighter pen in hand, and note your progress or any unresolved issues.

▶ Strategy 16: Enjoy yourself!

'Looking back, I'm sorry to say I think I forgot to enjoy myself! I'd tell anyone about to do a cert. to stop worrying and start enjoying.'

Participant, United Kingdom

'Got a real buzz from my class today. Enjoyed the lesson! And they seemed to enjoy me too! Now I'm driven to try even harder for them next time.'

Participant, Hong Kong

Former participants who have been particularly successful have often been those who have enjoyed the experience at the time. Their enjoyment improved their performance, and this was conveyed to fellow participants, which helped their teaching practice groups. Their enjoyment also positively influenced their learners' experience, and this reinforced their pleasure in teaching. A positively reinforcing cycle can be created:

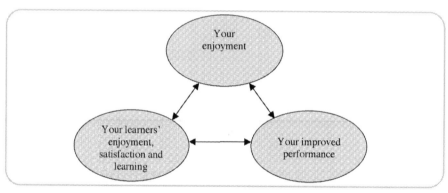

Figure 9.1 The enjoyment – improvement – satisfaction cycle

16: Enjoy yourself!: Steps to help you

You may like to identify your own set of steps to help you to remember to have a good time! Try brainstorming this with some of your fellow participants.

Succeeding: Key points to take away with you

- It is recommended that you take away a few strategies and steps from this chapter that you personally would like to develop further.

- To do this, follow the instructions provided in the section at the start of this chapter 'Using the sixteen strategies for certificate success'.

- It is also recommended that you return to this chapter at regular intervals both during and after your course, to update your personal selection in the light of your teaching experience.

- Use this space for your notes:

Notes

Notes

_____

_____

_____

_____

_____

_____

_____

_____

_____

_____

_____

_____

_____

_____

_____

Notes

- -

- -

- -

- -

- -

- -

- -

- -

- -

- -

- -

- -

- -

- -

www **Check your understanding** of Chapter 9 by completing the quiz available on the companion website at: www.sagepub.co.uk/brandt

Chapter 10

Being qualified

In this chapter, you can learn about:

- a certificate course graduate's search for employment in ELT/TESOL
- a course graduate's experience of the first few weeks in the workplace
- issues to consider when looking for employment
- how to identify a reputable employer
- some things to think about when starting a new job
- tips to help you to survive those first few weeks in your new job
- suggestions to help you to continue to develop your new career.

▶ EARLY DAYS IN THE LIFE OF A TEACHER IN ELT/TESOL

Below, you can read about the experience of Jean, a participant on a course in South-East Asia, as she ended her course and began looking for a job as a teacher in ELT/TESOL.

Jean had kept a journal throughout her 12-week part-time course, and she had found it so useful to reflect in this way that she continued to write for a few weeks while she made the transition from course participant to salaried teacher.

The extracts from Jean's journal below provide an overview of her experience. As you will see, the British Council (which she refers to as 'the BC') is one of the main employers of teachers in ELT/TESOL in the city where she had taken her course. As you read, you might like to make three lists: (a) what Jean wanted, (b) the problems she faced, and (c) the steps she took to address the problems.

Extracts from Jean's diary (1)

Week 12: the last week

So it's all over now bar the shouting. Two of us still to teach on Friday … then a short input session on Saturday. Then that's it!! …

Would love a job with the British Council – great place to start out with lots of support, resources and a super building. If not, who knows? I don't fancy teaching children – been there, got egg on the T-shirt. So, I'll watch the newspapers and listen to friends and hope that I can get employed somewhere.

POST COURSE

Thursday

Cold reality is setting in, in the job hunt … didn't really expect to get a contract job with the British Council here – they told me that it was unlikely for people straight from a cert. course to get one.

Far too many people are now chasing too few jobs. Had an interview today with the British Council … I will know by Monday. I did say that I was willing to work any hours, any age, any place …!

Went for several other interviews over the past week – but all for state schools. I'm not really interested – I want adult hours to go towards experience for my diploma, but I will take any job in the end because I need teaching experience … I'll know soon … I can always go back to nursing, I guess!

Wednesday

Sat hunched by the phone on Monday – nuffin.

Then S. rang on Monday to say that two others in our group had managed to get jobs at the BC and that was all there was going.

Fed up.

Sat by the phone all Tuesday – just in case – nothing.

Weds. morning I decided to ring the BC and be a bit pushy. They offered me 2 classes – one on-site, one off – GREAT!! A foot in the door!

So I went in for the workshops on Wednesday, having missed the induction and I hung around the person who allocates classes until she gave me 2 more!! Both off-site.

Then all hell let loose.

(to be continued)

If you made three lists as suggested above, you might like to compare them with these:

(a) What Jean wanted

Jean considered the following aspects of a new job important:

- a contract (ideally)
- employment with a reputable organization such as the British Council
- classes of adults, in particular (so that she can gain experience that will help her to get, eventually, a place on a diploma course)
- support
- resources
- good premises.

(b) The problems she faced

Jean experienced the following difficulties:

- competition
- disappointment
- missing the induction for new staff (because she was offered work at the last minute, after the induction had been held).

(c) The steps she took to address the problems

To address the difficulties listed above, Jean took the following steps:

- networking and watching out for advertisements in the local press
- being 'pushy' – more assertive, perhaps, than she was accustomed to being
- showing flexibility
- being willing to accept a less preferred teaching job (e.g. in a state school).

Each point that Jean raises in the lists above is discussed next.

▶ THE JOB HUNT: ISSUES AND STRATEGIES

1. Getting a contract

Jean recognized that, in her context, a full-time contract was unlikely for someone with no experience who has just completed a certificate course. This is because she took her course in her home city, in a region in which there was a great deal of competition for work in ELT/TESOL, and she was seeking a job with a particularly well-known and reputable organization. You may not have the same difficulty: it is possible to be offered either a part-time or a full-time contract with a certificate and no, or little, experience. It will depend largely on local market conditions: on the demand for, and availability of, teachers in ELT/TESOL in your area. This

> 'Oman is a haven for English Language instructors, with a wide variety of opportunities for teachers at all levels of experience. If you take a CELTA course in Oman, you may well find yourself with job offers before you have even completed it.'
>
> Baguley and Greenwood, 2005

may be a consideration, along with timing, if you have a choice of location in which to take your certificate course.

You can also increase your chances of finding work upon qualifying by taking a course that ends just prior to the start of a busy period for the centre or country. The months of April or May are good times to be coming to the end of a certificate course in the United Kingdom, for example, because many language centres become extremely busy over the summer as they seek to accommodate an influx of learners from other countries who want to improve their English during their summer vacations. Such work may be full-time, although temporary; it could nevertheless provide you with some useful experience and future contacts.

> 'I made a huge mistake in not starting to teach right after my course. I was too busy with other things and it just didn't happen. I've lost a lot of the confidence I had, and would only feel happy teaching one-to-one now. I'd advise anyone not to do what I've done – and to remember that the longer you leave it the harder it gets to go back in.'
>
> Participant, New Zealand

This last point relates to a consideration that Jean implies but did not make explicit. This is the need to teach as soon as possible after qualifying with a certificate course. Former graduates have said that the longer the break taken between your course and employment, the harder it is to begin teaching again.

2. Employment with a reputable organization

Jean had her sights set on a position with the British Council, partly because she knew that such a position would be likely to provide her with some of the other things she sought, such as support and good resources. You can use such criteria as these to help you to identify reputable centres. It is also the case that centres offering one of the three certificate courses referred to in this book (the CertTESOL, CELTA and School for International Training TESOL Certificate) will by definition meet minimum standards in terms of resources and premises, and so such a centre will represent a good employment choice. This area is dealt with in greater detail in the section 'Finding a reputable employer' below.

3. Classes of adults

Jean realized that, while her ideal employer (the British Council) offered classes to young learners as well as adults, ideally she needed experience with the latter. There were three reasons for this: the first is that her certificate course was concerned with teaching adults, rather than children; while some of the skills may be transferable, she wanted to develop and build upon the specific skills she had acquired during her course. The second reason is that she knew she needed to start to accumulate hours of experience of teaching adults, in order to eventually qualify for a place on a diploma course (she planned to take a Cambridge ESOL Diploma in English Language Teaching to Adults, as soon as she could); and thirdly, she had less interest in working with children, having, it seems, already done so.

4. Support

Jean understood that the course is a springboard. She knew that she would need support, particularly in the first few weeks. A good employer will also recognize this and will make arrangements for you to be provided with support, which could take some or all of the following forms:

- the provision of a mentor
- paid non-teaching time which you can use to prepare lessons and/or observe other teachers
- an induction programme
- professional development workshops, possibly open to all staff, including those who are part-time
- a staff handbook which contains information about the centre and its courses, staff contact details and systems of communication, the locations of resources, procedures, and so forth.

In identifying a good employer, you may wish to enquire about these forms of support. If you are fortunate enough to have a choice of employer, select the one that can offer you the most support.

5. Resources

Centres differ of course in terms of the quality and quantity of available resources. Jean described her preference to work in a centre that was well equipped, as clearly this would make her life as a new teacher easier.

As a minimum you should look for a well-stocked resource centre which might include lesson plans, visual aids, worksheets, audio and video equipment that can be borrowed for class use, games, current newspapers, and local information (brochures, leaflets, etc.).

In larger, more affluent centres you may find some or all of the following:

- a computer-assisted language learning laboratory (often known as a CALL laboratory)
- a self-access centre for learners (this may be known as an independent learning centre, or a learning resource centre)
- classrooms with interactive whiteboards
- a café or canteen
- a bookshop.

6. Good premises

The premises in which her future employer were located mattered to Jean; they may be less important to you. If you have little choice of employer, which is often the case for those who have just qualified, then the quality of the premises may not be a priority for you. A consideration may nevertheless be your work station and its surrounds. Particularly if you are offered part-time work, you may find that:

- You are expected to share a workstation. If so, find out where you can leave your books and materials so that they are secure.
- Your workstation is located in a busy, noisy staffroom. If so, find out if there is somewhere you can go to study and prepare with no distractions.
- You have to share a computer and printer with several teachers. If so, identify the 'quiet' times – periods when the hardware is less likely to be in use – and take advantage of them.
- You have to travel from the main centre to your teaching site (this is known as 'offsite' work; for a number of reasons your employer may offer classes in other parts of the city or town, and you may be expected to travel to such classes). If so, you may want to ask about a travel allowance; whether or not you can have a workstation on the offsite premises or at least somewhere you can leave your materials from one lesson to the next; facilities (can you get a glass of water there? Is there a photocopier you can use?); and access (for example, if your classes are being held in a local secondary school in the evening, who will open the building for you? Will there be someone on duty in case of an emergency? Are you expected to lock up?).

7. Competition

Jean's part-time course was a large one – there were 18 participants. As she might have expected, several fellow participants, living in the same town, were also looking for work at the same time. It may therefore, depending on local demand (which can be influenced by factors such as the time of year), be to your advantage if you are free to travel to another location to seek work. However, Jean adopted an assertive strategy, discussed below, and was eventually successful in finding employment.

8. Disappointment

Finding employment of any kind can of course be fraught with failure and disappointment. In Jean's case, she was disappointed when the employer did not call her when they said they would, on the Monday after her interview. But she was hoping to be offered work at one of the busiest times of the year, and although she had had an interview, it may be that awareness of her availability had yet to reach the person whose job it was to allocate classes to teachers. Jean therefore did exactly the right thing, when she physically visited that person (rather than phoning) and made her availability – and face – known.

9. Missing the induction for new staff

The timing of Jean's offer of work meant that she had already missed the induction that the centre offered to new teaching staff. Jean's journal does not suggest that she did anything about this (other than worry), but there are a number of positive steps she could have taken:

(a) Find someone who did attend the session, and copy their notes.
(b) Ask the staff member who ran the session for a copy of all handouts, or possibly of his or her presentation materials.
(c) Ask the staff member who ran the session to summarize the main points, over a coffee.

10. Networking and watching out for advertisements in the local press

While looking for work, Jean stayed alert to opportunities that might be advertised (in the local press; she may also have used the internet, although she does not mention this) and that might be passed on by word of mouth. As a result she appears to have succeeded in getting several interviews with potential employers.

11. Being 'pushy' – more assertive, perhaps, than she was accustomed to being

Jean found that she needed to be quite assertive (she used the word 'pushy') in order to get her first teaching job. It may be however, as suggested above, that she simply needed to make herself known to the people who were making the decisions. The larger the centre, the more likely it may be that you will need to 'push' a little to make yourself known. Centres can employ in excess of 50 or 60 teachers, and offer a range of classes in different locations: reflect for a minute on the work entailed for the person whose job it is to coordinate and timetable all the resources needed, human and physical alike. You can see that sometimes it will be a case of being in the right place at the right time: that is, being in or near the room where allocation is taking place, just as an additional class is created or as a teacher drops out.

12. Showing flexibility

Jean knew that being flexible would improve her chances of finding a teaching job. She therefore stated her willingness to teach at any time of day, in any location, and with any age group. This is a good strategy for anyone just starting out in ELT/TESOL. First of all, you can significantly increase your changes of finding work. Secondly, such flexibility can help to ensure that you are given a range of classes to teach, which provides you with excellent experience. Having taught a range of classes can serve you very well when it comes to finding your next position; it can also help you to establish your areas of particular interest.

13. Being willing to accept a less preferred teaching job (in a state school)

Jean seems to have recognized that immediate experience was important, and was prepared to work in a local secondary school rather than have no immediate teaching experience. This was a sensible decision and, although she did not need to accept such work, it would have been an acceptable alternative.

▶ A VIABLE POSITION WITH A REPUTABLE EMPLOYER

Above, I mentioned that centres running certificate courses such as the CertTESOL, the CELTA and the School for International Training TESOL Certificate represent good employment choices. However, if the centre you are considering does not run such courses, how can you be sure that you would not end up working for a so-called 'cowboy' organization (that is, one that is badly run, with a poor reputation in the local community)? In

> 'Korea to expel ESL cowboys.'
>
> Front page headline of *EL Gazette*, Issue No. 304, April 2005

the United Kingdom, you can consider centres that are accepted by the British Council or by the Association of British Language Schools. The British Council also runs its own language teaching centres in many countries outside the United

Kingdom, and it accepts other centres. While some countries have their own comparable accreditation organizations, many do not, and as yet no international organization has oversight of the profession. It can therefore be difficult to distinguish a well-run, professional centre from a 'cowboy' organization. It would be impossible to provide details here of all accreditation organizations in countries where these exist. It is not impossible, however, to provide a list of issues to consider when looking for a job in ELT/TESOL, and so this is the approach taken here. The main issues to consider are:

1. the centre
2. the job
3. the country
4. the practicalities.

You may find that some of the issues and suggestions below will not apply to your circumstances or stage of career. Nevertheless, a full list is provided in the belief that a significant proportion of what is described below will be of immediate relevance, while the remainder is likely to be useful at a later stage in your career. For the moment, a productive strategy would be to read the list below and highlight those points that are applicable to you, given your own particular set of circumstances.

The centre

Find out everything you can about it. You can:

- Visit the centre's website, if it has one. Visit as many other sites that make reference to the centre as you can, including, for example, chat rooms and professional associations such as TESOL (see the contact information provided on www to help you here).

- Enquire about the reputation of the centre in the local community, or speak to teachers already working there, if you can.

- Ask to be sent copies of centre literature (for example, the brochure of the centre) that will tell you a little about the facilities and work environment.

- The Department, or Ministry, of Education in the country you are interested in may also be able to advise you, if the centre you are considering is part of the state-run education system. If the centre is privately owned, try contacting the Chamber of Commerce or its equivalent. You can also approach consulates, high commissions or embassies: for example, if you are in the United Kingdom and considering employment in Thailand, you could visit the Royal Thai Embassy in London.

- Get references: ask to be put in touch with an existing or former employee, someone who has worked there for a reasonable period.

- Do not accept at face value any apparent affiliation, accreditation, certification, recommendation, validation or evaluation. A centre may appear to be accredited or in some other way validated by, for example, a university or a professional organization. You should not only confirm this with the affiliating organization itself, but also consider the affiliating body's credentials. This is because centres have been known to create their own 'affiliating body' with the intention of giving the impression that the centre has the necessary accreditation or validation.

The job

Find out about the job and working conditions. Ask questions about:

- the type of courses you will be teaching and the age range of your learners
- any social events you will be expected to take part in. (For example, you may be asked to escort students to places of interest. This is not always made clear on appointment. You may want to find out what your responsibilities will be and whether or not you will be paid for these extra-curricular duties.)
- who you would report to and the staff structure (are there Senior Teachers, for example, and/or will you have an (Assistant) Director of Studies?)
- the availability of teacher development and the culture (is it one of sharing ideas and materials?). Will you be able/encouraged to observe other classes?
- your employment status. Make sure that your new employer will arrange for you to be issued with an employment visa if you need one. Find out if there are costs involved in this and if so, who pays
- the job description
- how you will be paid – hourly, weekly, or monthly
- the number and timing of working hours per day. Will you be asked to work in the evenings, for example? If so, when would you be required to begin work the next day?
- the number of contact (teaching) hours per day
- the number of working days per week
- when the weekend falls and when your days off will be
- the location – will you be expected to work off-site?
- the class length (for example, in some places a teaching hour equals 50 minutes), and length of breaks between classes
- the expected number of contact (teaching) hours per year
- whether or not you will be expected to substitute for other teachers during their absence and if so, how many hours per week this accounts for

- the arrangements for covering your classes in the event of your absence. For example, are you expected to 'make up' classes missed through absence or public holidays?

- leave for medical reasons: how many days can you take per annum? Is it paid?

- whether or not it is possible to work overtime and, if so, what payment is offered for this

- contract length

- the number of days' leave per year, and whether or not they are paid

- any benefits you might be entitled to receive. Any or all of the following are possible: a gratuity, an annual bonus, medical insurance, housing, a relocation allowance, return annual airfares. Find out which, if any, of these apply to your dependents. In relation to this point, you may wish to find out if a contract you are being offered is on single or married status

- medical costs: find out if your employer will pay for these, if no insurance is provided or available. It is possible that, in some countries, access to the government health service will be provided. In either case, find out if you would be required to make any financial contribution to your costs

- the teaching resources. Find out what will be available, because different countries and cultures have different expectations of teachers. Ask what will be provided and what you will be expected to provide.

The country

Find out what you can about the country if you are unfamiliar with it. You might want to ask questions about:

- its economic development

- approaches to education

- attitudes to learning English

- the status of English in the country

- when English is taught in school and with what methods

- the status of teachers

- the attitudes to foreign workers and foreign teachers.

To find out about such areas, you could:

- speak to people who have visited the country you are interested in, if you can

- visit the consulate, high commission or embassy of the country in question and collect any literature they may have

- buy a guide book

- visit the website www.worldfactsandfigures.com for facts and figures on a range of relevant topics such as climate, health care and population size
- find out about the culture, in particular any norms of dress or behaviour that may affect you.

The practicalities

Find out about:

- your visa status with regard to the country you are considering (make sure you get reliable information about this)
- any vaccinations that might be recommended or required for the region
- getting there: will the employer pay for, or contribute towards, your ticket?
- accommodation: will you be expected to provide it, or will it be provided for you? If it will be provided, will you be expected to share? Will you be expected to make a financial contribution towards the rent? If provided, find out also how large it will be, whether or not it will be furnished, and where relevant, about heating or air conditioning. If accommodation is not provided, find out about costs and location in relation to your workplace

> 'I was completely confident that I would be able to do the job when I walked into my first class of students. It was well worth the time, effort and cost!'
>
> Participant, Hong Kong

- transport: make sure that you will be able to afford to live near your workplace, or, alternatively, that you can afford the daily travel costs involved in getting to and from work
- utilities: you should consider the cost of electricity, gas, water, telephone and internet access, for example
- the local banking system.

Jean's story continues below, as she moves from the job hunt to the workplace.

YOUR NEW TEACHING JOB: HOW TO SURVIVE THE FIRST WEEKS

In the extracts that follow, Jean describes her experience of the first few days in her new job:

Extracts from Jean's diary (2)

(continued)

Sunday

The next two days – Thursday/Friday – were a mad panic of discovery. How do you look for a course file when you don't know that one exists or that the worksheets you need for your course are in the 'Guide to Secondary Teaching' and not in the course file, neither of which you knew about anyway?

Friday

My first class – luckily, having already planned a 45 min GTKY (Getting To Know You) lesson, I was told to give them a test – that took 45 mins – so that was that lesson over with.

My next class had a grand total of 5 students. Out the window went the planned lesson. And in any case they all knew each other, having been together for a year already, so no chance of GTKY mingles there. One hour forty minutes of improvisation instead!

Sunday

Had some success today!

- I got awarded a shelf *and* a locker! (admittedly they are in different teachers' rooms but that's life)
- I found out the term dates
- I got a pigeon hole, an email address, a pay claim form, and a contract for the term!!
- I found out who my line manager is – I'm lucky – he's on planet earth!
- I found out the times of the teacher development workshops

Having got all that out of the way, all I need to do now is … teach!

Wednesday

I am really enjoying my classes, especially the Saturday class onsite.

I spend hours preparing for my business English class – they are a lovely group but hard work.

My classes are all so different – I hadn't expected that at all. I have a class from heaven and another from hell – what a learning curve. Getting used to saying 'I don't know, I'll find out for you!'

And what a great resource other teachers are. I was tearing out my hair and some ancient guy with a ponytail put me straight – 'they're just people like you and me', 'this happens to everyone', 'you'll get through it' – it was just what I needed to hear.

Although I'm part time it's obvious that I need to be 'around' quite a lot to find out what's going on.

(continued)

Saturday, 3 weeks after starting work

Well, I have now settled into the hours etc. but am still putting in a huge amount of preparation time before each lesson. I reckon I'm spending 4 or 5 hours preparing for each 1 in the classroom! But I'm really enjoying the teaching – my classes are not without their problems but I feel they are surmountable.

Have had my probationary observation – dreaded it but he was <u>very</u> positive in feedback – nuffin much wrong! He came up with a few helpful suggestions and that was that.

I'm a teacher now!

Jean's journal entries draw attention to a number of issues. Her comments fall into four main areas:

1. administration
2. resources
3. planning and preparation
4. teaching.

For each area that Jean writes about you can read a number of tips to help you to survive:

1. Administration

Some jobs will be administratively more demanding than others, particularly those in large centres. Jean had found work in a large centre, which can make communication more complex, as she discovered. Her situation was made even more difficult by the fact that she had little time before she started work in which to attend to administrative matters.

Tip 1: Ask your new employer for a list of administrative matters that you will have to attend to.

Tip 2: Attend to as many administrative matters as soon as you can, <u>before</u> you start teaching.

Tip 3: Spend time 'around' your new place of work. This will help you to acquire all sorts of information, from practical matters such as where the photocopier is to issues that may not be stated quite so explicitly, such as the dress code.

2. Resources

Jean's frustration increased when she failed to find the resources she needed, or when she discovered that they existed later rather than earlier.

Tip 4: Find out if the centre uses course books, and if your course syllabus is based on one. Make sure you are given a copy, with the supporting teacher's guide and any other components that you need, such as a practice or test book. Establish to what extent you are expected to follow the course book. Find out if a course outline is available – this will tell you exactly what you are required to cover on the course.

Tip 5: Even if it seems there are no resources for a course to which you have been assigned, make enquiries. Double-check the information you receive by asking the same question of more than person.

Tip 6: Find out who taught the course before you, and approach him or her for advice, support, and information about the students, if they are the same group.

Tip 7: Improve your self-reliance and begin to develop your own resource bank using a computer. Create worksheets, scan in documents and photographs: and save your work for future use or adaptation with another class, possibly in another centre, possibly in another country. Develop an approach to organizing your work on your computer at the very beginning (for example, a folder for grammar; another for reading skills; another for pronunciation work, and so forth). Purchase a memory stick (also known as a pen drive) with the highest available capacity so that you can easily transfer and transport your work: from home to the centre, and from one country to another. This initial effort and expenditure could serve you well for many years to come.

3. Planning and preparation

Jean found that she had planned a lesson for more students than were on the register for her class. She had assumed that the students, being new to her, would also be new to each other. Class size can affect the speed with which you are able to move through your plan as well as practical aspects of a lesson such as setting up pair and group work. Other contingencies to bear in mind include discovering that students have already covered the material or topic that you have planned, and having an odd number of students when you are planning pairwork.

Tip 8: Beware of your expectations and assumptions, such as the one that students in a class to which you have been assigned do not already know each other.

Tip 9: Always have a lesson 'up your sleeve'. Update this lesson as needed and make sure that it is suitable for any age range, any time, any place.

Tip 10: Keep a few short activities 'up your sleeve' too, for those few minutes of class time left at the end of a lesson.

Have something up your sleeve in case things don't work out

Tip 11: Expect to spend many hours preparing in the first few months of your first post-certificate teaching job. Remember two things: it is well worth the investment; and it gets easier quite quickly as you learn more.

4. Teaching

Jean enjoyed her classes, although she was surprised to find considerable variation between them. She identified some problems but was reassured by the fact that she could see how to overcome them. By the end of the three weeks, she felt she had become a fully-fledged teacher.

Tip 12: Expect your classes – even the 'same' class (that is, in terms of level, age range, syllabus, and so forth) to be quite different.

Tip 13: Use other teachers for advice and support. Many experienced teachers are more than willing to help out a less experienced colleague. They have been through it too!

Tip 14: Do not be afraid to tell students you do not know the answer – but do tell them that you will find out and let them know in their next lesson.

▶ CONTINUING TO LEARN

'I believe it's what comes after as much as the training on the certificate course which matters.'

Tutor, United Arab Emirates

In previous chapters I have emphasized the extent to which a certificate course is a springboard and a foundation. Alison, an experienced teacher, agrees. Reflecting upon her certificate course, she describes how it taught her the 'basics' but that she was unable to take everything in at the time. It was not until after her course was over, she felt, that everything she had studied began to make sense:

My Experience of the CELTA Course (continued)

Alison Standring

It was not until the end of my first year of teaching that I really felt I truly had the right to call myself a teacher. However, doing the CELTA course gave me an awareness of the basics of English Language Teaching and it also gave me the confidence to stand in front of a class. At the time, I couldn't digest all the information I was given but later it began to make sense and it has certainly helped me progress as a teacher.

It wasn't perfect, but then – nothing ever is.

The end

Ten steps can help you to foster your development and progression once you are in the workplace. These are:

1. Take advantage of having a mentor, if you have been assigned to one.
2. Observe other classes.
3. Set out to gain a variety of experience.
4. Participate in and contribute towards in-service development.
5. Read and research.
6. Aim to take further qualifications.
7. Join a professional association.
8. Attend conferences.
9. Network.
10. Practise 'good practice'.

Each step is considered in more detail below.

1. Take advantage of having a mentor, if you have been assigned to one

Your mentor – an experienced teacher who is familiar with the centre and its systems – will be an invaluable resource. Remember that you will not always have such a person dedicated to supporting you, so take full of advantage of the opportunity to ask questions and seek his or her advice and guidance as you need it.

2. Observe other classes

The opportunity to observe other classes tends to be more readily available to the inexperienced teacher than to the experienced teacher, unless it is a required part of a course leading to a further qualification. This is because being observed by a new teacher can be less intimidating than being observed by a fully-fledged peer. So take advantage of being 'green', if you like, and ask your director of studies to set up observations for you. Try to observe the full range of class type that is available at your centre (that is, observe different levels, different class sizes, different course books in use, and so forth). Remember to ask the teacher you have observed to set aside a little time to talk to you, ideally both before and after his or her class, in order to give you an idea of his or her plan, and then to discuss with you how the class went.

3. Set out to gain a variety of experience

It is a very good idea to try to ensure that, in the year or so immediately after taking a certificate course, you gain a variety of different teaching experience. If any of these choices are open to you, think about teaching:

- at a range of levels
- with a different set of materials and syllabus
- classes of different sizes (for example, you may be able to teach one-to-one, small groups of learners – perhaps no more than 6–8 learners; or larger groups of up to, say, 20 or 25 in a class)
- on part-time courses as well as on full-time intensive courses.

Such experience can help you to find out where your interests and preferences lie, and it can also help you to develop a variety of skills that will be of interest to your next employer.

4. Participate and contribute to in-service development

As Jean was fortunate to discover in her first three weeks in her new job, a reputable employer will offer in-service teacher development workshops on a regular basis. Such workshops may involve a variety of topics, from those of direct relevance to the field (such as teaching grammar) to those aimed more at personal development (such as training in the use of computer software, or the development of interpersonal skills). These workshops can take many forms including:

- An experienced member of staff runs a workshop, or a series of workshops, that he or she has developed around his or her particular interests.
- A member of staff reports on the highlights of a conference that he or she has attended, or presents the paper that he or she presented at the conference.
- A 'special interest group' (a 'SIG') has been set up (for example, you might find ESP or Phonology SIGs) and members meet on a regular basis to discuss matters of common interest, such as a particular issue or a new publication.
- A visiting well-known writer or researcher in ELT/TESOL is invited to deliver a lecture or series of lectures.

These are just some examples of different in-service development workshops that may be available to you. You may also be able to request particular sessions (for example, you may feel that developing writing skills is an area you need to know more about). Ask your director of studies if this is a possibility.

5. Read and research

Use your resource centre or staffroom, and the internet. Read or browse the full range of available materials. These include:

- course books, particularly recent ones
- reference books
- teachers' resource books
- files containing course materials
- journals such as the *ELT Journal* or *TESOL Quarterly*
- the *EL Gazette*
- websites (see **www** for some suggestions)
- *IATEFL Voices* and also the IATEFL Special Interest Groups Newsletters
- local journals/magazines/newsletters.

6. Aim to take further qualifications

It is likely that your director of studies will eventually encourage you to take a further qualification, such as the Cambridge ESOL Diploma in English Language Teaching to Adults (DELTA), or the Trinity College London Diploma in TESOL (DipTESOL). To be eligible for either, you need at least two years of experience of teaching ESOL; in relation to DELTA courses, this is further defined as needing to have gained at least 1200 hours of teaching experience. This may sound a great deal, but in fact, assuming two teaching years of 42 weeks each, it represents a reasonable average of just under 15 contact hours a week.

7. Join a professional association

The practice of teaching English in its many contexts has led to various associations and movements, the purpose of which is to support practitioners by enabling networking and the communication and promotion of ideas and research through journals, conferences, seminars, and workshops, for example. You should find one and join.

Based in the United States, you will find TESOL, a professional association that has several chapters, or affiliations, around the world. For example, there are 'TESOL Arabia' and 'Thailand TESOL'. (The term TESOL, therefore, has two uses, being used to refer to the field or subject, as well as the professional association. Check the context in which the acronym is being used to establish exactly what is being referred to.)

In the United Kingdom, on the other hand, you will find 'IATEFL', (the International Association of Teachers of English as a Foreign Language), among others. Many other countries have either their own professional associations in ELT/TESOL, or one that is affiliated to one of those above, and it is worth making enquiries to find one that relates both to your areas of interest and is active in your context. Ask your colleagues for advice here. See **www** for details of IATEFL and TESOL.

8. Attend conferences

As soon as you begin work in your new position, make enquiries about forthcoming conferences. Check notice boards, TESOL websites (see **www**) and contact any professional association you have joined. Ask your director of studies if you can be given time off in which to attend a conference; alternatively you may find that you are able to attend one that is held over a weekend. Attending conference presentations is an excellent way of staying up-to-date with current developments, and it is also a very good place for networking.

9. Network

The contacts that you make through networking can prove to be an invaluable resource. Such people can help you with a number of aspects of your career, including:

- ideas and resources for use in your current position
- information about future job opportunities
- first-hand experience of a job you are considering taking
- research or study that you may undertake.

You can network in a number of different ways, including:

- in your current position (you may wish to stay in touch with someone who leaves)
- at conferences

- through chat rooms available on ELT/TESOL websites (see **www** for some suggestions in this area)

- through professional associations (by joining a Special Interest Group, for example).

It is likely that you will quickly build up a collection of name cards as a result of such networking and it is recommended that you purchase a name card holder and organize the cards you receive according to the job you hold at the time. So, for example, I have a set of cards from the time I spent at International House in Hastings, in the United Kingdom; and I have another set for each of the other places in which I have worked. While some of these are of course now long out of date in terms of the person's contact details, the details of the centre or organization where he or she worked will often remain valid for many years.

Of course, networking is nothing if not reciprocal, so have your own name cards printed too for distribution.

10. Practise 'good practice'

As you begin your new job, it is a good idea to start thinking about what might constitute 'good practice' in the field. Being certain that what you are doing is ethical and represents current understandings of 'good practice' in ELT/TESOL can improve both your levels of confidence, and your job satisfaction.

Areas to reflect upon at this stage include:

- how to avoid discrimination in the classroom (think about gender; sexual orientation; race; age; those who are physically or mentally challenged)

- understanding that English is not inherently superior in any respect, but that it currently enjoys its international status because of historical accident

- the need to respect other peoples' cultures, religions, values, and traditions

- respecting publishers' and authors' rights with regard to photocopying (ask your director of studies for guidelines that apply to your context)

- understanding that a lack of proficiency in English does not equate to a lack of intelligence.

These are interesting, complex areas, ideal for discussion, and you might like to consider suggesting one or two of them as topics for an in-service workshop or discussion group at your centre.

Being qualified: Key points to take away with you

When looking for a position in ELT/TESOL, make enquiries about:

- the reputation of the organization
- the opportunities that you will have for teaching classes of adults, in particular, in order to gain experience of direct relevance to your qualification
- the support that will be available to you if you accept the position
- the quality of the centre's resources and premises
- whether or not an induction programme is available for new staff.

When trying to find suitable work, consider being:

- a little 'pushy', particularly if you are entering a highly competitive context
- flexible with regard to hours, timing, and type of class
- willing to accept a less preferred teaching job in order to get immediate experience.

When starting your new job:

- Ask your new employer for a list of administrative matters that you will have to attend to, and sort as many of them out as you can before you start teaching.
- Spend time 'around' your new place of work to help you to acquire a range of information.
- Even if it seems there are no resources for a course to which you have been assigned, make enquiries.
- Find out who taught the course before you, and approach him or her for advice and support.
- Begin to develop your own resource bank using a computer and store this on a memory stick to facilitate transferring and transporting your work.
- Always have a lesson 'up your sleeve'. Update this lesson as needed and make sure that it is suitable for any age range, any time, any place
- Keep a few short activities 'up your sleeve' too, for those few minutes of class time left at the end of a lesson.

- Expect to spend many hours preparing in the first few months of your first post-certificate teaching job.

- Use other teachers for advice and support.

- Do not be afraid to tell students you do not know the answer – but do tell them that you will find out and let them know in their next lesson.

To continue to develop professionally:

- Take advantage of having a mentor, if one has been assigned to you.

- Observe a range of classes.

- Set out to gain a variety of experience.

- Participate in and contribute towards in-service development.

- Read extensively.

- Aim to take further qualifications.

- Join a professional association that is active in your region.

- Attend conferences.

- Network: collect name cards and distribute your own.

- Always practise 'good practice'.

www **Check your understanding** of Chapter 10 by completing the quiz available on the companion website at: www.sagepub.co.uk/brandt

Endword

This book provides a great deal of information about some of the things that can be done on a short, intensive course that is designed to help you to become a qualified teacher in ELT/TESOL.

Real learning comes from doing those things.

Feedback

Did you find this book helpful? I would welcome your comments.

Please visit **www** where you will find an email address that you can use for your feedback

References

Aitken, R. (2002) *Teaching Tenses: Ideas for presenting and practising tenses in English.* United Kingdom: ELB

Baguley, N. and Greenwood, L. (2005) 'Oasis of opportunity'. In *EL Gazette*, November 2005.

Bolitho, R. and Tomlinson, B. (2002) *Discover English.* United Kingdom: Macmillan ELT

Brandt, C. (2006) 'Allowing for Practice: A Critical Issue in TESOL Teacher Preparation'. *English Language Teaching Journal,* Volume 60, Issue 4, October 2006

British Council (2005) 'TEFL Certificate Level Qualifications: Initial Training for EFL Teachers'. http://www.britishcouncil.org/teacherrecruitment-tefl-qualifications-certificates-2.htm
Retrieved, 29 October 2005

Cambridge ESOL (2004) 'Certificate in Further Education Teaching Stage 3'. http://www.cambridgeesol.org/teaching/cfet.htm
Retrieved, 23 March 2006

Cambridge ESOL (2005a) 'CELTA Syllabus (Course Aims)'. http://www.cambridge esol.org/teaching/celta8_251103.pdf
Retrieved, 2 April 2005

Cambridge ESOL (2005b) 'CELTA: Frequently Asked Questions'. http://www. cambridge-efl.org/about_us/faqs/celta_centres_faqs.htm#5
Retrieved, 10 April 2005

Cambridge ESOL (2005c) 'Certificate in English Language Teaching to Adults'. http://www.cambridgeesol.org/teaching/celta.htm
Retrieved, 1 May 2005

Close, R. A. (1992) *A Teacher's Grammar: the central problems of English.* United Kingdom: Language Teaching Publications

Cunningham, S. and Moore, P. (2003) *Cutting Edge: A Practical Approach to Task Based Learning, Advanced Student's Book.* United Kingdom: Longman

Doff, A. and Jones, C. (1994) *Language in Use Intermediate Classroom Book.* United Kingdom: Cambridge University Press

Downing, A. and Locke, P. (1992) *A University Course in English Grammar.* United Kingdom: Prentice Hall International Ltd

Education Guardian, TEFL (6 April 2004) 'Career doctor'. http://education.guardian.
co.uk/tefl/story/0%2C5500%2C1186300%2C00.html
Retrieved 16 December 2004

Education Guardian, TEFL (27 September 2004a) 'TEFL courses – a guide to what's
available'. http://education.guardian.co.uk/tefl/courses/story/0,15084,1312211,00.html
Retrieved 16 December 2004

Education Guardian, TEFL (27 September 2004b) 'TEFL courses – how to choose a
course'. http://education.guardian.co.uk/tefl/courses/story/0,,1313767,00.html
Retrieved 16 December 2004

Gray, P. X. (1997) 'The formation and development of TESOL: a brief history'.
International Education, Volume 27, Number 1. Fall, 1997. pp.71–83.

International House (2006) 'About IH: International House Background'. http://www.ih
world.com/background/index.asp
Retrieved April 3 2006

Kay, S., Vaughan, J. and Hird, J. (2001) *Inside Out Intermediate Student's Book*. United
Kingdom: Macmillan ELT

Lewis, M. (1986) *The English Verb: An exploration of structure and meaning*. United
Kingdom: Language Teaching Publications

Lewis, M. and Hill, J. (1985) *Practical Techniques for Language Teaching*. United Kingdom:
Language Teaching Publications

Longman Active Study Dictionary (2000) United Kingdom: Longman Group Ltd.

Murphy, R. (1997) *Essential Grammar in Use with Answers: A Self-study Reference and
Practice Book for Elementary Students of English*. United Kingdom: Cambridge
University Press

Oxenden, C., Lathan-Koenig, C. and Seligson, P. (1999) *English File Intermediate
Student's Book*. United Kingdom: Oxford University Press

Oxenden, C., Lathan-Koenig, C. and Seligson, P. (2001) *English File Upper-Intermediate
Student's Book*. United Kingdom: Oxford University Press

Polster, E. and Polster, M. (1974) *Gestalt Therapy Integrated*. London: Vintage.

Pugsley, J. (2005a) Trinity College London, by email, *'Your enquiry'*. Received 3 May 2005

Pugsley, J. (2005b) Trinity College London, by email, *'Re: Our correspondence re
CertTESOL'*. Received 28 October 2005

Pugsley, J. (2005c) Trinity College London, by email, *'Re: your book, Chas 2, 3'*. Received
7 November 2005

Richards, J., Platt, J. and Weber, H. (1985) *Longman Dictionary of Applied Linguistics*.
United Kingdom: Longman

School for International Training (2005a) 'TESOL Certificates: Frequently Asked
Questions'. http://www.sit.edu/tesolcert/faqs.html#6
Retrieved 1 May 2005

School for International Training (2005b) 'The SIT TESOL Certificate Course, AUA Language Centre, Bangkok and Chiang Mai, Thailand'. http://www.auathailand.org/sit/index.html Retrieved 25 March 2006

School for International Training (2005c) 'TESOL Certificate Course Goals and Objectives' http://www.sit.edu/tesolcert/docs/goals_objectives.pdf Retrieved, 2 April 2005

Scrivener, J. (2005) *Learning Teaching*. United Kingdom: Macmillan ELT

Soars, J. and Soars, L. (2003) *New Headway English Course, Student's Book, Advanced Level*. United Kingdom: Oxford University Press

Soars, J. and Soars, L. (2000) *New Headway English Course, Student's Book, Pre-Intermediate Level*. United Kingdom: Oxford University Press

Swan, M. (2005) *Practical English Usage*. United Kingdom: Oxford University Press

Swan, M. and Smith, B. (2001) *Learner English: A Teacher's Guide to Interference and Other Problems*. UK: Cambridge University Press

Trinity College London (2005a) 'Certificate in Teaching English to Speakers of Other Languages (CertTESOL), A summary of course content and key information for course members, from April 2004' http://www.trinitycollege.co.uk/resource/?id=695 Retrieved 10 March 2006

Trinity College London (2005b) 'Certificate in Teaching English to speakers of other languages (Cert Tesol). Validation requirements for validated and prospective course providers, from April 2004'. http://www.trinitycollege. co.uk/resource/?id=695 Retrieved 25 March 2006

Trinity College London (2005c) 'CertTESOL, FAQs.' http://www.trinitycollege.co.uk/site/?id=704 Retrieved 25 March 2006

Tusting, K. and Barton, D. (2003) *Models of Adult Learning: a literature review*. The National Research and Development Centre for Adult Literacy and Numeracy. http://www.nrdc.org.uk Retrieved 14 August 2005

Ur, P. (1999) *A Course in Language Teaching Trainee Book*. United Kingdom: Cambridge University Press

Index